Buffett
Beyond Value

Buffett Beyond Value

Why Warren Buffett Looks to Growth and Management When Investing

Prem C. Jain

WILEY

John Wiley & Sons, Inc.

Published by John Wiley & Sons, Inc., Hoboken, New Jersey.
Published simultaneously in Canada.

For general information on our other products and services or for technical support, please
contact our Customer Care Department within the United States at (800) 762-2974,
outside the United States at (317) 572-3993 or fax (317) 572-4002.

Wiley also publishes its books in a variety of electronic formats. Some content that appears
in print may not be available in electronic books. For more information about Wiley
products, visit our web site at www.wiley.com.

Library of Congress Cataloging-in-Publication Data:

Jain, Prem C. 1950–
  Buffett beyond value : why Warren Buffett looks to growth and management when
investing/Prem C. Jain.
      p. cm.
  Includes bibliographical references and index.
  ISBN 978-0-470-46715-2 (cloth)
  1. Investments. 2. Investment analysis. 3. Buffett, Warren. I. Title.
  HG4521.J264 2010
  332.6–dc22

                                                       2009041474

Printed in the United States of America
10 9 8 7 6 5 4 3 2 1

Contents

Preface

This book is for everyone with a serious interest in learning about stock market investing using principles espoused by Warren Buffett. Just over 20 years ago, while teaching at the Wharton School, I stumbled upon an essay by Warren Buffett that motivated me to carefully investigate his investment style.[1] I was intrigued when I realized that there was a fundamental difference between Buffett's attitude toward investing and the academic approach. While academics generally anchor on the impossibility of making above-average returns, Buffett proposes just the opposite. He argues that with a careful study of company fundamentals and management quality, investors definitively can earn above-average returns. His outstanding long-term record supports his claim. When faced with Buffett's record, most academics either dismiss it as an outlier or brand him a genius who cannot be copied or explained. I wanted to know if there was a systematic way of understanding and emulating his investment philosophy.

Most authors, including academics, characterize Buffett as a value investor. Buffett is not just a value investor—at least not in the popular sense that the "value" moniker is used. Buffett's publicly traded company, Berkshire Hathaway, has grown at an annualized rate of about 20 percent in assets, revenues, net worth, and market value for 44 years. His performance is closer to what would be expected from a successful growth investor. Unlike other businessmen who may have also amassed great fortunes, Buffett stands alone because his long-term success reflects growth of his business and investments in several different industries without ever riding a hot trend. There is another major difference between Buffett and other successful investors, which is actually the main reason I chose to study him diligently. Warren Buffett is a man of the highest level of integrity. He knows that he has a special gift, and instead of keeping it to himself, he has chosen to share his immensely valuable experiences with anyone who cares to do some research. A remarkable teacher, Buffett has written a considerable body of material on his ideas and principles, which allows for careful examination of his strategies and motivations.

The key reason for Buffett's unparalleled success is not only his ability to stay resolute with the primary value investing principle of maintaining a low downside risk but also his skill at pairing it with the growth investing principle of putting money into companies with sustainable growth opportunities. Thus, he combines the principles of both the value and growth investment strategies. Yet, he does not invest in high-tech companies, as so many growth investors do. His growth strategy is best understood by studying the businesses he has purchased at Berkshire Hathaway. Buffett buys good businesses that already possess outstanding, high-integrity management. He relies on the same principles for investing in common stocks. I elaborate on his investment principles throughout the book along with the specific topics covered in each chapter. These principles are useful whether you are investing in a bull market or a bear market.

Buffett and Contemporary Teachings at Business Schools

My goal as a teacher-researcher is not only to explore what Buffett practices but also to find answers to *why* his practices are successful. In 1997, my desire to understand *why* Buffett's investment style works and *how* his strategies blend with the lessons from contemporary finance led me to develop a new course at Tulane University. This course took a new approach to finance, where students studied Buffett's writings and decisions in conjunction with modern finance research. The students also analyzed a large number of businesses. In 1999, Tulane contributed $2 million from the university's endowment fund to create a portfolio to be managed by students under my guidance. I left Tulane in 2002 for Georgetown University, but Professor Sheri Tice continues to teach the increasingly popular course at Tulane.

From the outset, it is important to recognize that Buffett's ideas are not always at odds with modern finance theories. For example, the concepts of discounting cash flows and net present value are taught in all business schools. Resembling the net present value concept, concepts like intrinsic value and margin of safety are at the core of Buffett-style investing. Furthermore, the much-talked-about concept of diversification is discussed in a somewhat similar, although not identical, fashion both by investment texts and by Buffett. There is plenty of commonality between the business school curriculum and Buffett's approach. However, this book covers ideas from Buffett that go beyond what professors generally offer. My goal is to provide additional insights to lead you toward a more practical approach to investing in the stock market.

Focus on Important Questions

One key trait that makes Buffett successful is his ability to focus. To remain focused, I present many sections of the book in a question-and-answer format. This Socratic style forces one to pinpoint important questions that fellow investors, students, and colleagues have asked me over the years. At Berkshire Hathaway annual meetings, many of which I have attended over the past 20 years, Warren Buffett and Charlie Munger (chairman and vice chairman of Berkshire Hathaway, respectively) answer questions from the audience for several hours. Buffett also used a question-and-answer format in 2003 when he accepted my invitation to address Georgetown University MBA students and faculty.

Although this book concentrates on Buffett's investing style, I bring in related ideas from other investors and academic research to help improve your investment strategies. For example, no discussion on investing is complete without incorporating the pioneering and still relevant works of Benjamin Graham and David Dodd. Similarly, I draw from the thoughts of Philip Fisher and Peter Lynch to discuss growth investing strategies.

No one can teach Buffett's ideas better than Buffett himself. Clearly, he knows a thing or two about investing. In March 2008, *Forbes* magazine ranked Buffett as the world's wealthiest man with an estimated personal wealth of \$62 billion.[2] I wrote him a letter in 1997 suggesting that future generations would thank him if he were to write a book. He responded, "I definitely have a book in mind, though much of what I have to say has been covered in the annual reports." While we wait for Buffett to write his investment book, I decided to share my own analyses. To unmask his thoughts, I carefully studied Berkshire Hathaway's annual reports from the past 50 years, his 1958 to 1969 partnership letters, and as many of his other writings as I could find. I have benefited immensely from this effort and have done my best to capture Buffett's investment ideas in this book.

How Much Background Do You Need to Understand Buffett's Principles?

Buffett does not recommend sophisticated mathematical models. He writes, "To invest successfully, you need not understand beta, efficient markets, modern portfolio theory, option pricing, or emerging markets."[3] With this sentiment in mind, I have made certain that you do not need any knowledge of mathematical finance to benefit from this book. Consistent with Buffett's teachings, my experience tells me that the use of mathematical models to pick individual stocks is not particularly helpful. It may even be harmful because it can lead you to become overconfident in your abilities. As the financial crisis in 2008–2009 has shown, over-reliance on mathematical models can result in a false sense of security in the understanding of risk and return.

Some knowledge of accounting and finance is essential to follow this book, but most people investing in the stock market already understand such terms as *earnings*, *dividends*, and *return on equity*. My objective is to show how to interpret those terms so that you can use them effectively to improve your investing style. If you have no knowledge of basic investment terms, you may find some sections of this book a little advanced. Even then, you will see that there is more to picking a stock than being a whiz in manipulating numbers. If stock picking could indeed be formulated as a mathematical model, mutual fund managers could simply hire a bunch of rocket scientists and earn superior returns. But the evidence is just the opposite: It appears that investors who use simple principles generally do better than those who rely heavily on mathematical models.

To concentrate on Buffett's investing principles, I restrict my discussion to Buffett's investment-related ideas, how we can learn from them, and why they work. Others have already reviewed his interesting life story.[4] I doubt that you need to be as fascinated by bridge or baseball as he is to become a successful investor. Similarly, you need not have been born in Omaha, Nebraska, or share his taste in food. Even his friend and business partner Charlie Munger does not agree with all of Buffett's philosophical ideas. While Buffett is a Democrat, Munger is a Republican. You need not be either. By keeping the book focused on Buffett's investment philosophies, I highlight only the issues relevant to investing.

What Can You Learn from This Book?

This book is divided into nine parts and 30 chapters. There is continuity across chapters, but you can read most of them independently.

In Part I (Chapters 1 and 2), my main objective is to convince you that investing is like searching for buried treasure. One reason Buffett is successful is that he enjoys this process, and you are more likely to be successful if you treat it as a game and have fun with it. Next, I chronologically outline several important events in Berkshire's history to draw insights into Buffett's philosophy. Such a historical background is useful to keep the remainder of the book in perspective.

Part II (Chapters 3 to 6) explains basic investment strategies, so-called *value investing* and *growth investing*. Using concrete examples, I explain how you may compute *intrinsic value* and *margin of safety* before you invest. Particularly in Chapter 6, I explain why Buffett's strategies should *not* be classified as value investing in the traditional sense. He does what is most logical and frequently combines value and growth investing strategies effectively. In general, it is a mistake, and would limit your imagination, to pigeonhole Buffett's approach into any single investing style. He does what is most rational to create value in the long run. For lack of a better term, I simply call him a renaissance investor.

In Part III (Chapters 7 to 9), I look at how Buffett uses insurance to generate cash flows for other investments. To understand Buffett, you must have some understanding of the insurance business, which is the mainstay of Berkshire Hathaway.

In Part IV (Chapters 10 to 13), I discuss several of Buffett's investments in retailing, utilities, and manufacturing. These examples provide further insight into his emphasis on growth and management quality. In Part V (Chapters 14 to 17), I emphasize Buffett's opinions concerning several classic topics, such as diversification and risk.

In Part VI (Chapters 18 and 19), I discuss Buffett's thoughts on market efficiency and the ways in which you may incorporate his thoughts into your decision making.

In Part VII (Chapters 20 to 24), I review several important issues related to profitability and accounting. Although these chapters will not make you an accountant, they will provide you with a perspective that is not common in investing circles.

In Part VIII (Chapters 25 and 26), I focus on psychology because to be a successful investor, you must understand yourself and the biases that play a role in your decision making and the decision making of others.

Part IX (Chapters 27 to 30) is devoted to corporate governance, Buffett's thoughts on CEOs and other managers, and why he emphasizes appropriate compensation structure throughout a firm. The conclusion of the book discusses Buffett's emphasis on developing a suitable temperament for winning in the market, just as a baseball player needs to develop a temperament for winning on the diamond.

Overall, the book will allow you to discover that Buffett has achieved success by emphasizing the importance of high-quality managers more than any other metric. He calls his managers the "All-Stars" and discusses their accomplishments lavishly in Berkshire annual reports. By contrast, most research and teachings in business schools use financial numbers as the key metric for financial success and understanding businesses. My objective is to develop your understanding beyond the ideas you may have learned in your college courses, gleaned by reading articles in the popular media, or picked up through any other outlets. My motivation is not just to provide rules for investing but also to help improve your mind-set for investing. Having the right mind-set is pivotal, whether you are an individual investor, a student, an academic, or a professional portfolio manager.

PREM C. JAIN

Acknowledgments

When I initially narrated Warren Buffett's success story, my father, always a philosopher, reminded me what I frequently asked him when I was a child: "Why?" The answer is that I am grateful. I am grateful to my students at Wharton, Tulane, and Georgetown over the past 25 years who asked innumerable questions and helped me focus my thoughts. My colleagues, ever skeptical as professors are, gave me the benefit of their explanations and understanding of differences between how academics think and how businessmen and money managers think. I am sincerely grateful to my longtime friend Larry Weiss, who read an early version of the entire book and went through several chapters over and over again as I developed my ideas. My special thanks go to my friends Valentin Dimitrov, a careful reader and a trusted co-author, for his discussions with me for many years about Buffett's principles and for his ongoing comments on the manuscript at different stages, and Nancy Pitts, who read every word with a critical eye, asked many questions, and helped improve the manuscript. I thank Elisa Diehl and Cindy Leitner for carefully copyediting the entire manuscript at different stages.

I have benefited from my colleagues' and friends' knowledge about investing and Buffett. They listened patiently, sometimes argued and discussed, gave detailed comments, and contributed to the book in many ways. For this, I thank Reena Aggarwal, Bill Baber, Dale Bailey, Gary Blemaster, Jennifer Boettcher, Jim Bodurtha, Randy Cepuch,

Preeti Choudhary, George Comer, George Daly, Hemang Desai, Bill Droms, Jason Duran, Allan Eberhart, Patricia Fairfield, Therese Flanagan, Aloke Ghosh, Jack Glen, Zhaoyang Gu, Ingrid Hendershot (babyb), Jim Heurtin, Manish Jain, Saurabh Jain, Varun Jain, S. P. Kothari, Amit Kshetarpal, Subir Lall, Charles Lee, Jeff Macher, Ananth Madhavan, Jim Marrocco, Jerry Martin, Alan Mayer-Sommer, John Mayo, Chuck Mikolajczak, Vishal Mishra, Lenka Naidu, Kusum Narang, Keith Ord, Sandeep Patel, Lee Pinkowitz, Dennis Quinn, Sundaresh Ramnath, Korok Ray, Pietra Rivoli, Srini Sankaraguruswamy, Carole Sargent, Missie Saxon, Jason Schloetzer, Pamela Shaw, Paul Spindt, Emma Thompson, Sheri Tice, Cathy Tinsely, Joaquin Trigueros, Joanna Shuang Wu, and Teri Yohn. I am certain I have not included everyone, and I apologize to those whose names should also appear here.

I thank Warren Buffett for allowing me to use copyrighted material from his letters to shareholders and other sources. For my initial education and ensuing gifts in life, I credit my teachers in an elementary school in a small town in India. All my earnings from this book will be donated to children's education. Most important, I am especially grateful to my parents, my brother Subhash, and my three sisters Gunmala, Kanak, and Manju and their families for their unwavering love and support.

P. C. J.

Part One

INTRODUCTION AND BACKGROUND

In Chapter 1, I explain why it is easy to beat the professional mutual fund managers and how, with some effort, you can also outperform the market as a whole. I demonstrate that in the long run, rewards from playing the game of investing are large. In Chapter 2, I use important events from Berkshire Hathaway's history as a backdrop for various investing lessons that can be learned from Warren Buffett.

Chapter 1

The Thrill of Investing in Common Stocks

It's not that I want money. It's the fun of making money and watching it grow.[1]

—Warren Buffett

Warren Buffett has often mentioned that he enjoys running Berkshire Hathaway and has fun making money. I assume that you too want to earn high rates of return on your investments while having fun doing it. It is not difficult to do if you master certain principles that Buffett follows. You play baseball, golf, bridge, or the stock market because it is enjoyable. But you enjoy the game even more when you defeat the opponent, especially when you beat a seemingly superior player. Can you win in the game of investing? Yes, you can, so long as you are willing put some effort into it. And not only can you win; the thrill of the game arises because you can win often. You have weak opponents: "Mr. Market," who suffers from up-and-down moods, and professional money managers, who can be outperformed just as easily.[2] This game is not as difficult as most people think. It is as much fun as a treasure hunt. Berkshire Hathaway is just one of the treasures I have discovered. This introductory chapter will convince you that the rewards from becoming a better investor are enormous. Later in the book, I explain Buffett's principles and why they work, so that you may use them to earn those rewards by investing in the stock market.

How a 1 Percent Advantage Becomes a 100 Percent Gain

Only one in five actively managed mutual funds beats the Standard & Poor's (S&P) 500 index. Thus, if you invest in actively managed mutual funds, your odds of beating the market are only one-in-five. These odds are indeed low. A very simple approach to improve your odds is to invest in index funds because their returns will be close to the market returns. By investing in index funds instead of mutual funds, your odds of beating the market improve from one-in-five to four-in-five. But why stop there? If you have some money to invest for the long run, why not invest in common stocks? With common stocks, you can improve your returns even more, especially if you enjoy the process and put some effort into learning the principles that master investors like Buffett have laid out. Another great investor, Peter Lynch, echoes this viewpoint: "[A]n amateur who devotes a small amount of time to study companies in an industry he or she knows something about can outperform 95 percent of the paid experts who manage the mutual funds, plus have fun doing it."[3]

How much skill do you need to be much better off than investing in actively managed mutual funds? In the long run, not much! Let me explain. Based on a long historical record, the expected return on the market is about 7 percent to 10 percent per year. For simplicity, let's use 10 percent as a benchmark. Then, your return from an average mutual fund will be only 8 percent because about 2 percent goes toward expenses in running the mutual fund, which includes the management fees. If you invest $1,000 with a mutual fund and the mutual fund gives you a return of 8 percent per year, your initial investment of $1,000 will become $6,848 in 25 years; that is, you will have a net gain of $5,848.

Assume that you are able to develop just a 1 percent return advantage over the market in the game of investing or picking stocks. Remember that you also do not incur the 2 percent expenses in fees and charges when you invest in mutual funds. With 1 percent above the market, or

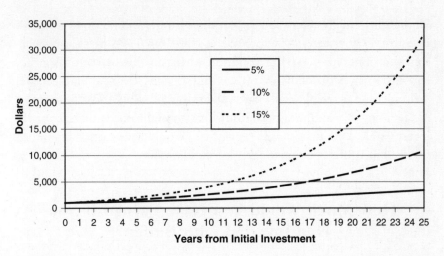

Figure 1.1   Growth of $1,000 after 25 or Intermediate Years at Different Rates of Return

11 percent per year, your initial $1,000 investment will become $13,585 at the end of 25 years, which is a net gain of $12,585. Thus, your net gain is more than twice what you would have had if you had invested in mutual funds. It is almost unbelievable, but the numbers do not lie. Even if you decide not to put all your money under your own management and invest all of it in individual stocks, you may find it worthwhile to take charge of some of your own investments. If nothing else, it will be a great learning experience and a new source of excitement.

An additional advantage of investing in individual stocks is that you will pay lower taxes. If you pick your investments carefully and do not sell them for a long time, you pay substantially less in taxes than if you had invested in mutual funds. Thus, even if you do not develop a 1 percent advantage over the market, you will come out substantially ahead when you judiciously invest in individual stocks rather than mutual funds.

Figure 1.1 shows what $1,000 will become in 10, 15, 20, and 25 years if you earn 5 percent, 10 percent, or 15 percent per year. Note that if you can earn 15 percent per year, your advantage over the market is enormous. A $1,000 initial investment will become $32,919 in 25 years at a 15 percent annual rate of return.

The 2008–2009 stock market crash may have made you pessimistic about investing. However, history tells us that you have an advantage.

This event actually offers you a great opportunity to find good stocks to invest in. Buffett recently wrote in the *New York Times* that for his personal account, he is buying common stocks in this market.[4] Another legendary investor with an outstanding record over several decades writes, "One principle that I have used throughout my career is to invest at the point of maximum pessimism."[5] So, spend some time learning to invest wisely. Let's first look at returns you would have earned if you had invested in Buffett's company, Berkshire Hathaway.

How Much Would You Have Earned If You Had Invested with Buffett?

In the past 30 years ending in 2008, Berkshire Hathaway has given an annualized return of over 23 percent per year. This is twice the rate of return you would have earned with the Dow Jones Industrial Average or the S&P 500 index. Obviously, Warren Buffett's performance is incredible. In terms of dollar amounts, if you had invested $1,000 in Berkshire Hathaway about 30 years ago, your investment today would amount to about $500,000. The lesson is clear: Learn from Warren Buffett's investment philosophy, which is described throughout this book. You may not be able to attain his level of success, but you do not have to be Warren Buffett to earn respectable returns in the stock market. If you can replicate even, say, one-fourth or one-third of the advantage he has over the market, you will earn very high long-term returns. The average investor is likely to be a relatively small investor. It is easier to beat the market with smaller amounts of money than with large investments. When Buffett ran his partnerships in the late 1950s to late 1960s, his returns were even larger. Now, Buffett cannot invest in smaller companies because the Berkshire portfolio is so large. But a small investor has the advantage of being able to invest in smaller companies. For Berkshire as a whole, returns were higher when the company was smaller, but even over the past 15 years, the average annualized return has been 12 percent compared with only about 6 percent for the S&P 500 index.

You never know: You might have the skills to pick the right stocks and become as good an investor as Warren Buffett. As long as you are not reckless, there is little downside in trying to find out whether you have some of the skills to be successful. One great thing about Buffett is that he has written generously about what he does and how he does it. If you have patience and the willingness, let's start learning about businesses and investing from the master.

Conclusions

Buffett has often described his investing philosophy as simple but not easy. It is simple in the sense that all you need to do is to identify outstanding businesses that are run by competent and honest managers and whose common stock is selling at a reasonable price. But how do you that? This book makes the process of discovering those businesses as easy as possible.

Chapter 2

1965–2009: Lessons from Significant Events in Berkshire History

History is philosophy teaching by examples.
—Thucydides, an ancient Greek historian

When Warren Buffett took control of Berkshire Hathaway in 1965, it was a small textile manufacturing company in New England. The prospects of the textile industry at the time were rather bleak. Buffett has transformed Berkshire into a large insurance, utility, manufacturing, and retailing conglomerate. In 44 years, the company's book value has grown from $19 to $70,530 per class A share, and the stock price has correspondingly grown from about $8 to $96,600. The following list of significant events in Berkshire history serves two purposes. First, it is important to learn from the examples others have set; and second, it presents a quick look at many of Buffett's principles. In later chapters, we will explore these principles further.

1965: Not Throwing Good Money after Bad

Event   Warren Buffett is listed as a Berkshire director for the first time, although he is not yet the chief executive of the company. Starting to accumulate Berkshire shares in 1962 at $7.60 per share, Buffett acquired a controlling interest in the company by 1965 with an overall average cost of $14.86 per share.

Lesson   Revenues at Berkshire have been declining, from $64 million to $49 million, in the prior 16 years. However, the company did not invest much to prop up the declining textile business. The decision not to invest in a declining business is a good example of the often-used maxim: "Don't throw good money after bad." Berkshire's cash flows are instead used for buying its own shares back in the open market and for investing in other securities. The main lesson is that one should be careful in investing in a company that is using its cash flows to sustain a dying business.

1967: Invest in Your Circle of Competence

Event   Berkshire makes its debut in the insurance business by acquiring two insurance companies for $9 million: National Indemnity Company and National Fire and Marine Insurance Company. Both companies are based in Omaha where Buffett lives.

Lesson   Buffett probably had a long-term plan to slowly develop the insurance business. This is a nearly perfect example of how a long journey starts with a small first step. He invests within his circle of competence: insurance.

1973: Cash Flow Is King

Event   Berkshire increases its investment in Blue Chip Stamps.

Lesson   In the trading stamp business, the company receives cash in advance for stamps: an IOU. The company does not have to pay interest on these IOUs, and it can use the cash thus received for investments in other businesses. This is a good example of Buffett's philosophy of generating cash flow with little risk. The insurance business has similar characteristics.

1977: Successful Growth

Event The insurance business continues to grow at a fast pace through expansion and acquisitions. Buffett reports that in the prior 10 years, insurance premiums grew by about 600 percent, from $22 million to $151 million.

Lesson Buffett's excellent knowledge of the insurance industry helps him to identify top managers and then delegate them to run individual units. Note that insurance was not a fast-growing industry. Outstanding managers are the key to successful growth. Invest with them when you find such opportunities.

1980: Buying Shares after Prices Fall

Event Berkshire initially invested in GEICO in 1976 when GEICO was close to bankruptcy. Berkshire increases its holding in GEICO to 7.2 million shares, equal to an equity interest of about 33 percent.

Lesson Buffett explains his investments in GEICO and American Express as follows:

> GEICO's problems at that time put it in a position analogous to that of American Express in 1964 following the salad oil scandal. Both were one-of-a-kind companies, temporarily reeling from the effects of a fiscal blow that did not destroy their exceptional underlying economics. The GEICO and American Express situations, extraordinary business franchises with a localized excisable cancer (needing, to be sure, a skilled surgeon), should be distinguished from the true "turnaround" situation in which the managers expect—and need—to pull off a corporate Pygmalion.[1]

Buffett has emphasized that most turnaround candidates do not succeed. However, GEICO and American Express are exceptions because the underlying businesses were healthy. You should buy shares after a precipitous fall in prices *only* when you can assess that the company's problems are temporary.

1984: Reported Versus True Financial Results

Event Buffett describes how estimates of losses in the insurance business can be substantially different from the final tally, and, therefore, reported earnings are subject to change. In 1983, reported underwriting results, based on estimates in 1983, indicated a loss of $33 million; but a year later, corrected figures turn out to be $51 million, about 50 percent more than the original estimate.

Lesson The following story explains that when managers plan to manipulate earnings, it is not difficult.

> A man was traveling abroad when he received a call from his sister informing him that their father had died unexpectedly. It was physically impossible for the brother to get back home for the funeral, but he told his sister to take care of the funeral arrangements and to send the bill to him. After returning home, he received a bill for several thousand dollars, which he promptly paid. The following month, another bill came along for $15, and he paid that, too. Another month followed, with a similar bill. When, in the next month, a third bill for $15 was presented, he called his sister to ask what was going on. "Oh," she said. "I forgot to tell you. We buried Dad in a rented suit."[2]

Preparation of financial statements requires a large number of estimates. When analyzing a company, you should examine several years' worth of financial statements, not just the recent ones.

1985: Capital Expenditures

Event Berkshire Hathaway closes its textile operations, which was its main business when Buffett took control of the company in 1965.

Lesson Buffett writes: "It [is] inappropriate for even an exceptionally profitable company to fund an operation once it appears to have unending losses in prospect."[3] As an example, Buffett states that Burlington Industries, another textile company, unsuccessfully invested more than $200 per share on the $60 stock. He writes, "When a management with a reputation for brilliance tackles a business with a reputation for poor fundamental economics, it is the reputation of the business that remains intact."[4] When you see a company making new investments in a dying business (e.g., the auto industry in the United States in recent years), you should not invest in that company.

1986: Corporate Jets and Other Luxuries

Event In small print, Buffett writes, "We bought a corporate jet last year."[5]

Lesson Corporate jets are very expensive and cost a lot to operate and maintain, or, as Buffett puts it, "cost a lot to look at." While it seems appropriate for Buffett to acquire a corporate jet, he clearly feels uncomfortable. As Benjamin Franklin said, "So convenient a thing it is to be a reasonable creature, since it enables one to find or make a reason for everything one has a mind to do."[6] As an investor, you can learn about a company's true culture from its spending practices.

1988: Holding Period of an Investment

Event Berkshire buys 14.2 million shares of Coca-Cola for $592 million. With respect to this first major purchase of Coca-Cola stock, Buffett states that his favorite holding period is forever. He further states, "We continue to concentrate our investments in a very few companies that we try to understand well."[7] He also recalls Mae West, "Too much of a good thing can be wonderful."[8]

Lesson In about 10 years, the market value of the Coca-Cola stock holding will increase tenfold. One reason Buffett can hold investments for long periods is that he invests only in companies that he understands and that have outstanding management. With respect to Coca-Cola's CEO, Buffett writes:

> Through a truly rare blend of marketing and financial skills, Roberto [Goizueta] has maximized both the growth of the product and the rewards that this growth brings to shareholders. Normally, the CEO of a consumer products company, drawing on his natural inclinations or experience, will cause either marketing or finance to dominate the business at the expense of the other discipline. With Roberto, the mesh of marketing and finance is perfect and the result is a shareholder's dream.[9]

Excellent investment opportunities are few and far between. When you find such stocks, you should buy a lot and hold them for a long time.

1989: Looking Foolish Versus Acting Foolish

Event In 1989, two natural disasters affected the insurance industry significantly. First, Hurricane Hugo caused billions of dollars of damage in the Caribbean and the Carolinas. Second, within weeks, California was hit by an earthquake causing insured damage that was difficult to estimate, even well after the event.

Lesson Before the 1989 natural disasters, premiums in the insurance industry were inadequate. Unlike many others, Buffett stayed away from unprofitable businesses. Immediately after the earthquake, the tables were turned. Given its strong financial position, Berkshire Hathaway offered to write up to $250 million of catastrophic coverage, advertising the offer in trade publications.

As Buffett explains: "When rates carry an expectation of profit, we want to assume as much risk as is prudent. And in our case, that's a lot."[10] Taking large risks with adequate premiums is profitable in the long run but may *appear* foolish. To this, Buffett responds: "We are willing to *look* foolish as long as we don't feel we have *acted* foolishly."[11] The key lesson is to act rationally, regardless of how it appears to others.

1990: Pessimism Is Your Friend

Event   For the banking industry, 1990 was a disastrous year. Fears of a California real estate disaster caused the price of Wells Fargo stock to fall by almost 50 percent. Buffett purchased an additional 4 million shares in Wells Fargo, increasing Berkshire's holding to about 10 percent of the bank's outstanding shares.

Lesson   Buffett writes: "The most common cause of low prices is pessimism—sometimes pervasive, sometimes specific to a company or industry."[12] But you also need to be careful, Buffet cautions: "None of this means, however, that a business or stock is an intelligent purchase simply because it is unpopular; a contrarian approach is just as foolish as a follow-the-crowd strategy. What is required is thinking rather than polling. Unfortunately, Bertrand Russell's observation about life in general applies with unusual force in the financial world: Most men would rather die than think. Many do."[13] In 2008–2009, when the stock market was down by about 40 percent, Buffett writes, "When investing, pessimism is your friend, euphoria the enemy."[14]

1991: Risk

Event   Midway, Pan Am, and America West enter bankruptcy, making 1991 a disastrous year for the airline industry. Buffett estimates that Berkshire's investment of $358 million in U.S. Air had declined by 35 percent to $232 million. Only a year earlier, Buffett had written that the U.S. Air investment "should work out all right unless the industry is decimated during the next few years."[15]

Lesson   There is always risk in investing, whether you invest in airlines or AIG. It is possible to lose a significant percentage even in fixed-income securities, although they are generally less risky. There is yet another lesson about the airline industry: "Despite the huge amounts of equity capital that have been injected into it, the industry, in aggregate, has posted a net loss since its birth after Kitty Hawk,"[16] writes Buffett. After his experiences with U.S. Air, Buffett seems to have decided that investing in the airlines industry is not in his circle of competence. If you invest in your circle of competence, you are likely to avoid highly risky investments.

1992: Stock Splits

Event Berkshire's stock price crosses the $10,000 mark for the first time.

Lesson A stock price level should not be used as an indicator of potential returns. A stock split is not helpful for a long-term investor. Buffett states, "Overall, we believe our owner-related policies—including the no-split policy—have helped us assemble a body of shareholders that is the best associated with any widely held American corporation."[17] In the end, what matters is the performance of the company. Do not invest in a company just because it has had a stock split. In 2009, Berkshire announced that it would split its class B shares for 50:1 in connection with its acquisition of Burlington Northern Santa Fe. Without the split, small Burlington shareholders would not receive Berkshire shares in a tax-free exchange.

1993: Identifying Excellent CEOs

Event Buffett's admiration for Mrs. B, Nebraska Furniture Mart's CEO, is well-known. In admiration, he writes the following:

Mrs. B—Rose Blumkin—had her 100th birthday on December 3, 1993. (The candles cost more than the cake.) That was a day on which the store was scheduled to be open in the evening. Mrs. B, who works seven days a week, for however many hours the store operates, found the proper decision quite obvious: She simply postponed her party until an evening when the store was closed.

She came to the United States 77 years ago, unable to speak English and devoid of formal schooling. In 1937, she founded the Nebraska Furniture Mart with $500. Last year, the store had sales of $200 million, a larger amount by far than that recorded by any other home furnishings store in the United States. Our part in all of this began ten years ago when Mrs. B sold control of the business to Berkshire Hathaway, a deal we completed without obtaining audited financial statements, checking real estate records, or getting any warranties. In short, her word was good enough for us.

Naturally, I was delighted to attend Mrs. B's birthday. After all, she's promised to attend *my* 100th.[18]

Lesson Buffett has often emphasized the importance of a sound track record. Obviously, Mrs. B did not need a high-level university degree to run a business successfully over a long period of time. Buffett saw a great opportunity in her abilities and did not hesitate to become her partner. Invest with CEOs who have an excellent track record.

1994: Extraordinary Results in Ordinary Businesses

Event Buffett discusses the extraordinary success of Scott Fetzer, a Berkshire subsidiary that was acquired in 1986 for $315 million. He writes, "Had Scott Fetzer been on the 1993 500 list—the company's return on equity would have ranked fourth. You might expect that Scott Fetzer's success could only be explained by a cyclical peak in earnings, a monopolistic position, or leverage. But no such circumstances apply."[19] Then what does explain Scott Fetzer's success?

Lesson Buffett offers this explanation: "The reasons for Ralph's [Scott Fetzer's CEO] success are not complicated. Ben Graham taught me 45 years ago that in investing it is not necessary to do extraordinary things to get extraordinary results. In later life, I have been surprised to find that this statement holds true in business management as well. What a manager must do is to handle the basics well and not get diverted. That is precisely Ralph's formula."[20] Once again, similar to the example of Mrs. B, learning to identify excellent managers through their track record will help you a great deal in earning superior returns.

1995: Corporate Acquisitions

Event In 1995, Berkshire acquires Helzberg's Diamond Shops. In this connection, Buffett writes,

Jeff was our kind of manager. In fact, we would not have bought the business if Jeff had not been there to run it. Buying a retailer without good management is like buying the Eiffel Tower without an elevator.[21]

Lesson Unlike Buffett's acquisitions, most acquisitions do not work well because they do not come with excellent management and good underlying business economics. The mergers are often motivated by hubris so aptly explained by Peter Drucker: "Deal making beats working. Deal making is exciting and fun, and working is grubby. Running anything is primarily an enormous amount of grubby detail work ... deal making is romantic, sexy. That's why you have deals that make no sense."[22] Buffett has regularly questioned the acquisition practices of most managers, and so should you.

1996: Selling Too Early

Event Berkshire Hathaway becomes the 100 percent owner of GEICO when it purchases the shares—about 50 percent—that it did not already own. Although Buffett first purchased GEICO shares in 1951 on his personal account, he sold those shares in 1952, only to lament his decision later. He bought back into the company over the years starting in 1976.

Lesson Buffett explains that although he made a profit when he sold his GEICO shares for $15,259 in 1952, "in the next 20 years, the GEICO stock I sold grew in value to about $1.3 million, which taught me a lesson about the inadvisability of selling a stake in an identifiably wonderful company."[23] On a personal account, I first purchased my Berkshire shares in 1987 and sold within a year, only to regret that decision later. I have since purchased more of Berkshire shares, and it is currently my largest holding. Do not sell a good stock for a small profit.

1996: Hiring Practices

Event The 79-year-old founder and CEO of FlightSafety International, Al Ueltschi, sells his company to Berkshire Hathaway. Al has had a life-long affair with aviation and actually piloted Charles Lindbergh. Buffett explains his hiring practices as follows:

An observer might conclude from our hiring practices that Charlie and I were traumatized early in life by an EEOC bulletin on age discrimination. The real explanation, however is self-interest. It's difficult to teach a new dog old tricks. The many Berkshire mangers who are past 70 hit home runs today at the same pace that long ago gave them reputations as young slugging sensations. Therefore, to get a job with us, just employ the tactic of the 76-year-old who persuaded a dazzling beauty of 25 to marry him. "How did you ever get her to accept?" asked his envious contemporaries. The comeback: "I told her I was 86."[24]

Lesson What matters is the performance of the individual, and only on that basis should a person be judged, not on the basis of age. As Buffett further explains, "Al may be 79, but he looks and acts about 55. He will run operations just as he has in the past: We never fool with success. I have told him though we don't believe in splitting Berkshire's stock, we will split his age 2-for-1 when he hits 100."[25] Ignore age and other prejudices when evaluating those with whom you should invest.

1997: Patience

Event Berkshire reports a large nontraditional investment of $4.6 billion in long-term zero-coupon treasury bonds. If interest rates were to rise, Berkshire would lose heavily; and if the interest rates were to fall, Berkshire would make outsized gains. Why did Buffett make such an unconventional investment?

Lesson Buffett first explains the need for discipline when there is exuberance in the stock market.

Under those circumstances, we try to exert a Ted Williams kind of discipline. In his book, *The Science of Hitting*, Ted explains that he carved the strike zone into 77 cells, each the size of a baseball. Swinging only at balls in his "best" cell, he knew, would allow him to bat .400; reaching for balls in his "worst" spot, the low outside corner of the strike zone, would reduce him to .230. In other words, waiting for the fat pitch would mean a trip to the Hall of Fame; swinging indiscriminately would mean a ticket to the minors.[26]

Buffett decided not to swing—that is, not to make additional investments in the stock market in 1997. However, he also makes it clear that
"just standing there, day after day, with a bat on my shoulder is not my
idea of fun."[27] Patience, although not easy, is necessary for success in
investing. When stock price appears high relative to fundamentals, stay
away from investing.

1999: Taking Responsibility

Event Berkshire has the worst absolute performance of Buffett's tenure
to date and, compared with the S&P 500 index, the worst relative performance as well. Buffett gives himself a D in capital allocation.

Lesson It is an everyday matter to see corporate managers blaming
others when their company's performance is below par. If not other
individuals, the guilty party is frequently the climate or the interest rates.
Instead, with respect to the 1999 results, Buffett writes:

> Even Inspector Clouseau could find last year's guilty party: your Chair-
> man. My performance reminds me of the quarterback whose report
> card showed four Fs and a D but who nonetheless had an understand-
> ing coach. "Son," he drawled, "I think you're spending too much time
> on that one subject." My "one subject" is capital allocation, and my
> grade for 1999 most assuredly is a D.[28]

Do not blame others. When you take responsibility for your failed
investments, as Buffett often does, it is easier to learn from your mistakes
and avoid repeating them in the future.

2000: Selling in Euphoria

Event Buffett mentions that the "long-term prospect for equities in
general is far from exciting."[29]

Lesson With hindsight, one can conclude that Buffett should have
sold some of the holdings before the stock market started to decline

in 2000. The Coca-Cola shares traded at prices as high as $85 per share in 1998. Ten years later, in 2009, Coca-Cola stock price is about $45 per share. As Buffett has recognized, the stock market does become euphoric periodically, and the main lesson is that an investor should sell in those circumstances.

2001: Not Losing Focus When Disaster Strikes

Event On September 11, 2001, terrorists attack the World Trade Center in New York and the Pentagon in Washington, DC.

Lesson Buffett estimated that insurance losses surrounding the events of September 11 were $2.2 billion, one of the largest in Berkshire history. Even Berkshire did not anticipate a terrorist attack and had not protected itself from such a megadisaster. On September 26, he wrote to his managers: "What should you be doing in running your business? Just what you always do . . . almost all operating decisions that made sense a month ago make sense today."[30] Essentially, Buffett suggests that such disasters could actually present opportunities for managers to expand their businesses.

2002: Financial Weapons of Mass Destruction

Event Using Enron as an example, Buffett discusses possibilities of huge losses from derivative contracts and his decision to close down the derivative business that came with the acquisition of General Re in 1998.

Lesson Buffett writes, "We try to be alert to any sort of megacatastrophe risk, and that our posture may make us unduly apprehensive about the burgeoning quantities of long-term derivatives contracts." He was remarkably prescient in stating, "In our view, derivatives are financial weapons of mass destruction, carrying dangers that, while now latent, are potentially lethal."[31] Investors in large companies like Enron, WorldCom, AIG, Bear Stearns, Lehman Brothers, Freddie Mac, and Fannie Mae lost all or most of their investments because these companies indulged heavily in derivatives that they could have done without. The important lesson for an average investor is that one should avoid investing in companies with difficult-to-understand business models or financial statements.

2008–2009: Market Crashes

Event During a span of six months from September 2008 to March 2009, Berkshire stock class A experiences prices as high as $150,000 per share and as low as $75,000, representing a decline of 50 percent. The market as a whole experiences a similar downturn.

Lesson As Buffett points out: "Amid this bad news, however, never forget that our country has faced far worse travails in the past. . . . Without fail, however, we've overcome them."[32] This is not the first time that Berkshire's stock price has gone down by 50 percent. It has happened three other times since Buffett took control over the company in 1965. In recent years, from 1998 to 2000, Berkshire's stock price dropped by about 45 percent, from $79,000 to $44,000. Berkshire was a good buy after such a decline. While I recommend that you do your homework, late 2009, in my opinion, is still a good time to buy Berkshire stock and stocks in other conservatively financed, prominent companies.

Conclusions

From its first acquisition of two small insurance companies in 1967, Berkshire Hathaway has expanded its insurance business and become one of the largest insurance operations in the world. The events and milestones of the past 44 years discussed in this chapter reflect many of Buffett's decisions and practices. His long and successful track record and his willingness to share his thoughts make it possible for us to study his ideas in depth. The rest of the book is devoted to developing a good understanding of the investing principles that Buffett both espouses and exemplifies and why those principles work.

Part Two

BUFFETT INVESTING = VALUE + GROWTH

The phrase *value investing* popularly means an investing style based on financial ratios such as price-to-earnings or market-to-book. By contrast, in *growth investing,* one seeks to discover companies that are likely to grow at a fast pace in the future. In Chapters 3 and 4, I discuss value investing and growth investing, respectively. Both investing styles have merits. Chapter 5 focuses on the concept of intrinsic value, the value you assign to a stock based on its assets and earnings. In Chapter 6, I explain how we can best learn from Buffett by viewing him as an integrator of both value and growth investing principles.

Chapter 3

Value Investing—It's Like Buying Christmas Cards in January

[W]e had learned from Ben Graham that the key to successful investing was the purchase of shares in good businesses when the market prices were at a large discount from underlying business values.[1]

—Warren Buffett

I f you love bargains, you will love value investing. *Value investing* is regarded as the cornerstone of Buffett's investing strategy. Value investing is similar to buying something while it's on sale. An everyday example of value investing is buying Christmas cards in January at about half the price of the same cards a month earlier, in December. If you buy Christmas cards in January and use them the following Christmas, you will have implicitly earned a return of about 100 percent on your investment. If you tend to come up with such ideas, implement them, and compute your potential returns, you are a natural value investor. For value investing in the stock market, you buy when prices are low relative to fundamentals (e.g., earnings and book value), and then wait for prices to move up.

Most stocks do not sell for bargain prices, just as most items in the local mall do not sell for bargain prices. Good deals are not available every day. An investor must be patient and wait for such opportunities to arrive. You need patience to wait for a truly outstanding value opportunity, and you need even more patience after you purchase a stock. It often takes time for price to reflect value. In the case of Christmas card investing, you need to wait about a year. In the stock market, the wait is often even longer.

The stock market also has complications that do not arise in Christmas card investing. We know that Christmas arrives faithfully every December and that an opportunity to invest in Christmas cards arrives soon after. On the other hand, good opportunities in the stock market do not announce their arrival. Nor can you always anticipate the industry or geographic location in which opportunities might arise. Furthermore, you will never know for sure that an opportunity is staring at you. There is no guarantee: You always have some chance of ending up with a bad outcome. While value investing is not as easy as it looks at first glance, you can become a good value investor with time as long as you carefully follow the philosophy developed by Benjamin Graham.

Value Investing and Two Essential Principles

Benjamin Graham developed the core principles for investing in financial securities. To the best of my knowledge, he never used the term *value investing* to describe his approach. From what I can determine, he did not give any name to the investing principles he developed. No matter what he called it, he is generally known as the father of value investing. Much has been written about value investing in the past few decades, but authors define it in different ways. The common elements across various definitions from both practitioners and academics suggest that value investing implies an investing style that emphasizes using financial ratios such as the price-to-earnings or market-to-book ratios. The term *value investing* is also commonly invoked when one does not invest in fast-growing companies or sticks to conservatively financed companies. A value investor is someone who focuses first and foremost on preserving capital. Earning high returns is desirable but secondary.

How effective is value investing as a means for generating high returns? Does this style generate above-market returns? Buffett's inordinate success is generally attributed to value investing. However, as I will discuss in the next few chapters, Buffett's investing style does not fit the popular, but limiting, definition of value investing. Furthermore, we should not rely on evidence from a few success stories to conclude that value investing generates high returns. Anecdotal evidence does not prove a proposition; it can only offer examples. Without the scientific evidence provided by research, we can be incorrectly convinced by anecdotes. Academic research, as we will see in this chapter, strongly supports value investing, and thus, there is more than anecdotal evidence to support the merits of value investing. But for now, let's focus on the two most significant principles emerging from the value investing literature, primarily from Graham's voluminous writings and in particular from his famous book *The Intelligent Investor*.[2] I explain why these principles work and what makes them important.

Principle 1: Price Should Not Be High Relative to a Company's Average Earnings over a Number of Years

The first principle essentially relates to the most often discussed ratio in the financial world, the price-to-earnings ratio, or simply the P/E ratio. The market P/E ratio rose from 18 in the early 1990s to about 30 in the early 2000s as interest rates declined steadily during the same period. As interest rates increased starting in the early 2000s, the market P/E ratio declined back to below 20. During the mid-1970s to early 1980s, the market P/E ratio went down to as low as 7 to 9 because of high interest rates and economic slowdown. In terms of specific numbers, after evaluating the current conditions in 1972, Benjamin Graham states, "We suggest that this [P/E] limit be set at 25 times average earnings, and not more than 20 times those of the last 12-month period."[3]

There are two lessons that we can learn from history. First, it is generally a good idea to avoid investing in stocks when the market P/E ratio is high, say higher than 20. Second, we can extend the same argument to individual stocks, with one caveat. You should examine a company's P/E ratio over a number of years, by looking, perhaps, at the price in relation to the past five to 10 years' earnings. If you use only recent earnings,

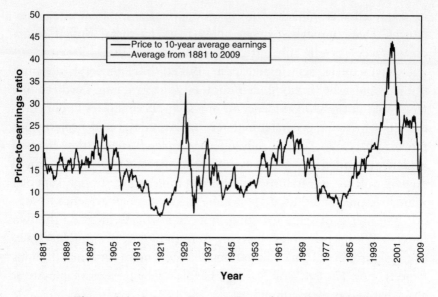

Figure 3.1 Price-to-Earnings Ratio from 1881 to 2009

a company may have a low P/E ratio because earnings are temporarily high, or it may have a high P/E ratio because earnings are temporarily low.

Figure 3.1 shows the history of the market's P/E ratio where earnings are defined as the average of the past 10 years' earnings. The average ratio over the entire time is 16.3.[4] The latest ratio of 18.9 at the end of October 2009 is slightly higher than the average. You can see that when the ratio is very high, it reverses toward the average and frequently goes substantially below the average. Just because the ratio is currently near the average does not imply that it cannot go any lower or higher. Overall, this chart suggests that if the ratio is very high, as it was in 2005–2007, it is not a good time to invest. On the other hand, when the ratio is very low, it is a good time to invest.

Several successful investors have used the P/E ratio as the core of their investment strategy, including John Neff, who is well known for successfully managing billions of dollars through the Vanguard Windsor Fund for more than 30 years—a very long time in the mutual fund management business. Very few mutual fund managers have managed large portfolios successfully for such a long period. Why was John Neff so successful? "We relied on relentless applications of low P/E sympathies, abetted by attention to fundamentals and a liberal dose of common sense."[5]

Investors may also use other valuation ratios such as the market-to-book or the S&P 500 earnings as a fraction of gross domestic product (GDP), which Buffett has referenced in his writings. At the aggregate level, it does not matter which ratio you examine. The results are similar. At the individual stock level, whether you use the P/E ratio or the market-to-book ratio or another ratio entirely, you should depend on the nature of the company's business and the availability of suitable data.

Principle 2: Each Company Selected Should Be Large, Prominent, and Conservatively Financed

This principle is straight from Graham. He recommends investing in large and prominent companies because it is not easy to evaluate small and less-known companies. Their financial statements are less reliable, and they may be more easily affected by unforeseen circumstances. In other words, the risk involved in investing in small and less-known companies is high. "Where should I start to look for worthwhile common stocks?" you may ask. Buffett often recommends that an average investor may start with the *Value Line* sheets. *Value Line* usually does not follow small companies. Thus, the first criterion of investing in large companies is easily met. *Value Line* also provides a stock's historical record over the prior 20 years. The availability of a long track record is useful because you can decide whether the company is prominent. You may read the *Value Line* description of the company and then decide whether you want to conduct additional research.

Regarding Graham's position that a company should be conservatively financed, it is possible to discuss at great length what exactly this term means. However, whether the company is conservatively financed will be immediately clear from a cursory examination of its short- and long-term debt levels in relation to its total assets, or its debt-to-equity ratio. To make life simple for investors, *Value Line* ranks stocks on a scale of safety, from one to five. Coca-Cola, a major holding of Berkshire Hathaway, usually has the highest safety ranking of one. A large, established company such as Coca-Cola, with a market capitalization of about $100 billion at the end of 2008, has only about $3 billion of long-term debt. It is not difficult to conclude that the company is conservatively financed.

Berkshire Hathaway has always been conservatively financed. Why is conservatism important? Because it is difficult to predict when funds will be suddenly needed for profitable investments or for claims. A conservatively financed company can raise funds in short order, and a liquidity crisis in the economy would not affect the company. For example, in 2008, large and prominent (but *not* conservatively financed) companies such as Citicorp, Goldman Sachs, and General Electric suffered significantly, and several others were merged, declared bankruptcy, or were on the verge of bankruptcy. On the other hand, Berkshire Hathaway used this as an opportunity to invest in companies such as Goldman Sachs and General Electric. Thus, in the long run, conservatively financed companies are likely to produce higher returns as they are in a position to take advantage of such opportunities.

While I consider these two principles or guidelines to be most important, they are principles and not specific rules. For example, not all large companies may lend themselves to sound financial analysis because of the complexity of their business. It may not be easy to define which company is prominent and which is not. Thus, you will have to use a fair amount of judgment in selecting your investments even in your application of these principles.

Other Helpful Guidelines for Value Investing

To help you with narrowing your field of inquiry, I discuss some of the more common concepts that Buffett and other value investors have relied on over the decades, concepts that have withstood the test of time.

A Sharp Decline in the Stock Market

A sharp decline in the stock market generally presents a good investment opportunity. In mid-1973, after the market had declined dramatically,

Berkshire Hathaway bought a large stake of 1.9 million shares in the Washington Post Company (WPC). You might think that only Buffett could see that the company offered such a good opportunity. He suggested just the opposite: "Calculating the price/value ratio required no unusual insights. Most security analysts, media brokers, and media executives would have estimated WPC's intrinsic value at $400 to $500 million, just as we did. And its $100 million stock market value was published daily for all to see."[6] In 2009, even after a 50 percent decline in its price in recent years, WPC is trading at about $400 per share, and it has paid regular dividends. Berkshire's investment translates into an annualized return in excess of 15 percent per year including dividends, an excellent return compared to about 9 percent in the market during this period.

Depending on your level of risk tolerance, it is reasonable to argue that you should increase your investment in the stock market whenever there is a 20 percent correction from reasonable price levels. It is not the price decline per se that is important; it is the price in relation to earnings, as the second principle mentioned earlier requires. Perhaps a market P/E of about 12 suggests opportunities based on the fact that the long-run market P/E average is about 16. Of course, such an investment should not be for the short term because the decline could continue for a considerable time. You should certainly gauge the valuations of the market as a whole in relation to its fundamentals. If the decline continues, you may think about increasing your investment. Thus, in some cases, you will have to wait a long while for the stock market to come back. Patience, once again, is a prerequisite for earning superior returns.

In 2008, the S&P 500 index declined by about 37 percent and even Berkshire Hathaway's stock price declined by 32 percent. Are there opportunities in this market? Buffett thinks so. In an op-ed article in the *New York Times,* October 17, 2008, he wrote: "I've been buying American stocks. This is my personal account I'm talking about, in which I previously owned nothing but United States government bonds." Of course, no one—not even Warren Buffett—can time the stock market perfectly. Since October 17, when the S&P 500 index stood at 940, it declined to as low as 676, or a decline of 28 percent, by early March 2009. These are trying times for investors all over the world. It is difficult to be optimistic in recessionary times. However, "when investing, pessimism is your friend, euphoria the enemy."[7]

The Industry That Leads the Decline

The stock market decline in 2008 and 2009 was pervasive across many industries, although financial stocks have been hit especially hard. Such pervasive slides are uncommon. Usually, a 10 percent to 20 percent decline is led by one or a few industries. In those instances, the industry that leads the decline may lead the recovery and offer early investing opportunities. For example, in the fall of 1998, Russia faced a payment crisis and defaulted on its debt. The U.S. stock market went down by about 20 percent, led by the financial and technology sectors. The same sectors then provided the most gains in the following year. In general, when a market decline is led by one or two industrial sectors, it is worthwhile to pay special attention to good companies in those sectors. Even in these situations, it is important to keep in mind that you should invest only if you are comfortable with the fundamentals of the company.

During the Russian default crisis, the stock price of Merrill Lynch declined from a high of $102 per share in July 1998 to $42 per share in October 1998, a 60 percent drop. In my view, it was a substantial decline and offered an opportunity for higher returns in the future. The following year, Merrill Lynch's stock price went up by about 100 percent. Merrill Lynch's business was not difficult to analyze at the time. (Its business became more complex several years later.) It was not the only company that offered this wonderful opportunity. You could have bought into any of the well-known financial companies and done well. The average decline in the well-known stocks of Citigroup, Chase Manhattan, and Bank of America was about 50 percent. And each one of them served up a 100 percent return in 1999. Although it is not easy to time the market, opportunities like these are large enough to offer a substantial margin of safety. During 1998, Berkshire purchased about 1 million additional shares of American Express, increasing its holding to 50.5 million shares. The decision to purchase was probably influenced by the decline in the share price of American Express. During the 2008–2009 market crash, American Express, once again, went down from $60 per share to about $10 per share, only to rebound to $40 per share within a year.

Watch Out for Temptations

Value investing does not suggest that one should invest indiscriminately when a company's stock price declines and the stock looks cheap relative to its price a few months earlier. If you start buying things every time you walk into a store that is having a 50 percent off sale, you will soon be in debt or bankruptcy. All items on sale are not true investment bargains but are instead invitations to collect junk, only to be sold at your next garage sale for a fraction of what you paid. Beware of these tempting, yet misleading, so-called bargains.

Kmart has often appeared as a bargain stock. The rise of Wal-Mart as a successful retailer led to the decline of Kmart's stock price in the early 1990s. At every stage of Kmart's price decline, the stock appeared to be a bargain if you looked at its P/E ratio. After almost a decade, the stock price was only about $9 per share, having declined from a high of $27 in the early 1990s. It continued to look inexpensive relative to its earnings per share—and unfortunately, I invested in Kmart. I proved Graham right: "Observation over many years has taught us that the chief losses to investors come from the purchase of *low-quality* securities at times of favorable conditions."[8] During the time that Kmart's stock price was declining, the market went up about 300 percent, and Wal-Mart was a phenomenal success, amassing a gain of about 700 percent. If I had made a few trips to Kmart stores and dug deeper into its financial statements, it would have occurred to me that Kmart was a low-quality company relative to Wal-Mart. And low-quality companies such as Kmart do not survive. In 2002, Kmart went bankrupt.

Often, companies get into trouble and their stock prices fall significantly. They appear to be good turnaround candidates. Most turnarounds, however, do not end up successful, and you should not be tempted to invest in them. Thus, a low price is not a good indicator for investing. Outstanding turnaround stories, such as that of Chrysler in the 1970s, give investors hope that other companies in trouble may turn around in the same manner. However, unless you are in a position to see that the turnaround is indeed highly probable, you should not invest in turnarounds.

The principle of avoiding turnarounds is like avoiding Christmas tree (as opposed to Christmas card) investing. Toward the end of December,

Christmas trees are available at throwaway prices, if not for free. From an investment perspective, buying a Christmas tree at the end of the season is a waste of money. The price is low, but the value is even lower. In a few days, when the tree has turned brown and shed its needles, it will have to be thrown away.

Does Value Investing Really Work?

After this discussion of value investing, you might ask if there is reliable evidence in support of value investing. Academics have asked this question for a long time because they are usually not satisfied by anecdotal evidence. Buffett has addressed this issue head-on. Speaking at Columbia University in 1984, he presented the performance records of seven disciples of Benjamin Graham. He also included the performance of two pension funds for which he had helped select managers with value orientation. The results show that value investors do very well. Buffett writes: "[I]f you found any really extraordinary concentration of success, you might want to see if you could identify concentrations of unusual characteristics that might be causal factors. Scientific inquiry naturally follows such a pattern."[9] In this case, the main common characteristic was the value investing approach that all the Graham disciples had followed.

It is not surprising that Buffett's findings did not have any effect on the general academic opinion, at least until recently. Academics usually rely on evidence from very large data sets and are convinced only when a strategy has been shown to work over long periods. In other words, an academic study would conclude in favor of an investment strategy only if even a monkey (computer) could replicate the strategy. In my opinion, this is not necessarily a very good approach to advance our knowledge, but it is the academic standard. Nevertheless, recent academic research seems to have turned the corner in favor of value investing.

Academic Research Evidence

Academic research is based on analyzing large sets of data using extensive computer power. We should keep in mind that it is almost impossible to program a computer to identify what Benjamin Graham calls "large, prominent, and conservatively financed" companies or identify high-quality management. For example, how would a computer know that the CEO of Berkshire Hathaway is a good manager? For this reason, qualitative variables are all but ignored in most academic studies or their treatment is simplistic. In defense of academic studies, the good news is that those studies meet the highest possible standards of any studies of large data sets, and everything about the methodology is clearly laid out. Hence, they do provide us reliable statistical results to ponder.

Research has shown that even simple value investment strategies, such as investing in low P/E stocks, produce outstanding returns over a number of years. These results have been replicated by many researchers over different periods and are, thus, reliable. Therefore, it can be concluded that an investor who implements simple value investment strategies and uses other discerning qualitative variables should obtain even better returns. Graham points out that "[an] investor should start with the low-multiplier [i.e., low P/E] idea, but add other quantitative and qualitative requirements thereto in making up his portfolio."[10] Many apparent low P/E stocks such as Kmart and Bethlehem Steel would not have been selected by careful value investors because the companies were neither prominent nor conservatively financed. In the next section, I discuss two sets of studies. I first present a discussion of studies that compare performances of portfolios constructed by high versus low P/E stocks, and then I compare performances of portfolios constructed by high market-to-book versus low market-to-book stocks.

Performance of High versus Low P/E Stocks

The most prominent of recent studies on value investing was conducted by Professors Joseph Lakonishok from the University of Illinois and Andrei Shleifer and Robert Vishny from the University of Chicago.[11] They formed portfolios based on P/E and several other ratios to examine annual stock returns from 1963 to 1990. In Table 3.1, I present results from a similar analysis I conducted that includes return results until 2007. The table first shows returns to 10 different portfolios of stocks formed annually on the basis of P/E ratios. Portfolio 1 is composed of 10 percent of the stocks with the highest P/E ratios, or the extreme-glamour stocks.[12] Similarly, Portfolio 10 is composed of stocks with the lowest P/E ratios, or the extreme-value stocks.

Table 3.1   Evidence That Value Investing Works

	Returns on Portfolios of Stocks Based on Price-to-Earnings (P/E) Ratios		Returns on Portfolios of Stocks Based on Market-to-Book (M/B) Ratios	
	Portfolio number	Return (% per year)	Portfolio number	Return (% per year)
Highest P/E stocks	1	9.4	Highest M/B stocks	1	9.5
	2	10.4		2	11.5
	3	12.1		3	12.3
	4	11.8		4	12.6
	5	11.3		5	12.0
	6	12.9		6	12.5
	7	14.4		7	13.5
	8	14.2		8	13.5
Lowest P/E stocks	9	13.8	Lowest M/B stocks	9	14.5
	10	15.9		10	16.0

The portfolios of the lowest P/E stocks beat the portfolios of the highest P/E stocks by a considerable margin. The corresponding returns are 15.9 percent versus 9.4 percent per year. Lakonishok and colleagues show that over a five-year period after formation of the portfolios, the extreme-value (lowest P/E) stocks earn a 138.8 percent return in comparison to a 71.1 percent return for the extreme-glamour (highest P/E) stocks. Thus, over a five-year period, the lowest P/E stocks outperform the highest P/E stocks by a factor of almost two to one. Even if you did not invest in only the lowest P/E portfolio, the performance is generally better for the lower P/E stocks than for the higher P/E stocks. These results support Benjamin Graham's ideas on value investing, which should encourage you to follow his approach.

Performance of High versus Low Market-to-Book Stocks

The accounting value of a company's common stock as reported on the balance sheet is known as the *book value*. It is based on accounting rules and procedures. On the other hand, the price per share, or the *market value*, receives a lot of attention and is determined by the market. Generally, if a company's earnings are expected to increase at a high rate, the market price is substantially higher than the book value. An investor should ask: "How high should the market price be in comparison to the book value in order to invest?" There is no general formula to answer this question. Therefore, an investor should examine the historical ratios of the same firm as well as the ratios of other firms in the same industry. If the market price is substantially higher than the book value, it is likely that the price is too high for a value investor to choose the stock. On the other hand, if the market price is not very high, the value investor should look favorably and possibly invest in the stock—keeping in mind Graham's view that the company should be large, prominent, and conservatively financed.

The results of a comprehensive study conducted by Eugene Fama and Kenneth French of the University of Chicago support the idea that investing in low market-to-book ratio stocks results in higher returns.[13] Fama and French examined monthly returns for a large number of stocks from July 1963 to December 1990, a period of more than 27 years. I replicate their analysis using recent data, and those results are presented in Table 3.1. The extreme-value portfolio includes 10 percent of the lowest market-to-book stocks, whereas the extreme-glamour portfolio consists of 10 percent of the highest market-to-book stocks. The difference in returns across the two extreme decile portfolios is about 6 percent. Using the market-to-book metric, Lakonishok and colleagues also report results for a five-year strategy in which the stocks are held for five years once the portfolios are formed. They find that for a five-year holding period, the extreme-value portfolio earns 146.2 percent as opposed to only 56.0 percent for the extreme-glamour portfolio. The conclusion from these studies is that the value investment strategy works well enough that you should be able to beat most of the professional money managers who focus on short-term results.

The Power of Multiple Variables

Beyond the P/E strategy or the market-to-book strategy, researchers have examined portfolios formed on the basis of several other variables. In particular, portfolio formations based on cash-flow-to-price and growth in past sales or assets support the value investing approach. It is better to buy high cash-flow-to-price than low cash-flow-to-price stocks, and similarly, it is better to buy stocks with low past growth in sales than high past growth in sales. In addition, when two ratios are used simultaneously, the results are even stronger.

Using two variables (e.g., growth in sales and P/E), Lakonishok and colleagues form nine stock portfolios. The stocks are independently sorted, in ascending order, into three groups of bottom 30 percent, middle 40 percent, and top 30 percent based on each of the two variables. Returns presented are compounded five-year post-formation returns and assume annual rebalancing of these nine portfolios. The important conclusion from this analysis is that a value investment strategy based jointly on past performance (growth in sales) and expected future performance (P/E or market-to-book ratio) produces higher returns than strategies based exclusively on one variable, such as the P/E ratio.

Frequently Asked Questions

Any investing strategy that has been shown to work should be looked at more carefully through probing questions. In this section, I discuss three frequently asked questions, which are relevant whenever an investment strategy is being evaluated. This discussion should help you better appreciate the evidence and help you think about evaluating other strategies that you develop yourself.

How Long Does It Take for Value Investing to Yield Superior Returns?

The results show that while returns are not outstanding in the first year after the portfolios are formed, they are not discouraging. The value strategy does work in the first year, but the difference of about 4 percent to 6 percent (depending on the study) is not remarkable. In subsequent years, the difference is larger. Lakonishok and colleagues show that by the fifth year, the difference is almost 8 percent per year, which is substantially larger than the first-year figure.

These results show that it takes several years of patience to benefit fully from the value strategy. An investor needs to be extremely patient after the portfolio is formed. The analyses performed are based on the assumption that the portfolios are not balanced frequently. One important point to remember is that if an individual stock in the portfolio goes up in price and no longer qualifies as a low P/E stock, it should not be sold immediately. It should be held at least until such time as the entire portfolio is reevaluated. By no means am I suggesting that you should put all your hard-earned money in such a strategy in one go. As with any strategy, you should slowly learn the ins and outs, invest a little at a time, and develop your skills.

One nice side effect of this analysis is that once a portfolio is fully formed, you need not monitor the portfolio on a regular basis. Ideally, the investor should not come back to evaluate the portfolio for several years. I have often described this strategy as "less effort is better than more effort," or, succinctly, "less is more." A value investor should spend more time at the beach than at the office. Is value investing really as easy as it sounds? Yes, it is, but it won't be if you do not have the psychological resolve to refrain from touching the portfolio for a long time. To develop the psychological resolve, you probably need to analyze by yourself the historical data of the stocks in your portfolio to become comfortable with their past performance and the results presented here.

Such an analysis will also make you more comfortable with the value strategy. Then, you will indeed enjoy the time you save by not watching your portfolio constantly. Overall, to truly benefit from the value investment strategy, you should *not underestimate* the effort needed to learn about the strategy. You need to practice a lot. If it were possible to develop the psychological resolve by reading a few articles or books, enough investors would have followed the value investment strategy to make its benefits go away. That prompts the question: Do you have the right temperament for value investing? There is only one way to find out. Practice.

Are the P/E and Other Value Strategies Likely to Work in the Future?

An investor should also ask or think about whether a strategy that has worked in the past will continue to work in the future. No one can guarantee that. However, given that people generally get excited about glamour stocks and new investors continually come to the market, such strategies *are* likely to work in the future. As mentioned before, enough people will lack the psychological resolve to hold the same portfolio and not trade often. David Dreman wrote a book in 1977 that explains the P/E strategy in detail. Before that, Graham and Dodd discussed this topic in their books. At all these points, a reader would have wondered if the strategy would work in the future. As shown by Lakonishok and colleagues' research, a reader would have done very well indeed if he or she had adopted the value strategy even after the publication of the Dreman book. Dreman eventually wrote another book, published in 1998, that confirmed his earlier findings.[14]

Clearly, there will be years in which the P/E or other value investment strategies will not work. The investor has to have patience in those years and remain invested. Another main problem lies in the fact that if you were to examine the types of stocks that are in the extreme-value portfolios, you would find them highly unattractive. Often, the so-called extreme-value stocks defined in these studies are small and have high financial leverage. Thus, even these academic studies do not do full justice to what Graham proposes you should do as outlined in the principles discussed earlier. Overall, it is gratifying that Graham's principles are vindicated by modern academic work. If you are a value investor, you may continue to practice your strategy and try to make it better by reading Buffett and other disciples of Graham.

Are Value Investment Strategies Riskier?

This is a legitimate question because, as the old saying goes, if a deal looks to be too good to be true, it probably is. The deals explained in the previous section in terms of value investment strategies seem to be too good to be true. A thoughtful investor needs to take into account the possibility that the reason that value investment strategies offer such excellent returns is that they are riskier. If that were true, a scientific inquiry would show that. If value investment strategies were more risky and produced high returns, the investor should at least be aware of that possibility and, indeed, be more careful.

Benjamin Graham addressed the issue of risk in his book *Intelligent Investor*. He states that "if a group of well-selected common-stock investments shows a satisfactory overall return, as measured through a fair number of years, then this group of investments has proved to be safe."[15]

Lakonishok and colleagues address the notion of risk by examining five-year returns to portfolios formed in each year starting in 1968. In a five-year holding period, the average difference between the returns on the extreme value and glamour portfolios is 84.2 percent.[16] What is also remarkable is that in each five-year period for which this study was conducted (1968 to 1985), an investor would have been better off using a value strategy. In other words, it does not matter when you start on the value investment strategy as long as you wait at least five years before you compare the results of a value investment strategy against other strategies. Furthermore, Lakonishok and colleagues also show that while value investing does somewhat better during the down-market months, it does not do appreciably worse in the up-market months. Overall, evidence shows that value investing does not expose an investor to excess risk in the long run.

The modern risk-based models in the academic literature are unable to explain why value investment strategies are superior to others. The most commonly used academic model, popularly known as the Sharpe, Lintner, and Black (SLB) model, describes beta as the most appropriate risk measure. As I mentioned before, Fama and French show that the results cannot be explained using the risk measure beta. They state: "We are forced to conclude that the SLB model does not describe the last 50 years of average stock returns."

There is no reliable evidence to prove that the traditional value investing strategies are riskier than investing in the stock market as a whole. Value investing yields higher returns because these strategies are contrarian to the behavior of the typical investor.[17]

Conclusions

The basic idea behind value investing is to purchase a stock at a sensible price using benchmarks such as earnings, assets, dividends, and others that you may develop. In addition, the company should be conservatively financed. A number of scientific studies show that even the use of easy-to-follow basic financial ratios can reward you well.

Value investing strategies probably work because so many investors, some of whom may even start investing according to value investing criteria, abandon their disciplined approach and give in to the attraction of glamour stocks. The value investor needs to have sufficient patience to investigate the company and also to wait for a few years for the strategy to work. Many investors probably do not have the patience. If human behavior is not likely to change, superior returns will continue to flow to those who invest based on fundamentals, have patience, and do not give in to the latest fads. So, you have to ask yourself a difficult question. Are you really any different from the average person who claims to be a value investor but fails to practice the basic principles? *Well, are you?*

Chapter 4

Growth Investing

[T]he greatest investment reward comes to those who by good luck or good sense find the occasional company that over the years can grow in sales and profits far more than the industry as a whole.[1]

—*Philip Fisher*

Warren Buffett freely acknowledges that Philip Fisher's teachings influenced his investment philosophy. Fisher's philosophy, usually referred to as *growth investing,* is based on finding outstanding companies and staying with them through all the fluctuations of a gyrating market. Growth investing is investing in stocks of companies whose earnings are expected to grow at a higher than normal rate over a long time, not only for the next quarter or the next year.

When people think of growth stocks, they usually think of Microsoft, Intel, Cisco, and others. While many of the growth stocks come from high-tech industries, not all of them do. Coca-Cola, Wal-Mart, and Starbucks are but a few examples of non-high–tech growth stocks. Thus, investing in the high-tech sector is not synonymous with growth investing. Buffett invested in Coca-Cola when it was more of a growth stock than a value stock.

Coca-Cola as a Growth Stock

At the end of 2008, Coca-Cola was the single largest common stock holding in Berkshire's portfolio, amounting to 16 percent of the common stock portfolio. Most of the purchases were made in 1988 and 1989. At the end of 1988, Coca-Cola's book value per share was $1.07, whereas the stock price was $5.70 (split adjusted), giving it a market-to-book (M/B) ratio of 5.32. Also, from the price-to-earnings (P/E) perspective, Coca-Cola was about 35 percent more expensive than an average stock in the S&P 500 at the time (16.8 for Coke compared with 12.4 for the S&P 500). Prior to Buffett's purchase, the stock price had gone up 200 percent from 1978 to 1988. Buffett did not buy Coca-Cola stock because it was inexpensive relative to its earnings or book value or because its price had fallen significantly owing to some problem at the company.

In Table 4.1, I present Coca-Cola's earnings per share and book value per share to examine its historical growth before Buffett decided to purchase the stock. Because of frequent share repurchases by Coca-Cola, the growth in unadjusted book value is substantially understated. To account for this, the last column presents the growth in Coca-Cola's book value per share after accounting for the company's repurchases of its own shares.

During the 10 years prior to Buffett's purchase, Coca-Cola's earnings per share grew at the rate of 11.1 percent, and book value grew at the rate of 10.7 percent. Coca-Cola's earnings-per-share growth rate was impressive: Earnings for the S&P 500 firms in the same period grew at the rate of only 7.1 percent. Therefore, Coca-Cola's earnings grew almost 50 percent faster than those for the S&P 500 firms. Its stock price grew similarly, as mentioned earlier. Coca-Cola at that time already had a proven track record, and, obviously, a stock like that does not trade at a low P/E or M/B ratio. An investor would buy a stock like Coca-Cola only if he were convinced of its continued growth.

When an investor buys a stock primarily because of his conviction that a company would grow for many years in the future, he is a growth investor. Buffett's purchase of Coca-Cola seemed to be the result of a growth investing strategy. It worked out well for Berkshire. Many investors and writers think that when value investing works, growth

Table 4.1 Growth in Coca-Cola's Earnings and Book Value per Share before Berkshire Purchased the Stock

Year	Earnings per share	Percent growth in earnings per share	Book value per share as stated	Percent growth in book value per share	Growth in book value per share after adjusting for the accounting effects of share repurchases
1979	$1.13	11.9%	$5.18	10.5%	9.3%
1980	1.14	0.9	5.60	8.1	8.1
1981	1.21	6.1	6.12	9.3	8.3
1982	1.32	9.1	6.82	11.4	8.0
1983	1.37	3.8	7.14	4.6	6.7
1984	1.59	16.1	7.08	–0.1	9.4
1985	1.72	8.2	7.72	9.0	10.3
1986	2.07	20.3	9.13	18.3	13.3
1987	1.43	17.4	8.66	–5.1	14.3
1988	2.85	17.2	8.58	–0.9	19.1
10-year average		11.1%		6.5%	10.7%

investing does not work, and vice versa. Such misguided thinking has come about because of a tendency in the profession to divide a group of stocks into two, and only two, categories. This type of mechanical division of a group of stocks leads to erroneous inferences. For example, it is not uncommon to divide the 500 stocks in the S&P 500 index into two categories—value and growth—where the value category includes 250 stocks with a book-to-market ratio that is higher than the median. The remaining 250 stocks are put into the growth category. In such a system, when one category outperforms the overall index, the other category, by virtue of design, will underperform the overall index.

Growth investing is harder because it is not based on quantitative formulas such as the P/E or M/B ratios. Benjamin Graham points to two reasons why growth investing is difficult. First, the price may already reflect the potential growth. In fact, in most cases, when the market senses growth, the price goes up quickly. In early 2009, even after a price decline of over 30 percent, Google's P/E ratio is about 30. For the better part of the previous three years, the ratio has been much higher. Second, the investor's judgment of the future may prove wrong.[2] However, if an investor selects stocks based on an accurate assessment of the company's future, growth investing can be very lucrative.

How to Identify Growth Stocks

Wal-Mart has been a great growth stock, giving an 80,000 percent return over a 38-year period since 1970, when shares first became publicly available, or an incredible 35 percent per year. How did Sam Walton do it?

According to Sam Walton: "There is only one boss—the customer. And he can fire everybody in the company from the chairman on down, simply by spending his money somewhere else."[3] The success of a business, and hence its growth, depends primarily on its customers. To find a great growth business, you need to evaluate it from a customer's point of view. Once you are satisfied that the company's sales and earnings will continue to grow and that you can buy the stock at a reasonable price, buy and hold it for a long time.

I start with how *not* to identify a growth stock because it is especially important if you have been considering value investing. You should not examine the financial fundamentals immediately after you have discovered a company that may grow in leaps and bounds for many years. Do not emphasize the fundamentals much. In other words, when you start thinking about a growth stock, do not start thinking about the historical P/E ratio or, for that matter, any other quantitative measure that you might have learned in business school. If you start thinking about traditional financial ratios, you will start thinking of value stocks, and you will probably never pick a great growth stock. You would never have picked shares in Microsoft, Wal-Mart, or Home Depot if you had looked at the fundamentals soon after the companies went public. Even if you knew these were incredible companies, you would have missed their tremendous potential. I'm not suggesting that traditional financial ratios are not important; I'm simply suggesting that you should not try to identify a growth stock using financial ratios alone.

Importance of Track Record: Sales and Earnings

The most important driver of growth in stock price is growth in earnings. Future earnings growth frequently depends on past earnings growth. To convince yourself that you must look at the track record, think about fellow students or colleagues at work. With high probability, you will discover that students who get consistently good grades for a number of semesters continue to get good grades for many more semesters to come. Similarly, people who do well in a job continue to do well for many years to come, although good grades do not necessarily predict who will do well in a job! This correlation also applies to corporations. Companies that have had positive results for a while are likely to exhibit that kind of performance for years to come, especially when the management team remains in place. Once in a while, this may not work, but on average you will come out a winner if you play the game by emphasizing a company's track record of earnings.

A short record of, say, less than five years is probably a dangerous way to identify the future growth of a company. It is important to focus on a longer time span. Great growth companies remain outstanding for many years after their initial spurt in growth. Unless you know a lot about the company, it is best to avoid initial public offerings (IPOs). While IPOs are often marketed as growth stocks, their long-run performance has been dismal. Professors Jay Ritter and Ivo Welch show that for more than 7,000 IPOs made over 1980 through 2005, the average three-year post-IPO performance is 20 percent *below* the corresponding market returns.[4] Generally speaking, IPOs are anything but growth stocks.

Growth in earnings does, however, depend on growth in sales, especially in the long run. I mentioned Sam Walton's focus on the customer because the customer is the main driver for growth in sales. In general, it is best to keep both sales and earnings in mind when thinking about growth investing, not just one or the other. One good approach to finding growth stocks is to identify some great products and services, as Peter

Lynch has often emphasized. Still, you must ask several questions before you actually buy stock in such companies. You can afford to take your time. Great companies will give you returns of several hundred percent, and if you miss some of it in the beginning, you should still do well. Here are some qualitative questions that you should take time to ask and answer before you decide to invest in a growth stock.

Is There Potential to Grow Sales and Earnings for Several Years?

This is the most important question. You should bother to investigate a company thoroughly only if it has the potential to grow for several years. You could have bought shares of an outstanding company such as Starbucks almost any time from 1992 to 2000 for impressive returns. It seemed clear that Starbucks would continue to grow for a long time because customers seemed highly satisfied. Of course, when either the price becomes excessive or when it is apparent that growth has slowed, you should sell the stock.

One-time events that help grow companies for a short period usually affect prices significantly, but such changes are often temporary. In the mid-1970s, again in the mid-1990s, and once again in the mid-2000s when oil prices went up quickly, many companies supplying oil-drilling services became high-growth companies. However, they could not sustain their growth. For example, Global Marine, an otherwise well-managed company, was trading at around $35 per share in late 1997, but oil prices went down in 1998, and Global Marine's stock price quickly retreated to less than $8 per share. A careful investor looking for an outstanding long-term growth company would have avoided Global Marine because the growth was from a one-time event.

This concept could also be applied to the Internet craze of the 1990s. At that time, it was difficult to know which companies would have sustainable growth. Unless you were in a position to determine long-term growth with some degree of confidence, you should have avoided Internet companies. Note that at the time of going public, even Microsoft was not an outstanding growth stock because it was not clear that the company could sustain its growth. However, over time, it became clear that Microsoft's products were immensely successful, Microsoft was a near monopoly, and the number of customers for those products would increase for many years to come. At that point, it was a good growth stock worth investing in.

How Are Relations with Employees?

Good employee-management relations lead to high customer satisfaction. A company may have fine products, but unless the company's employees are happy, customer satisfaction may disappear with time. A conversation with the employees—or some other source—would reveal a great deal about employee-management relations. Wal-Mart did not succeed only because it had lower prices, but because of outstanding management-employee relations. In 1999, I attended the Wal-Mart shareholders' annual meeting in Fayetteville, Arkansas. Joining me in attendance were more than 10,000 Wal-Mart employees who are also shareholders. I have never seen such enthusiasm from the employees of a company. They cheered often and ended the meeting with the well-known Wal-Mart cheer that starts, "Give me a W!" I talked to a few of the employees and realized that the unbelievable enthusiasm was genuine.

The advantages of enthusiastic employees are immense: The company's expenses are lower because its employees pilfer less, customers are happy and keep coming back, and inventory does not stay on shelves for long (inventory turnover is high). Sam Walton called employees "Wal-Mart associates," and most are shareholders.[5] In 2005 and 2006, Wal-Mart's management-employee relations deteriorated over employee healthcare benefits. This probably was one reason for a decline in the company's growth in 2006. However, Wal-Mart has responded vigorously to correct this problem and improve its image.

Is Research and Development Important?

Research and development (R&D) is needed in *all* companies—not only high-tech ones—to improve their products and services. Companies such as McDonald's and Home Depot constantly improve themselves through customer surveys, research in human relations, market research, and sociological research. Home Depot would not be a great success story without its research efforts into improving building materials or its surveys of customers on the quality of Christmas tree needles.

R&D in high-tech companies such as Microsoft, Cisco, and Intel is clearly even more important, and these companies can't sustain growth without a significant R&D effort. If a company has been successful because of past R&D, a simple but meaningful question to ask is whether it is continuing those efforts at the same level. When the personal computer industry was relatively new, a number of companies, including Kaypro and CompuAdd, were highly profitable but have since disappeared. Sometimes, companies are highly profitable because they copied others but are not innovative. With changing technology, these companies' growth falters at the next juncture of product development. Investors who extrapolate past sales growth into the future without understanding the need for R&D to sustain the growth are likely to suffer.

You might think that companies like Wal-Mart do not have significant R&D expenditures. That is not true. Wal-Mart has spent large sums of money developing its high-tech inventory control systems and one of the most up-to-date transportation networks. Determining which companies are savvier in using their R&D dollars is a difficult task for an investor. Merely because a company outspends other companies in R&D does not imply that it will bring more blockbuster products to the market. The only solution that I know of is to read about the company and learn as much as you can from various sources.

A case in point is Dell Computer, which spent substantially less on R&D per dollar of revenue than Compaq and IBM. Dell may not do basic research, but one should not immediately conclude that Dell is left behind in product innovation. This is because Dell depends more on licensing patents. It spends large sums of money on development and to maintain the best direct-to-customer model. Dell has been closer to Wal-Mart in its business plan than to Compaq or IBM. Michael Dell's book *Direct from Dell* describes Dell's R&D efforts to keep his company's cost advantage over IBM and others.[6] The focus was not on basic research. Instead of comparing R&D expenses across companies in an effort to pick the best companies, you should evaluate the qualitative nature of R&D expenses and evaluate whether they are keeping up with growth in revenues.

How Does the Company Respond to Challenges?

Because of their culture, some companies adapt to the changing world faster than others. For sustainable growth, it is necessary that companies rediscover themselves often. For most companies, it is not easy to change, and even some large firms fail when they encounter new technologies.[7]

IBM does not sell typewriters anymore. Did it surprise you when IBM sold its personal computer division to Lenovo in 2005? Not me. In fact, I wondered what took IBM so long. IBM is now a one-stop shop for all sorts of computer hardware, software, and services. Over time, IBM has rediscovered itself.

Wal-Mart is another company that seems to adapt to the times. Initially, it was only a discount store. Later, it added Sam's, which is a buyer's club, and then groceries. Wal-Mart has been expanding overseas and is highly successful in China and Mexico, but not in Germany, Japan, and Korea. In Mexico, Wal-Mart's subsidiary (Wal-Mart de Mexico) has entered the banking industry, opening branches inside its stores. Such ventures don't always have to be successful, but you need to monitor them for potential growth. Wal-Mart is pushing hard to be a successful Internet retailing company, and I will not be surprised if it becomes an Internet powerhouse in the future to compete against Amazon.com.

If a company has rediscovered itself a few times, its culture will probably allow it to continue doing so. Thus, it is necessary to take a long-term perspective in selecting a growth stock. A growth stock is not necessarily a young company. When the Internet first arrived, Microsoft did not consider it to be an important force. However, Microsoft changed its opinion quickly and remade itself. Today, it is working hard to compete with Google on Internet search and advertising. Finding out whether a company rediscovers itself often requires a considerable amount of research. Financial ratios just don't capture these qualitative aspects of growth companies. However, these efforts are necessary if you want to discover outstanding growth companies.

Is Management Quality Excellent?

Philip Fisher's approach is probably the best for judging the quality of a company's management. He suggests posing questions to the company's consumers, suppliers, and employees to get a good sense of the quality of its management. It is not impossible to discern that Wal-Mart, Google, and Southwest Airlines have excellent management. Also, each year *Fortune* publishes a list of the world's most admired companies and *Barron's* publishes a list of the world's best CEOs. You may know some of the companies in such lists well and select them for further investigation for investing.

To measure the commitment of a company's top management, find out whether the senior managers own company shares and whether they keep the shares they are awarded as part of their compensation. If the senior managers of a company sell their shares soon after the shares are awarded or after they exercise their stock options, you need to investigate the company carefully.

Why are some management teams better than others? I do not claim to know the answer to this question in most cases, but here is a thought. Every year I ask graduating students about their preferences for the companies they would like to work for. It has always amazed me how knowledgeable young people are. In the late 1990s, the company of choice was Microsoft. In the late 2000s, it is Google. If students, especially talented ones, choose Google over Microsoft, then Google's management culture will, over time, change to reflect the quality of the people it employs. Not surprisingly, various surveys reveal that many of the same companies are identified as having good management time and again over a number of years. Since high-quality managers have pride in their companies and themselves, they are likely to take steps to maintain the company's reputation.

Here is one more clue to management quality or lack thereof that comes directly from Buffett's principle of circles of competence. When a retail company appoints a new CEO without retail experience, it raises a red flag about his or her potential effectiveness. Such incongruous appointments are common. To the best of my knowledge, CEOs in Berkshire subsidiaries all have relevant experience and envious track records. Avoid company financial statements and other documents to decipher management quality. According to company reports, all managers are excellent! Thus, it is imperative to look at other sources for information on management quality.

How Important Are Profit Margins?

When profit margins are high and can be maintained at that level, growth in sales will produce better and better results as the company grows. Otherwise, growth in sales will not be highly valuable. As Philip Fisher points out: "All the sales growth in the world won't produce the right type of investment vehicle if, over the years, profits do not grow correspondingly. The first step in examining profits is to study a company's profit margin."[8]

Excellent growth companies almost always have high profit margins relative to other firms in the same industry. For example, one might assume that Wal-Mart probably has smaller profit margins than its competitors because it is well known for lower prices. That is one reason given for Kmart's loss of market share to Wal-Mart and finally going bankrupt in 2002. You may be surprised to know that Wal-Mart's profit margins were higher: 3.4 percent versus 1.8 percent before Kmart went bankrupt. An excellent company rarely competes on price alone. There are usually other reasons for its excellence. My analysis led me to believe that Wal-Mart's high profitability is partly due to its focus on high inventory turnover.

It is often argued that companies with high profit margins attract competition, and thus, their high profit margins will ultimately go away. The truth is not that simple. Companies with higher profit margins can always reduce their prices to drive the competition away and still remain profitable. While competitors such as Advanced Micro Devices try to copy Intel's products to compete on price, Intel lowers the price of its older-generation products and moves on to higher-margin products. In theory, it is possible for competitors to ultimately catch up with Intel, but it appears to me that, in practice, it is more difficult than it appears to an unconnected party. How can another company easily compete with a market leader and innovator like Intel, which is highly profitable and has deep pockets? The competition must also think of the possibility of losing billions of dollars, not being able to compete, and possibly even going bankrupt. Overall, high-profit–margin companies usually fall in the growth category.

What Is the Company's Achilles' Heel?

With many potential variables to examine, I do not recommend that you use a long list of variables to evaluate a company's growth prospects. How about looking at a company from another perspective? Where is the Achilles' heel? This will help you to not fall in love with the stock. If the situation deteriorates with respect to the important variables, you will be able to sell the stock before it is too late. If you fall in love, you sometimes miss the cues to sell.

Once, on a Yahoo! chat board, I asked what Berkshire Hathaway's Achilles' heel could be. The most frequent answer was Buffett's age (77 in 2007 when I asked the question). The question is clearly an important one. Without Warren Buffett, will the stock price tumble? In most cases, when the CEO of a great company retires or resigns, there is a vacuum at least for a while. After Sam Walton died, Wal-Mart's stock price was stagnant for a time. However, the company remained strong; and finally, after two or three years, the company resumed a path of growth.

One Example of a Non-Technology Growth Stock

There are innumerable examples of non-high–tech growth stocks, and depending on your skills, background, and commitment to acquire knowledge, you should be able to find some of them in the future. Recent examples are Wal-Mart, Home Depot, Starbucks, Chipotle, Danaher, and Eaton Vance. However, in this section, we are going to discuss one specific example of a non-technology growth stock: McDonald's.

In 1980, McDonald's stock price was about $1 per share (split-adjusted) compared with its price of about $45 per share in 2000. On average, the stock price rose by more than 20 percent per year or about twice as fast as the overall market. Even if you bought it in 1990 at about $7 per share, you would have enjoyed at least a sixfold increase in the stock price by 2000.

The question becomes whether you should have bought McDonald's common stock in 1990 after the company had experienced phenomenal growth. Over the prior five years, the earnings per share grew at a steady rate of about 14 percent per year, from $0.28 in 1985 to $0.55 in 1990. McDonald's was expanding overseas successfully. So, a person with a good knowledge of the fast-food industry and McDonald's would have, I believe, surmised that earnings would continue to grow steadily. The earnings per share grew from $0.55 in 1990 to $1.40 in 1999.

When you identify a company such as McDonald's that has grown steadily, you need to follow up by asking whether the current price is reasonable. In my discussion, I am not including IPOs, tiny companies, or other companies that are difficult to value. The P/E ratios of stocks like McDonald's are generally high in relation to their historical levels or the market, and they remain high for long periods. You should not immediately conclude that the stock is expensive and that you have missed the boat. It is uncommon for a growth stock to trade at a low P/E ratio. The stock is still worth buying as long as the price is not astronomical, say above 25 or 30 times earnings, and you are confident about future growth. Only in rare cases do stocks trading above a P/E of 30 generate high returns over a long period.

By 2000, McDonald's P/E was 32. A P/E of 32 was high in contrast to its median P/E of about 18 in the prior 10 years or the long-run S&P 500 P/E of about 16. This is when knowledge of the firm becomes important. It was still a good company and was expected to grow, albeit at a slower rate. It was just not a good time to buy.

From an investing point of view, one thing you can do is to wait for opportunities in good growth stocks once you identify them. With McDonald's, you would have done well if you had invested in 2003 when the stock hit a low of about $13 per share, primarily because of an outbreak of mad cow disease in the United Kingdom and isolated places elsewhere. The rumors of the demise of McDonald's proved to be wrong. What a bargain growth stock it was! In 2009, its stock price was around $53 per share.

Conclusions

To find a promising growth stock, I recommend that you start by examining earnings for several years because companies that have grown strongly for several years, on average, are sound candidates to generate good earn-ings in the future. You also need to examine qualitative variables, such as the quality of management and company culture, as they are the true underpinnings of future growth. Before you buy a growth stock, you should consider the possibility that the price may already be reflecting a high growth potential. You may do so by evaluating its P/E ratio or, preferably, computing its intrinsic value as I discuss in the next chap-ter. Overall, success in growth investing requires you to have a very good knowledge of the company's business and an ability to forecast its earnings well.

Chapter 5

Intrinsic Value

In general terms, it [intrinsic value] is understood to be that value which is justified by the facts, e.g., the assets, earnings, dividends, definite prospects, as distinct, let us say, from market quotations established by artificial manipulations or distorted by psychological excesses.[1]

—*Benjamin Graham and David Dodd*

Before you risk your hard-earned money on a stock, you probably want to know the value you can expect to get in return. The value you assign to a stock, or that stock's *intrinsic value*, is the maximum amount that you are willing to pay now for future benefits, which could come from dividends or the potential sale of the stock at a realistic future price. It makes no sense to buy a stock when its intrinsic value is smaller than the current price. Buffett cautions: "The calculation of intrinsic value, though, is not so simple . . . intrinsic value is an estimate rather than a precise figure."[2] In this chapter, I compute the intrinsic value of Wesco Financial, Coca-Cola, and Berkshire Hathaway to more thoroughly explain this concept.

Computing Intrinsic Value

Individuals differ from one another in assessing companies' future prospects. They also differ in their risk tolerance. Hence, it should be no great leap to accept that there is no unique intrinsic value that can be assigned to a common stock upon which everyone will agree. In computing intrinsic value, you should start by examining a company's balance sheet. Some assets, such as cash and investments in marketable securities, are reported at market value. As a first approximation, the intrinsic value of such items can be taken to be the same as their market values. For most companies, however, the major component of intrinsic value comes from their future earnings.

For valuation of future earnings, you can start with estimating a growth rate based on your evaluation of the company's past performance. Then you can apply the estimated growth rate to current earnings to approximate expected earnings for a future year, say, 10 years from the current year. Finally, apply a P/E multiple to the future earnings per share to estimate the value of those earnings in the future and discount them to their present value. In addition, dividends should be properly accounted for.

While it is a simple approach, it requires many assumptions. For example, you may have to adjust reported earnings in an attempt to obtain underlying or sustainable earnings. You also need to assume a growth rate, a P/E multiple, and a discount rate. With this approach, it is important to know the company's business well for you to come up with reliable estimates.

Let's examine three examples of evaluating common stocks. The first one, Wesco, is easy to evaluate because most of its assets are in marketable securities. Earnings play a limited role in Wesco's intrinsic value. In contrast, Coca-Cola's value is driven primarily by its earnings. Finally, I present an approach to estimating Berkshire's intrinsic value.

Wesco: Focus on the Balance Sheet

Wesco Financial Corporation is an 80.1 percent subsidiary of Berkshire Hathaway. Charlie Munger, vice chairman of Berkshire Hathaway and chairman of Wesco, has estimated the intrinsic value of Wesco in selected prior years. This analysis follows his arguments using data from the 2008 annual report.

Table 5.1 presents the Wesco balance sheet in a summary form. Wesco has total assets of $3,051 million, of which $298 million, roughly

Table 5.1 Wesco Financial Corporation Balance Sheet, December 31, 2008

Assets	
Cash and cash equivalents	$ 298
Investments	
Marketable equity securities	1868
Securities with fixed maturities	29
Other assets	856
Total assets	$3,051

Liabilities and Shareholders' Equity	
Liabilities	
Float (Insurance losses not yet paid)	$ 215
Income taxes payable, deferred	231
Other liabilities	227
Total liabilities	673
Shareholders' equity	2,378
Total liabilities and shareholders' equity	$3,051

Dollar amounts in millions.

10 percent, are in cash and cash equivalents. The marketable securities of $1,868 million are primarily in Procter & Gamble ($386 million), Coca-Cola ($326 million), Wells Fargo ($373 million), and Kraft Foods ($269 million). Thus, most of Wesco's assets (cash and cash equivalents, securities with fixed maturities, and investments of $298 million, $29 million, and $1,868 million, respectively), amounting to $2,195 million, are reported at market values and may be considered liquid assets.

We should subtract liabilities from these assets to the extent they are related to the assets. On the liabilities side, total reported liabilities are $673 million. There are only two meaningful items that are directly related to investments: the deferred income taxes payable of $231 million and the float of $215 million. Both are non-interest–bearing liabilities. The first amount is payable to the IRS only when the securities (such as Procter & Gamble) are sold. Thus, it is essentially an interest-free loan from the IRS to Wesco. You need to estimate the true value of this liability. If you assume that these securities will not be sold for a long time, the taxes will also not be paid for a long time. Then, most of this liability may be ignored for valuing Wesco. Thus, the true value of the liability is somewhere between zero and $231 million. I assume the true liability to be $115 million, halfway between zero and $231 million.

The second liability, *float*, is the term for money the company holds, and as long as insurance underwriting results are break-even, it costs the company nothing. I assume that the company will not have to pay this float for any foreseeable future and may even generate some income from the float. Thus, I will assume that the float from the insurance business is essentially free. Subtracting the liability of $115 million from $2,195 million equals $2,080 million as an estimated value of liquid assets.

If Wesco did not have any operating subsidiaries, we could stop here. Wesco's total net income for 2008 was $82 million. Out of this, $64 million came from investments, and the remaining $18 million came from operating businesses. Having already assigned a value to the investments, we should consider only the remaining $18 million. An examination of the earnings over the past few years suggests that these earnings are sustainable, as earnings have been similar in recent years. Because Wesco has no debt and earnings are likely to remain at least at this level and possibly grow, I use a simple approach to value these earnings. I assign a P/E multiple of 15 that results in a valuation of $270 million for the operating businesses. So, my estimate of intrinsic value of Wesco's common stock is $2,080 million + $270 million, or $2,350 million. Based on the number of shares outstanding (7.12 million), this translates into an estimated intrinsic value of $330 per share. In comparison, the market price at the end of 2008 was $288 per share. Note that we made several assumptions, and our estimate of intrinsic value would change if we used a different valuation for the float from the insurance business, the estimated P/E ratio, or the valuation of deferred taxes. Our estimate of intrinsic value is close to the book value per share of $334 reported by the company at the end of 2008.[3]

You have surely noted that Wesco's intrinsic value depends a lot on the valuation of its investments—that is, the market prices of Procter & Gamble, Coca-Cola, Wells Fargo, and Kraft Foods. As a first approximation, we have used market values of these investments as if they represent their intrinsic values. For a more elaborate evaluation, you may consider computing intrinsic values of these holdings. Remember that the intrinsic value is an estimate—even more important, it is just one person's estimate, which can vary widely across individuals. In this case, my estimate of $330 was not vastly different from the market price of $288 per share at the end of 2008. So, Wesco was not a buy.

Coca-Cola: Focus on Earnings

Unlike Wesco, Coca-Cola derives its value from its earnings. In the case of Wesco, we did not emphasize growth in earnings. Coca-Cola is different, and it presents a good example to discuss growth in earnings. I will use 1998 as the base year for this purpose because it gives us an opportunity to look at developments since then.

At the end of 1998, Coca-Cola's total assets of $19.14 billion were mostly represented by tangible assets. The company's liquid assets in the form of cash and marketable securities were only $1.81 billion. An 11-year history detailed in the annual report showed that Coca-Cola's cash and marketable securities in 1998, at about 10 percent of revenues, were in line with historical levels. Also, they were less than 1 percent of the market value of the company's shareholders' equity. Therefore, we need not treat them separately as we did for Wesco. I assume that this much cash and marketable securities are needed to run the company.

The next step is to think more clearly about growth prospects. In the 10 years before 1998, Coca-Cola's revenues grew at the rate of 8.8 percent per year, and its earnings per share grew at 14.5 percent per year. However, in the immediately preceding five years, the growth in revenues had slowed to 6.0 percent, and earnings per share to 11.2 percent.

The company's earnings for 1998 were $1.42 per share, which seemed sustainable because earnings per share for the prior three years were similar: $1.67, $1.40, and $1.18, respectively. It seemed reasonable to estimate the future growth in earnings to be 10 percent per year for the next 10 years, which was closer to the previous five years' growth in earnings. Under this assumption, in 10 years, expected earnings for 2008 (based on data in 1998) would be $3.68 per share. Next, we need to estimate a reasonable P/E multiple for earnings per share for 2008. For a low-debt, well-managed company, a P/E multiple of 15 to 20 appears reasonable. However, for the purpose of this computation, let's use a 15

P/E multiple that gives the expected value of earnings at the end of 2008 as 15 ×3.68, or $55.20 per share.

The present value of $55.20 depends on the discount rate assumed. I think of the discount rate as the minimum rate at which I would be comfortable owning a part of the company's business. The discounted value of $55.20 in 1998 at the discount rate of 7 percent (a low rate, but an assumption based on the mortgage rate I was paying at the time) is $28.06 per share. If Coca-Cola was not paying any dividends, that would be one estimate of the intrinsic value of Coca-Cola at the end of 2008 (or in early 1999 when 1998 year-end accounting data became available).

We should add the value of dividends at least for the amounts expected to be received during the following 10 years. The cash dividend in 1998 was $0.60 per share. Assuming a 10 percent growth rate in dividends (similar to the growth rate in earnings), an investor would have received $0.66 in 1999, and so on. Using a discount rate of 7 percent, the discounted value of the next 10 years' dividends is $9.83 per share. Therefore, my estimate of Coca-Cola's intrinsic value in 1999 was $28.06 + $9.83 = $37.89.

In the fall of 1999, when I made these calculations in a class I was teaching, the stock price was about $70 per share. Based on these calculations, Coca-Cola stock seemed overvalued by almost 100 percent. Note that we estimated that in early 2009, the Coca-Cola stock price would be around $55.20 per share. In early 2009, the Coca-Cola stock price was $45 per share; and the P/E multiple, based on trailing 12 months' earnings, was 18.

You can add many other changes and complications. For example, you could argue that we should value dividends differently from earnings because dividends are being paid out while earnings are not. You could have simply used the dividend discount model generally attributed to Myron Gordon.[4] Overall, depending on assumptions, you could have produced substantially different estimates of Coca-Cola's intrinsic value in early 1999.

A few additional comments on the analysis are worth making. Coca-Cola is a stable company, so it is relatively easy to estimate future earnings. The possibility of you going very wrong is low. Given that there are far too many uncertainties for high-tech companies, you should think more carefully about their future earnings before you compute intrinsic value in a similar manner.

Even Coca-Cola's stock price fluctuated by a factor of two between 1998 and 2009. It has seen a low of less than $40 per share and a high of more than $85 per share. So if you do not have a long-term view and do not have sufficient liquidity, you may not achieve your goal of reasonable returns with any company's stock. For example, if you suddenly need funds and are required to sell when the price is low, you might lose a substantial amount of your original investment even if you invest in Coca-Cola, let alone in stocks of companies with less predictable earnings. There is another advantage to computing intrinsic value. It keeps you grounded so that you do not become nervous when the stock price goes down. As a matter of fact, I considered buying Coca-Cola stock when the share price was around $40, down from $85. But I did not because intrinsic value estimates still did not justify buying.

A check: While I was assigning a 15 to 20 P/E multiple to Coca-Cola's stock, I wondered why the P/E multiple in early 1999 was $70/1.42, or about 49. It could have been 25 or even 30, but why did the stock command a high P/E of 49? Around then, the market was assigning high valuations not only to Coca-Cola but also to a host of other stocks, especially Internet stocks. These stocks were boats that were being lifted in a rising tide. What can we learn from this? You could say, "The market was wrong," but for me, unfortunately, that is never a satisfactory answer. I would ask, "Why was the market wrong?" I simply do not have a satisfactory answer to the question, "Why was Coca-Cola's stock price so high?" Nevertheless, when it does happen, it is best not to buy.

Berkshire Hathaway: Intrinsic Value

Let's compute Berkshire's intrinsic value. Buffett has never furnished his estimate of Berkshire's intrinsic value, nor has he suggested a well-defined approach. However, he has frequently discussed various inputs that may be considered by investors. My approach is based on Buffett's recent hints on how to compute Berkshire's intrinsic value. As mentioned in the preface, my objective here is to learn as much as we can from Buffett's writings.

Table 5.2 Berkshire Hathaway Data for Its Valuation

Year	Per-share investments	Pretax earnings per share (noninsurance businesses)
2000	$50,648	$ 848
2001	47,460	1,379
2002	52,705	2,215
2003	62,273	1,971
2004	66,967	2,148
2005	74,129	2,441
2006	80,636	3,625
2007	90,343	4,093
2008	77,793	3,921
2000–2008 compounded growth rate	5.50%	23.10%

One way to compute intrinsic value is to start by estimating expected future cash flows that can be taken out of a business. If cash flows are not taken out of the business (as in the case of Berkshire), they result in additional growth. We can then extrapolate past growth into the future with any adjustments that we deem appropriate. In the case of Berkshire, cash flows ultimately end up in one of two places.

1. Investments, such as stocks, bonds, and cash equivalents. These include equity investments American Express, Wells Fargo, etc.
2. Purchase of majority-owned or fully owned subsidiaries such as Dairy Queen, NetJets, etc.

By valuing these two items, we can value Berkshire. To value the investments (item 1), we will use their market values. To value subsidiaries (item 2), we will use their earnings. Buffett has periodically given numbers for both these items in Berkshire's annual reports. Let's examine the historical performance from Table 5.2.

1. Berkshire's investments per share grew from $50,648 in 2000 to $77,793 in 2008, a compounded growth rate of 5.5 percent per year. For the period 1995 to 2006, Buffett reports the growth to be

12.6 percent. The lower recent growth probably reflects additional investments in fully owned subsidiaries, the increasing size of the company, and especially the market crash of 2008.

2. The pretax earnings of noninsurance businesses have gone up from $848 per share in 2000 to $3,921 per share in 2008.[5] This growth rate in earnings amounts to 21 percent per year. For the entire period from 1965 to 2008, the compounded annual growth rate was about 17 percent. The recent high growth in earnings is primarily due to acquisitions, as Berkshire's focus shifted toward using more free cash flows for this purpose. Under the assumption that the recent pattern of using cash flows will continue, we will apply the growth rate of 21 percent to estimate future earnings.

Let's consider what the company will look like 10 years from now. Recall that we did not use such projections in computing Wesco's intrinsic value, as it did not seem important and it was not easy to do so. In the case of Berkshire Hathaway, there are at least three questions to consider.

- Is the growth rate going to be smaller or higher than the percentages we just computed, or the same?
- How long is the growth rate going to last?
- Finally, what discount rate should we use?

I didn't see anything in the various annual reports that suggests that we should not use the company's recent growth rates, so let's use 5.5 percent for investments per share and 21 percent for earnings of noninsurance businesses. The 5.5 percent growth rate for investments appears low and the 21 percent growth rate for noninsurance earnings appears high, but you can always use different rates and get different intrinsic value estimates. Also note that if there are no new acquisitions for growth, Berkshire's cash flows will be used toward a higher growth in investments. As before, I will use the discount rate of 7 percent for discounting future values to compute the current intrinsic value estimate.[6]

Based on these assumptions, 10 years from now—that is, at the end of 2018—the values are expected to be as follows:

Investments per share:	$132,882
Pretax earnings per share:	$ 26,379

Let's value investments per share at their reported value of $132,882 because they are essentially at market value. For earnings, I use a P/E multiple of 10 on pretax earnings (which is equal to a multiple of about 15 on after-tax earnings). If we do that, we get a per-share valuation of Berkshire's common stock, class A. The estimated value 10 years from now is $132,882 + 10(26,379) = $396,672. The present value of this depends on the discount rate you use. With a 7 percent discount rate, that gives a present value of 396,672 ÷ 1.97, or $201,356.

We are almost there. Similar to our approach to Wesco, if we assume that the cost of float is zero and use half the deferred tax liability amount, we end up subtracting about $3,300 per share from $201,356. Rounding it off, my estimate of Berkshire's current intrinsic value is $198,000 per share.

Wow! It seems that Berkshire was undervalued at the time of this analysis in early 2009 as the market price of the stock was around $90,000 per class A share. So, Berkshire stock was a buy and remains so in November 2009, with the stock price around $100,000.

This computation does not imply that Berkshire's stock price is likely to jump in the short run. It is difficult to know how and when prices will reflect value even if my estimates are correct. I don't know how other market participants are thinking and valuing Berkshire. This is just my estimate. As earnings go down in 2009 because of recession, it will not surprise me if Berkshire's stock price goes down or remains about the same in the short term. However, let's examine what the future values imply in terms of expected returns. If you purchase a Berkshire class A share at $90,000, the implied rate of return is 16 percent per year if the stock price does reach $396,672.

A check: Let's use the data from 2006 and 2007 to examine the validity of this approach. For 2006, the investments per share were $80,636, and the pretax earnings per share were $3,625. Ignoring additional minor estimates, this gives us a per-share value of $80,636 + 10(3,625) = $116,886. In early 2007, when the 2006 annual report became available, the stock price was about $110,000. So maybe our metric is slightly generous in valuing Berkshire common stock. But it is not dramatically different from the price in the market. Using the same metric for 2007 data, an estimated intrinsic value in early 2008 is $90,343 + 10(4,093), or $131,273. The stock price in early 2008 was $140,000. Berkshire's stock prices move considerably with the market because of its large investments in common stocks.

When to Buy Any Stock: Consider Margin of Safety

We computed intrinsic values of three companies, and we know that a stock should be purchased only if the market price is below the stock's intrinsic value. A question that you must ask is: "How *much* lower should the price be relative to the intrinsic value?" I think of margin of safety for any stock as the difference between a stock's intrinsic value and its market price. If you buy a stock at its intrinsic value, you will have no margin of safety. If everything goes as you assume in your calculations, you will earn an annual rate of return equivalent to the discount rate assumed. For example, if you assume a discount rate of 7 percent as we did in the examples and purchase the stock at intrinsic value, your annual rate of return will be 7 percent. If the same stock is purchased at 25 percent below the intrinsic value, the calculations show that the rate of return will be about 10 percent per year. And if the stock is at half the intrinsic value, the rate of return will be about 15 percent. So it seems logical that you should buy a stock with a large margin of safety. An alternate way of thinking about looking for a large margin of safety is to require a large discount rate.

A few points you should be fully aware of: First, in computations of Berkshire's intrinsic value, investments per share are based on market prices. As the market goes up or down, the value of investments per share will change accordingly. If the underlying stocks are overpriced or underpriced, the intrinsic value will also be biased upward or downward. Second, we relied on operating earnings of noninsurance subsidiaries to grow at the rate of 21 percent. With the November 2009 announcement of the Burlington Northern Santa Fe acquisition, the growth rate in earnings is now more likely to be accomplished.

Given that there are many assumptions involved in this process, you should compute different numbers based on those assumptions. The proportion you invest in an individual stock should depend on its margin of safety and your confidence in your computation of its intrinsic value.

Finally, you should learn about the management. If you have a Buffett or Munger type on your side, a smaller margin of safety should be adequate.

Conclusions

This chapter is devoted to explaining the methodology behind estimating the intrinsic value of a common stock to provide you with a guideline for a buy or sell decision. It is important to learn a lot about the company so that you may consider an appropriate method for computing its intrinsic value. You should invest only when the margin of safety is high.

Chapter 6

Buffett Investing = Value + Growth

[M]ost analysts feel they must choose between two approaches customarily thought to be in opposition: "value" and "growth." ... In our opinion, the two approaches are joined at the hip: Growth is always a component in the calculation of value.[1]

—*Warren Buffett*

Most people characterize Buffett as a value investor. The common usage of the term *value investor* connotes someone who invests in stocks that have such characteristics as low price-to-earnings (P/E) or market-to-book (M/B) ratios. It also refers to those people who buy stocks after the market prices have fallen substantially. Presumably, such investors have a sufficient understanding of the underlying businesses and expect the prices to recover. As Buffett's words clearly state, a smart investor should consider both value and growth investing simultaneously. Contrary to popular belief, Buffett is not a pure value investor. In this chapter, I illustrate the way Buffett combines value and growth investing strategies to earn high returns.

Berkshire Hathaway Is a Growth Stock

For each of the past four decades, Berkshire has outperformed the S&P 500 index. Table 6.1 presents the annualized rates of growth in Berkshire's book value per share, Berkshire's stock returns, and corresponding returns on the S&P 500 index. For the entire 40-year period ending in 2008, Berkshire's annualized growth in per-share book value is 20.7 percent and its annualized stock return is 21.8 percent. If you had invested $10,000 in Berkshire common stock at the beginning of 1969, your investment would have grown to $26.7 million. On the other hand, the annualized return on the S&P 500 index has been only 8.9 percent, which would have grown your investment from $10,000 to only $302,000. Clearly, Berkshire has been a long-term growth stock.

Berkshire's rate of growth seems to have slowed in recent years, maybe because of its large size and maybe because of events including the terrorist attack on the United States in 2001 and the market crash in 2008. Since 1965, Berkshire has suffered a decline in book value per share only in 2001 and 2008. Still, even in the most recent decade, Berkshire has generated 4.7 percent above the corresponding returns on the S&P 500 index.

Berkshire's results in Table 6.1 include those from its majority-owned or wholly owned subsidiaries and its minority holdings through common

Table 6.1 Berkshire's Performance versus the S&P 500

10-year periods and the 40-year period	Annual Change			Berkshire's stock performance relative to S&P 500 (2) − (3)
	In per-share book value of Berkshire (1)	In Berkshire stock price (2)	In S&P 500 (dividends included) (3)	
1969–1978	20.5%	15.9%	3.1%	12.8%
1979–1988	28.2	40.4	16.2	24.2
1989–1998	29.0	31.0	19.2	11.8
1999–2008	6.4	3.3	−1.4	4.7
1969–2008	20.7	21.8	8.9	12.9

stocks. Detailed data on purchasing and selling dates and prices on Berkshire's minority investments in common stocks are harder to collect. However, Gerald Martin from American University, Washington DC, and John Puthenpurackal from University of Nevada, Las Vegas, collected the detailed data on Berkshire's investments in common stocks and analyzed them carefully.[2] For 1976–2008, the Berkshire common stock portfolio generated an average return of 18.2 percent, handily beating the 10.6 percent that the investments would have generated if the investments had been made in the S&P 500 index.

It seems almost impossible to duplicate Buffett's track record. However, the good news is that over the years, he has provided an extensive body of written and spoken material on his ideas and principles. Even if we cannot duplicate Buffett's results, we should at least be able to learn from his own methods to improve our results. I begin with a brief discussion of why Buffett may have initially invested in GEICO in 1976, and later allude to some other acquisitions and draw some inferences on salient features of his investing style.

Value Plus Growth

GEICO's stock price soared from $5 in the late 1950s to more than $60 in 1972. Then, the Cinderella story ended. On the brink of bankruptcy, the stock traded near $2 per share in 1976. By 1977, Berkshire had purchased 1.29 million shares for $4.1 million, averaging $2.55 per share. In addition, Berkshire invested $19 million in a GEICO convertible preferred stock issuance of $75 million. By 1980, Berkshire's investment in GEICO was $47 million, which amounted to about a 33 percent equity interest in GEICO. As GEICO repurchased its own shares over the next 15 years, Berkshire's ownership of GEICO increased to 50 percent.

In value investing, the purpose of using the P/E ratio or another metric is not to benefit from some special quality of the metric per se. The underlying purpose of using such metrics is to warn the investor to invest only when the downside risk is low. At the time of the initial GEICO purchase, the company was incurring losses, and hence, the P/E ratio was meaningless. Because the company was about to declare bankruptcy, its book value also did not mean much. However, after raising additional equity from Berkshire and others, the company was saved from filing for bankruptcy. Consequently, Buffett's investment did not have a high probability of losing money. This *attention to downside risk* is the main ingredient that Buffett borrows from the value investing strategy.

If Buffett were just a plain vanilla value investor, he would probably have sold the GEICO shares after the price had gone up by more than 100 percent in less than a year of his initial purchase or within a few years thereafter. He understood GEICO well, as he had followed the company since 1951. Overall, he invested in GEICO for its potential long-term growth, just as a growth investor would. Berkshire's $47 million investment in GEICO grew by about 50 times, to $2.3 billion, by 1995 when he purchased the remainder of the firm. GEICO is a good example of how Buffett's success lies in identifying companies that are not just value investments but also have good growth potential. Buffett-style investing or Buffett investing is not just pure value investing; it is value plus growth investing.

The value investing approach is sometimes known as the *quantitative approach* because of its focus on mathematical variables such as the P/E ratio, while the growth investing approach is often referred to as the *qualitative approach* because of its focus on harder-to-calculate variables based on future estimates. Obviously, I am not claiming to have discovered the approach of combining value and growth as a superior approach to value investing; Buffett gets full credit for developing it. Buffett has described his investing approach in bits and pieces in many different places. The following statements taken from his 1967 letter to his partners probably give the best clues to his philosophical development in this regard. He writes:

> Although I consider myself to be primarily in the quantitative school, the really sensational ideas I have had over the years have been heavily weighted toward the qualitative side where I have had a "high-probability insight." This is what causes the cash register to sing. However, it is an infrequent occurrence, as insights usually are, and, of course, no insight is required on the quantitative side—the figures should hit you over the head with a baseball bat. So, the really big

money tends to be made by investors who are right on qualitative decisions, but, at least in my opinion, the more sure money tends to be made on the obvious quantitative decisions.[3]

Clearly, Buffett believes that a considerable emphasis on growth investing is necessary if one wants to earn large returns.

Implementing Value Plus Growth

To implement Buffett-style investing for common stocks, you may employ a two-step process. First, decide whether the downside risk, or the risk of losing your investment, is low. Often, low P/E or M/B metrics suggest a low downside risk. Second, after having judged that the downside risk is low, you should analyze the stock's growth potential and compute its intrinsic value and margin of safety. You should buy a stock if the margin of safety is high, even if its P/E is above the market P/E or above the company's historical average P/E. Not all your investments will turn out to be wonderful growth stocks. However, since you protected yourself by taking a low downside risk, you will not lose often and, when you do unavoidably lose, you will not lose much. As I explain next, your gains can still be very high if only a few of your investments turn out to be truly successful growth stocks.

The substantial benefit of investing in growth stocks can be illustrated by a hypothetical example. It shows that even if only one out of every five of your stock investments does well, your overall return can be high. Assume that the average market return is 10 percent. You invest $1,000 in each of five stocks for a total investment of $5,000 with a three-year horizon. If you earn 10 percent per year as expected, your $5,000 investment would become $6,655 at the end of three years. But if just one of your five stocks turns out to be a growth stock with a 200 percent return over the three-year period, your portfolio would be worth $8,324—a substantially higher sum than the $6,655. The annual compounded rate with one successful growth stock turns out to be 18.5 percent per year.

The value plus growth concept can be further illustrated using some of Berkshire's investments. From 1987 to 1991, Berkshire invested a total of about $2 billion in five convertible preferred stocks: Champion

International, First Empire State, Gillette, Salomon Inc., and U.S. Air. All these investments could be characterized as value investments because the downside risk was low. Large company preferred stocks, on average, are safe investments because they are not expected to default on their dividend payments or the principal amounts. Out of these five, only Gillette turned out to be a good growth stock. In 1990, Berkshire invested $600 million in Gillette, which was taken over in 2005 by Procter and Gamble, with Berkshire receiving about $5 billion in Procter and Gamble stock in exchange. Over the 15-year period, Berkshire earned about 16 percent per year, which was twice the rate on the S&P 500 index for the same period. The other four investments essentially generated normal returns. In 2008, Berkshire invested in three preferred stocks or convertible instruments that are similar to preferred stock. They are issued by Goldman Sachs ($5 billion), General Electric ($3 billion), and Wrigley ($6.5 billion). Even if one of them turns out to be a growth stock, returns to Berkshire will be high. If not, Berkshire will earn decent interest on these investments.

It is important to realize that low downside risk is very important. In the previous example of picking five stocks, if you were to pick them from a fast-growing high-tech industry, you would have probably lost all your investment in one or two stocks. Assuming that you make 200 percent on one stock as pointed out earlier, earn the market return on the remaining two, and lose all your investment in two stocks, your final sum will be $5,662, giving you an annual rate of only 4.2 percent on your initial $5,000 investment. This is substantially less than the 10 percent that you would have earned had you simply invested in the market.

At least two of Buffett's well-known practices can be directly linked to the two-step process I've outlined. First, consider his practice of investing only in his circle of competence. In the two-step process, you need to compute a stock's intrinsic value, which requires reliable earnings forecasts for several years in the future. You can forecast well only when you know the company well or when it is in your circle of competence. Second, Buffett rarely invests in high-tech or fast-growing industries. One possible reason may be that they are not in his circle of competence. But even if Buffett knew a lot about some fast-growing companies, he might avoid them because it is hard to find stocks with a high margin of safety in these industries. Often, investors have high expectations from such stocks and bid their prices very high. On average, they are overvalued; that is, there is no margin of safety. In Buffett-style investing or, in other words, if you are looking for stocks that Buffett would want to buy, you are better off looking in traditional industries.

Where Does Growth Come From?

As I said before, Buffett does not invest in high-tech or fast-growing industries. Then, how has he accomplished a high rate of growth (over 20 percent) for an extended period? The key seems to be his emphasis on quality of management. His philosophy is the same whether he acquires companies or invests in common stocks. There are several characteristics in his management philosophy that, combined, provide this outcome.

When a company is acquired by Berkshire, managers do not face financial analysts or worry about the stock price. Berkshire and its subsidiaries do not forecast earnings and do not conduct conference calls with analysts. The managers do not have to meet or beat the next quarter's or next year's earnings. This frees up their time and allows them to concentrate on the company's long-run operating performance. The compensation plans are also designed to accomplish what academics call "maximization of shareholder value." Value is further created with reductions in costs once a firm comes under the Berkshire umbrella. Berkshire does not lever up the acquired company. This has two advantages. First, in keeping with Buffett's philosophy, the downside risk is maintained at a low level, and second, employees are happier as they are more secure of their employment. Similarly, other input costs such as raw materials and rent are also lower because suppliers feel more assured of prompt payment. The main lesson from this is that after acquisitions, Buffett helps enhance management quality even though he emphasizes that good quality management should already be in place before he purchases a company.

One of Buffett's acquisition criteria is deceptively simple but very insightful. He acquires a company only if the current management comes with the acquisition. This is rather unique because most acquirers replace the incumbent management with a new team of their own. Why does

Buffett go against the norm in the business world? To start with, it is obvious that if the acquired business was successful under the existing managers, they should not be replaced. However, most other acquirers replace them anyway. Maybe, there is hubris lurking in the background. My guess is that most acquirers prefer to manage bigger companies. This helps their compensation package, their ego, and their influence in the business world.

Buffett's approach has additional advantages. If the acquired company was a private company, as is frequently the case, the CEO was probably also the owner. Under Berkshire, he is still the CEO of his unit but is now a manager under Buffett. Although he is now a manager rather than an owner, he is likely to behave as an owner because he was an owner before he sold his company to Berkshire. In economic parlance, this reduces the principal-agent, or conflict of interests, problem. If the manager behaves as an owner, there is no conflict. In most cases, the sellers are independently wealthy and more interested in successful growth of their companies than their own compensation. Additionally, since the seller gets to keep the company under his control, he may be willing to take a lower price. Finally, if some company management had manipulated earnings in the past to get a good price from selling the company, the seller probably would not sell it to Buffett. This is because Buffett would ask him to stay on and manage the company. Most hidden problems (for example, earnings management or off-balance-sheet debt) are likely to surface within a few years. No one would want to manage a company knowing that it has such a ticking time bomb. This reduces the likelihood of Buffett ending up with dishonest managers and solves the "let the buyer beware" problem.

Buffett also promises those who sell their firms to Berkshire that he will hold the purchased companies forever even if profitability declines. I do not know of any major acquisition that Berkshire later sold. Why is this important? It builds trust and security in the seller's mind about the future of the company, especially if the seller wants to be sure his business will prosper. As Buffett writes, "We have a decided advantage, therefore, when we encounter sellers who truly care about the future of their businesses."[4] Overall, Buffett's acquisition principles are designed to produce high earnings for a long time. In essence, growth is accomplished through good management.

Examples from Berkshire Investments

Over the past 44 years, Berkshire has acquired a large number of companies and has invested in common stocks of companies as a minority shareholder. Buffett has mentioned that the principles applied for these two types of investments are the same. While there is a common theme across his investments, no two investments are identical. To enrich our understanding of Buffett investing, I break down a few of his investment decisions.

Railroad: Burlington Northern Santa Fe

During 2006 to 2008, Berkshire acquired 70.1 million shares, or 20.1 percent, of Burlington Northern Santa Fe (BNSF), which operates one of the largest North American rail networks, with about 32,000 route miles across 28 states and two Canadian provinces. Berkshire paid about $78 per share for a total investment of $5.5 billion, making it the third-largest Berkshire common stock holding behind Coca-Cola and Wells Fargo. BNSF is, next to Union Pacific, one of the top two U.S. railroads, each bringing in about $18 billion in revenues. It was formed from a merger between Burlington Northern and Santa Fe Pacific in 1995. BNSF's financial statements provide insights into its valuation and the reasons for this large Buffett investment. The data from 1996 to 2008 (selected years for brevity) are presented in Table 6.2.

First, following the value investing principles, the downside risk is low. The long-term debt is only 25 percent of total assets which is reasonable for a company with large holdings in property, plant, and equipment. The company generates steady cash flows as the service it provides cannot be easily replaced by another vendor. From reading the annual reports of BNSF and other railroads, I gather that the company has a large market share in several regions. Furthermore, return on equity (ROE) has been stable at around 13.5 percent. Overall, the economics of the business seem good. Also, the railroad business is an easy one for investors to understand, a principle that Buffett emphasizes. Buffett did not pay a high price in relation to earnings. His purchase price-to-earnings (P/E) ratio based on the average earnings per share in 2005 and 2006 is 15.3. This is only slightly higher that BNSF's 13-year average P/E of 14.9 and is close to

Table 6.2 Burlington Northern Santa Fe Financial Highlights

	2008	2007	2006	2005	2004	2000	1997	1996	Average
Revenues	$18.02	15.80	14.99	12.99	10.95	9.21	8.49	8.19	11.11
Operating income	$3.91	3.49	3.52	2.92	1.71	2.11	1.77	1.75	2.36
Net income	$2.12	1.83	1.89	1.53	0.81	0.98	0.89	0.89	1.19
Total assets	$36.40	33.58	31.80	30.43	29.02	24.38	21.27	19.69	26.95
Long-term debt	$9.56	8.15	7.39	7.15	6.52	6.85	5.29	4.71	6.69
Shareholders' equity	$11.13	11.14	10.53	9.64	9.44	7.48	6.82	5.99	8.65
Number of shares (millions)	348	359	370	382	377	415	464	456	404
Earnings per share	$6.08	5.10	5.11	4.02	2.14	2.38	1.88	1.91	3.04
Dividends per share	$1.44	1.14	0.90	0.74	0.64	0.48	0.40	0.40	0.66
Capital expenditure	$2.18	2.25	2.01	1.75	1.53	1.40	2.18	2.23	1.85
Depreciation expense	$1.40	1.29	1.18	1.11	1.01	0.90	0.77	0.76	0.99
Operating income/Total assets	10.7%	10.4%	11.1%	9.6%	5.9%	8.7%	8.3%	8.9%	8.6%
Return on equity (ROE) (Net income/Shareholder's equity)	19.0%	16.4%	17.9%	15.9%	8.5%	13.1%	13.0%	14.8%	13.5%
Long-term debt/Total assets	0.26	0.24	0.23	0.24	0.22	0.28	0.25	0.24	0.25
Stock price at year-end	$75.71	83.23	73.81	70.82	47.31	28.31	30.98	28.79	
Price-to-earnings (P/E) (current year)	12.5	16.3	14.4	17.6	22.1	11.9	16.5	15.1	14.9
Dividend yield (Dividend/Price)	1.9%	1.4%	1.2%	1.0%	1.4%	1.7%	1.3%	1.4%	1.5%

Note: Dollar amounts in billions, except per-share numbers. For brevity, reported data are only for selected number of years.

the long-run S&P 500 P/E ratio of 16. While not cheap in terms of the P/E that a pure value investor may prefer, BNSF's valuation fits Buffett's approach of paying a reasonable price when the economics and growth prospects of the business are good. In his words, "It's far better to buy a wonderful company at a fair price than a fair company at a wonderful price."[5]

Second, the growth prospects are above average. A series of data spanning a long period allows us to estimate future growth with a reasonable degree of confidence. The growth rate in earnings over the past five years was 23 percent per year, but the growth over the past 12 years was only 10 percent a year. It appears to me that the recent growth rate is on the high side as the economy was doing well with demand for coal and agriculture transportation increasing at a faster-than-normal rate, probably because of high oil prices. BNSF's increased growth rate has driven its ROE to an unusually high rate of 19.0 percent. Will the growth continue, and at what rate? That is probably the most difficult question a Buffett-style investor faces.

BNSF has the usual sources of growth, such as revenues, acquisitions, and productivity. It has also increased earnings per share through share repurchases, which the firm is likely to continue because of its significant free cash flows. Share repurchases have slowly reduced the number of shares outstanding from 456 million in 1996 to 348 million in 2008 (a reduction of 24 percent over 12 years). Thus, a 2 percent growth rate can be expected based on share repurchases alone. For future projection, I start with the 12-year historical growth rate of 10 percent and reduce it by 1 percent to 9 percent to be conservative.

With a 9 percent growth rate, BNSF's expected earnings in 10 years will be $14.39 per share. Applying a P/E of 15, the expected price at the end of 2018 is $216 per share. The present value of $216 using a discount rate of 7 percent is $110 per share. In addition, an investor will get dividends, which I assume will also grow at the rate of 9 percent per year from the current level of $1.44 per share. The present value of the dividends is about $14, giving us an intrinsic value for BNSF of about $124 ($110 + $14) per share. In early 2009, the BNSF stock price was $68. It was a good investment at this price.

On November 3, 2009, Berkshire announced a plan to acquire, at $100 per share, the remaining 77.4 percent of BNSF's outstanding shares not currently owned by Berkshire. Based upon the number of shares remaining for Berkshire to acquire, the value of the aggregate consideration to complete the acquisition is approximately $26.4 billion. This will be the largest Berkshire acquisition ever. Overall, the downside risk is low, the price is not high, and growth potentials are good. It is a quintessential Buffett investment.

Training: FlightSafety International

In 1996, Berkshire Hathaway acquired FlightSafety International (FSI), a large company providing pilot, flight attendant, and mechanic training services in the United States, Canada, and Europe. In terms of the value investing principle of low downside risk, the most relevant fact was that the then CEO, A. L. Ueltschi, owned 31.8 percent of the company and elected to receive Berkshire shares in exchange for his FlightSafety stock. Thus, he was not selling the company because he did not believe in its future. He remained the CEO until 2003 and is still the chairman of the board. Bruce Whitman, an employee since 1961, became the CEO in 2003. A.L. Ueltschi founded the company in 1951 and its shares started trading publicly in 1968. Praising Ueltschi, Buffett wrote, "Al may be 79, but he looks and acts about 55. He will run operations just as he has in the past. We never fool with success."[6]

In the five-year period prior to the acquisition by Berkshire in 1995, FSI's revenues grew from $267 million to $326 million, an annualized growth rate of 5.1 percent, similar to what is expected in the traditional industries. FSI's net income grew a little faster at the rate of 6.5 percent, but no one would have classified FSI as a growth stock. The price of $1.5 billion paid by Berkshire was about 2.5 times the book value and 18 times earnings in 1995. Thus, Buffett did not pay a high price for the company, but it was not cheap either. As I discussed earlier, good companies are rarely available cheap, and in that sense Buffett is not a pure value investor.

How about growth? FlightSafety grew quickly after it was acquired. Buffett wrote in Berkshire's 1998 annual report, "FlightSafety's operating profits increased significantly over 1997 as a result of continued growth in all areas of its training business."[7] The capital expenditures at FlightSafety during 1997, 1998, and 1999 were about 20 percent of the identifiable assets at year-end. This was at least twice the rate of capital expenditures before it was acquired. Buffett made it possible for FSI to grow by keeping successful management in place. Company-specific data are not available since 1996, but the company remains one of the largest companies in its industry.

Aviation: NetJets

NetJets, formerly known as Executive Jet Aviation (EJA), was acquired by Berkshire in 1998 for $725 million. NetJets sells fractional shares of jets and operates the fleet for its many owners. NetJets does not own most of these airplanes; they are owned by customers. Warren Buffett was a satisfied customer for three years before he made this acquisition. NetJets, a private company, grew fast under its CEO and majority shareholder, Richard Santulli, who pioneered the fractional jet ownership concept in 1986. He stayed with his company just as most other CEOs of Berkshire acquisitions stay with their companies. I discussed earlier that managers are the purveyors of growth. However, when a long-term, successful CEO stays with the company, it is also an indication that the downside risk in the acquisition is low. When Richard Santulli resigned in 2009, David Sokol, CEO of Berkshire's subsidiary MidAmerican, took over as the new NetJets CEO.

What is the usual source of a high growth rate in the old economy or in a well-established industry? In some cases (recall Wal-Mart and GEICO), growth comes from taking market share away from other firms. In this case, NetJets grew by luring business and first-class travelers in traditional airlines and corporate jet owners.

Since Berkshire bought NetJets, growth in revenues has been well above the normal growth of about 5 percent to 7 percent in so-called traditional industries, which include aviation. As Buffett wrote in March 2000, "Currently, our customers own planes worth over $2 billion, and in addition we have $4.2 billion of planes on order. Indeed, the limiting factor in our business right now is the availability of planes."[8] In 2007, Buffett explained how growth may have been accomplished: "The NetJets brand—with its promise of safety, service and security—grows stronger every year. Behind this is the passion of one man, Richard Santulli. If you were to pick someone to join you in a foxhole, you couldn't do better than Rich. No matter what the obstacles, he just doesn't stop."[9] Once again, it appears that management quality is the way to growth.

It should not be assumed that growth is a sure thing even if an accomplished CEO is at the helm. In the case of NetJet's European expansion, the company incurred a cumulative loss of $212 million over its first 10 years in operation starting in 1996. However, Buffett reported in 2007 that the European segment was now doing well. Buffett gives credit to Richard Santulli, who appointed a new person to lead the European segment. This sequence of events suggests that experienced managers are helpful in maintaining a low downside risk in times of trouble.

Berkshire combines financial numbers on NetJets and FSI under one segment called Flight Services, and even then, data are available only for certain years. For the two companies discussed here, Buffett proudly states, "[A] common characteristic of the companies is that they are still managed by their founding entrepreneurs. ... These men are both remarkable managers who have no financial need to work but thrive on helping their companies grow and excel."[10]

For 1999, the first year both subsidiaries operated for a full year under Berkshire, revenues were $1.86 billion with identifiable assets of $1.79 billion. For 2005, the latest year for which data are available, revenues were $3.66 billion, and identifiable assets were $3.17 billion. In six years, revenues grew at a rate of 12 percent per year and assets at a rate of 10 percent per year. Because of continuing expansion, profitability has been erratic.[11] Operating profits in 2005 were only 3.8 percent of year-end identifiable assets. The discussion in the 2006 annual report suggests that the results have improved substantially. Berkshire did not present the details, but I estimate that operating profits were about 11 percent of the identifiable assets employed. From 1999 to 2007 (the last year for which earnings data are available), pretax earnings in the Flight Services segment have gone up from $225 million to $547 million, an annualized growth rate of about 12 percent.

NetJets also shows how a growth company's profitability is generally tied strongly to the economy. The global recession of 2008–2009 had a significant impact on NetJets. The company produced pretax losses of $531 million for the first nine months in 2009. Overall, NetJets is still an evolving story, but Buffett's emphasis on patience and high-quality management comes through.

High-Tech: BYD

On September 29, 2008, Berkshire announced plans to invest $230 million for a 10 percent stake in BYD (initials for the Chinese name), a fast-growing Chinese company listed in Hong Kong. The initials are now used for "Build Your Dreams." With 2008 revenues of $3.9 billion and total assets of $4.8 billion, BYD is one of the world's largest manufacturers of rechargeable batteries and handset components. It is also a successful car manufacturer. Since 2002, its revenues have grown about eight times from $500 million to the current level of $3.9 billion, most of the growth coming internally. It is a quintessential rags-to-riches Horatio Alger story for BYD CEO Wang Chuan-fu.

Based on 2008 reported earnings per share, BYD's P/E ratio at the time of Berkshire's purchase was about 14, in line with other Berkshire acquisitions. Furthermore, as Table 6.3 shows, BYD's earnings per share have been steady, if not growing consistently with revenues. The debt-to-total-assets ratio of 0.28 appears to be fairly conservative. Overall, the downside risk from this investment is not high. Soon after the Berkshire investment, in October 2008, the BYD stock price doubled and then moved steadily upward and doubled again over the next several months. If Buffett were a pure value investor, he would have sold his stake when the price quadrupled. However, during the Berkshire annual shareholders meeting on May 2, 2009, Charlie Munger made it clear that the BYD investment is for the long term.

You may wonder why Berkshire made a commitment to a long-term investment in a fast-growing high-tech company. The answer: BYD is a global leader in two of its three businesses (rechargeable batteries and handset components), Berkshire did not pay a high price for it, and Berkshire's subsidiary MidAmerican has incentives to help BYD succeed in producing inexpensive rechargeable batteries. MidAmerican's CEO David Sokol is now a nonexecutive director on the BYD board. As one of the largest wind power generators in the United States, MidAmerican can become a major user of rechargeable batteries to store energy from wind power generation. At a low price, the worldwide demand for rechargeable batteries is immense.

Combining its knowledge of rechargeable batteries and automobiles, BYD introduced a hybrid electric car in December 2008. If successful,

Table 6.3 BYD's Selected Financial Data

	2008	2007	2006	2005
Revenues	26.79	21.21	12.94	6.5
Total assets	32.89	29.29	16.39	11.21
Debt (interest bearing)	9.16	8.12	5.73	4.03
Shareholders' equity	11.28	10.71	5.29	4.18
Net income	1.02	1.61	1.12	0.5
Earnings per share	0.5	0.79	0.55	0.25
Debt/Total assets	0.28	0.28	0.35	0.36
Return on equity (percent)	9.0	15.0	21.2	12.0

Numbers are in billions of Chinese Yuan (RMB), except earnings per share and ratios.

it can be a world leader in electric car production. That may be the real growth story that has generated so much excitement for the firm.[12] At the Berkshire annual meeting in May 2009, large crowds gathered to see the prototypes, which are expected to be introduced in the United States in the near future.

From an investing point of view, even if the car project is not a big hit, the company is already generating satisfactory profits for the shareholders. Current levels of profits must have given comfort to Buffett to invest in this venture even if he did not completely understand the technology. After all, he did not have to fully understand the technology; David Sokol is Buffett's eyes and ears in this case. It also makes sense for MidAmerican to help BYD in launching an electric car in the United States as it will increase demand for electricity, replacing a corresponding demand for imported oil. Finally, again, for successful investing, Buffett has always emphasized the importance of management quality. Charlie Munger and Buffett have praised the BYD CEO highly on several occasions for his accomplishments. So, it appears that BYD is not a speculative investment even though it is in the high-tech field.

Overall, Buffett's investments are generally not driven by the concept of value investing alone. As a value investor, he keeps the downside risk low but is willing to pay a reasonable price for expected growth. The BNSF investment in a traditional company is a quintessential Buffett investment. The BYD investment, even though it is in a high-tech company, is a good example of Buffett-style investing in that it represents the way he blends value and growth investing principles together, and in the way growth is accomplished through high-quality managers.

Conclusions

The main message from value investing strategies is to invest with low downside risk. If a stock satisfies this criterion, you should then consider its growth in earnings to implement a value-plus-growth strategy that I call Buffett-style investing or simply Buffett investing.[13] The focus in value investing is on the past, the focus in growth investing is on the future, and the focus in Buffett investing is on both the past and the future. You should also pay special attention to management quality, because high-quality management is the source of growth in Buffett-style investing. To implement this strategy, you should compute the stock's intrinsic value and compare it with the stock's price. As a rule of thumb, if the price is about half the intrinsic value, it is worth investing in that stock.

There is more to Buffett than simply value and growth investing. Buffett engages in arbitrage investing, investing in silver futures, betting on oil, forward trading in foreign currencies, managing a large number of wholly owned subsidiaries, and writing derivative contracts. He frequently narrates investment-relevant stories from other fields such as psychology, sports, country music, and life in general. Given his broad knowledge and his deep understanding of investment-related topics, I prefer to call him a renaissance investor rather than attempting to pin him down under more limiting monikers. The rest of this book illustrates Buffett's method of extracting relevant investment information from so many seemingly unrelated fields.

Part Three

OTHER PEOPLE'S MONEY

Most companies sell products or services first and collect cash later. Buffett does the reverse through Berkshire's insurance companies. Insurance companies collect premiums in advance. Buffett then uses this cash, which is really other people's money, for investing. In Chapters 7 and 8, I focus on Berkshire's insurance businesses, which are the mainstay of his success. In Chapter 9, I discuss tax deferment, which is another source of other people's money.

Chapter 7

Insurance: Other People's Money

Our main business—though we have others of great importance—is insurance. To understand Berkshire, therefore, it is
necessary that you understand how to evaluate an insurance company. The key determinants are: (1) the amount of float that the
business generates; (2) its cost; and (3) most critical of all, the
long-term outlook for both of these factors.[1]

—*Warren Buffett*

B erkshire's main business is insurance, and Warren Buffett can
hardly hide his enthusiasm when he talks about GEICO, a
Berkshire-owned insurer that primarily provides auto insurance.
There is probably no better place to learn from Buffett about business and
investing than from his long and successful involvement with GEICO.
Buffett's professor and mentor Benjamin Graham at Columbia University was chairman of GEICO. A careful examination of Buffett's writings
tells us why he bought GEICO shares initially and why GEICO has been
successful. Buffett narrates the story of his desire to learn deeply about
GEICO:

[O]n a Saturday in January 1951, I took the train to Washington
and headed for GEICO's downtown headquarters. To my dismay, the

building was closed, but I pounded on the door until a custodian appeared. I asked this puzzled fellow if there was anyone in the office I could talk to, and he said he'd seen one man working on the sixth floor. . . . And thus I met Lorimer Davidson, Assistant to the President, who was later to become the CEO.[2]

Buffett reflects his enthusiasm in GEICO as he continues, "When I finished at Columbia some months later and returned to Omaha to sell securities, I naturally focused almost exclusively on GEICO." And when Buffett was running Berkshire, he said, "Berkshire purchased a large interest in the company during the second half of 1976, and also made smaller purchases later. . . . Then, in 1995, we agreed to pay $2.3 billion for the half of the company we didn't own." Thus, GEICO became a wholly owned subsidiary of Berkshire Hathaway, 44 years after Buffett first set foot in its office in Washington.

Insurance Companies as Other People's Money

The GEICO commercials beckon potential customers by claiming, "A fifteen-minute call could save you 15 percent or more." This resembles Wal-Mart's slogan, visible in every Wal-Mart store: "We sell for less." GEICO has the potential to become the Wal-Mart of the insurance industry. GEICO has been the engine of growth for Buffett's insurance business and has generated capital for Berkshire to invest in other opportunities. Unlike most other businesses, an insurance company makes money in two distinct ways: (a) underwriting profits, or operating profits, and (b) float.

GEICO's Revenues and Operating Profits

When you buy an auto insurance policy, you pay a premium. Subsequently, if you submit a claim, the insurance company pays you. The underwriting profits, or operating profits, are the difference between the premiums earned and the claims made in any given period.

GEICO's operating profits and revenues since 1996 are presented in Table 7.1. I have two main observations. First, GEICO's revenues

Table 7.1 GEICO's Revenues, Operating Profits, and Operating Profits

Year	Revenues	Float	Operating profits before taxes	Operating profits as a percentage of revenues
1996	$ 3,122		$ 171	5.5%
1997	3,482	$2,917	281	8.1
1998	4,033	3,125	269	6.7
1999	4,757	3,444	24	0.5
2000	5,610	3,943	−224	−4.0
2001	6,060	4,251	221	3.6
2002	6,670	4,678	416	6.2
2003	7,784	5,287	452	5.8
2004	8,915	5,960	970	10.9
2005	10,101	6,692	1,221	12.1
2006	11,055	7,171	1,314	11.9
2007	11,806	7,768	1,113	9.4
2008	12,479	8,454	916	7.3
Total	$95,874		$7,144	7.5

Dollar amounts in millions.

and operating profits have increased substantially over time—but what is even more impressive is that percentage profitability, or profits as a percentage of revenues, has also increased. In most cases, especially in a mature industry such as insurance, profits per dollar of revenues decline as the company grows by taking market share from others. A company has to be very well managed to increase revenues and simultaneously increase profitability.

My second observation is that operating profits can change dramatically from year to year. Competition in the insurance market in 1999 and 2000 drove down premium rates, which was the main reason that GEICO was close to break-even profits in 1999 and incurred losses in 2000. Since operating profits are volatile, it is important for management to focus on the long run—which many companies simply cannot do. As an investor, you should examine earnings for several years, especially when analyzing an insurance company. GEICO's operating profits as a share of revenues averaged 6.4 percent from 1996 to 2008 but are higher, at 10.1 percent, over the most recent five years.

Insurance is not a fast-growing industry, but GEICO has grown fast. Progressive Insurance competes with GEICO and is of about the same size, with $13 billion in 2008 revenues. Its operating profitability of 10.1 percent over the past four years is also similar to that of GEICO. From 2004 to 2008, while revenues at Progressive have remained stagnant, GEICO's revenues have increased by 40 percent. Buffett shares his insight into GEICO's growth: "At GEICO, Toney Nicely—now in his 48th year at the company after joining it when he was 18—continues to gobble up market share while maintaining disciplined underwriting. When Tony became CEO in 1993, GEICO had 2.0 percent of the auto insurance market, a level at which the company had long been stuck. Now we have a 7.7 percent share."[3] In other words, Buffett suggests that long-term profitable growth in a mature industry emanates from the work of excellent management.

Float: Other People's Money

Unlike most other businesses, an insurance company receives money from its customers, in the form of premiums, before spending money on the product. The company pays out only after claims are filed. Meanwhile, the company keeps the money and can earn a return on this money by investing it in bonds and stocks. This money is called *float* in insurance industry parlance.

Over the past 10 years, from 1998 to 2008, GEICO's revenues have increased from $4.0 billion to $12.5 billion, an increase of 212 percent, while float has increased from $3.1 billion to $8.5 billion, an increase of 174 percent. There are two distinct advantageous aspects of float in relation to other liabilities or debt. First, even though it is a liability, the company is not required to pay any interest on it. If the company faces financial hardship for some reason, the hardship will not be accentuated because of debt holders. In other companies, say manufacturing companies, the debt holders may bring additional hardship to the company in difficult times by asking for their money back or by not renewing their loans. Second, growth in insurance companies requires very little additional capital expenditure. If a company is well managed and grows, the level of float grows as the company grows. On the other hand, in manufacturing companies, growth usually requires substantial additional capital expenditures, which may necessitate issuance of new debt or equity. So, the benefits from growth in manufacturing businesses are not as high as those from growth in insurance businesses.

How has GEICO been so successful? The main reason is its focus on the long run which must be attributed to its high-quality management. For example, consider earnings volatility. While most companies regard earnings volatility to be a nuisance, a high-quality management team can actually *benefit* from earnings volatility. When companies encounter declining earnings, such as in the severe recession of 2008, most publicly traded companies reduce marketing efforts to trim costs. However, GEICO views times of economic downturn as opportunities to increase marketing efforts to capture market share from other companies. This may reduce earnings in the short term, but it is a good long-run strategy that GEICO can engage in but other companies that are worried about short-term earnings cannot. Buffett's philosophy of focusing on the long run and ignoring periodic volatility is advantageous to GEICO.

In Berkshire's 1998 annual report, Buffett explains this approach. "[C]ompanies that are concerned about quarterly or annual earnings would shy from similar [marketing] investments, no matter how intelligent these might be in terms of building long-term value. Our calculus is different: We simply measure whether we are creating more than a dollar of value per dollar spent—and if that calculation is favorable, the more dollars we spend the happier I am."[4] In 1995, GEICO spent $33 million on marketing, in 1999, it spent $190 million, and in 2009, it spent approximately $800 million. In the case of GEICO, Buffett sees the long-term benefits from capturing market share and does not worry about the short-term losses from increased marketing expenses.

GEICO's management has also been able to maintain or even increase its operating profitability as mentioned earlier. Operating losses, if any, may be viewed as the cost of generating float. On average, GEICO has been generating operating profits, not losses. Thus, there is no cost of float. In other words, GEICO's float or other people's money is free. For an insurance company, both the amount and the cost of the float are important. For GEICO's valuation, discussed next, we use these two variables.

GEICO's Valuation and Returns to Berkshire

Since 1996, GEICO has been a wholly owned Berkshire subsidiary. Berkshire paid $2.3 billion for about half the company, which suggests GEICO's market value to be $4.6 billion. There are two sources of intrinsic value for GEICO. First, GEICO's operating profits, according to my estimates from reading the financial statements, were about $100 million in 1995. Using a multiple of 10 to value this pretax income amount (which is about a P/E of 15), I estimated the value of operating profits to be $1.0 billion. Second, using GEICO's financial statements, I estimated the company's float to be about $3.1 billion. Since this float is an interest-free loan from policyholders, its value to GEICO can be assumed to be $3.1 billion. This gives us an estimate of GEICO's intrinsic value to be $4.1 billion. There were also some investments in excess of float. Hence, my estimate of GEICO's intrinsic value is conservative. Overall, Berkshire's acquisition price was in line or a little over GEICO's intrinsic value. The 1995 purchase of half of GEICO was not cheap as a pure value investor would like. However, consistent with the argument on Buffett-style investing in the previous chapter, it was acquired for its future growth potential.

How much was GEICO worth in 2009, based on end-of-the-year data in 2007 or 2008? As I did before, I use 10 times the underwriting profits and add float to it. This implies a value of $18.8 billion, given by $(10 \times 1.1) + 7.8$ for 2007 data. Based on 2008 data, which are influenced by the dramatic economic slowdown, GEICO's valuation is still $17.6 $(10 \times 0.9 + 8.5)$ billion. I prefer using 2007 data because 2008 is an unusual year, although the difference is not significant. Under Berkshire, GEICO's value has increased from $4.6 billion to $18.8 billion in 11 years. In addition, I estimate that in the meantime, GEICO generated about $4 billion of free cash flows. These may have been paid to Berkshire in dividends or held by GEICO as investments. Thus, GEICO's value of $4.6 billion at acquisition at the end of 1995 has now gone up to $22.8 billion, which works out to be a return of a little over 13 percent per year since 1995. In comparison, the annualized return on the S&P 500 index for the same period was only 4.8 percent. I do not know what to attribute GEICO's growth to other than high-quality management.

Prior Berkshire Insurance Businesses and Blue Chip Stamps

Berkshire's insurance business and Buffett's use of float did not start with GEICO. Buffett used other people's money from several prior businesses. In 1967, when Malcolm G. Chace was the chairman, and Buffett was a board member, Buffett's influence on Berkshire was clearly evident as Chace wrote, "We are highly pleased with the results of our insurance subsidiaries since their acquisitions in March 1967. . . . Our investment in the insurance companies reflects a first major step in our efforts to achieve a more diversified base of earning power."[5] It was the beginning of Buffett's long-term plan to transform Berkshire from a manufacturing company into an insurance giant. It is difficult to imagine that Buffett could have achieved what he has without a long-term plan.

After learning about the insurance business while he was a student at Columbia University, he probably thought it was better to acquire 100 percent of small insurance companies than to acquire shares in a large insurance company such as GEICO. By acquiring entire insurance companies, Buffett could influence the quality of insurance underwriting and the use of its float. After its initial entry into the insurance business in 1967, Berkshire acquired several smaller insurance companies and started new insurance businesses. By 1975, Berkshire's insurance segment constituted about 64 percent of the $255 million of Berkshire's identifiable total assets. By the time an opportunity arose to invest in GEICO in 1976, Buffett was savvy enough to handle a large company and acquired a significant stake.

Insurance is not the only business that generates float. As far back as 1972, Berkshire owned 17 percent of Blue Chip Stamps, which engaged in furnishing a trading stamp service in California, Nevada, and Oregon. In 1973, Blue Chip held $93.4 million of what can be termed other people's money—the money it collected that would be given back slowly to customers as they redeemed their stamps. The size of this float was almost twice the amount of its shareholders' equity of $53.1 million. In 1973, Berkshire increased its holding to 19 percent of the outstanding shares and, by 1980, owned about 60 percent. In 1984, Blue Chip Stamps was merged into Berkshire.

With time, trading stamp service revenues declined. Many businesses got into trouble as their revenues declined, resulting in a sudden loss

of shareholder value. However, in well-managed float-generating businesses, the transition is not as severe because the output is almost never
sold at a loss. As the demand for a product (trading stamps in this case)
declines, the company may reduce its size slowly without much pain and
suffering. The amount of float does not drop as fast as revenues decline.
With respect to float and declining business, Charlie Munger, chairman
of the Blue Chip board, wrote in 1981, "In our trading stamp business,
our 'float'—is large in relation to current issuances. (Trading stamp revenues peaked at $124 million in fiscal 1970, and our 1981 revenues of
$15.6 million therefore represent a decline of 87% from peak volume.)"[6]
Blue Chip's float has been a good source for Berkshire's growth. Using
this float, Berkshire acquired several companies including See's Candies,
Mutual Savings, Buffalo Evening News, and Precision Steel. Why did
Berkshire acquire these businesses that do not seem to have anything in
common? We get a good insight into Buffett and Munger's principles of
investing and running businesses from what Charlie Munger wrote[7]:

> Our five constituent businesses have more in common than might be
> noted by a casual observer:
>
> 1. They are all high-grade operations suffused to a considerable extent
>   with business ideas of Benjamin Franklin, manned by high-grade
>   people operating within a long tradition emphasizing reliable and
>   effective service.
> 2. When functioning properly, each business will usually generate
>   substantial amounts of cash not claimed by compulsory reinvest-
>   ment in the same business.

Buffett and Munger have emphasized the importance of cash flows
beyond the compulsory reinvestment in the same business because these
cash flows can help growth of Berkshire as a whole.

Conclusions

In your investments, you should follow Buffett's lead and stay within
your circle of competence, which in Buffett's case is insurance. Buffett's

in-depth understanding of insurance business has served Berkshire well. Its insurance business GEICO has done well, in part, because Buffett does not pay attention to short-term earnings volatility. Also, instead of borrowing in the open market, Buffett uses low-cost float, or other people's money, from the insurance business to invest in or acquire other companies.

Chapter 8

Reinsurance: More of Other People's Money

[W]e are a Fort Knox of capital, and that means volatile earnings can't impair our premier credit ratings. Thus we have the perfect structure for writing—and retaining—reinsurance in virtually any amount. In fact, we've used this strength over the past decade to build a powerful super-cat business.[1]

—Warren Buffett

If a hurricane hits Miami, an insurance company with a large number of policies in the area will be inundated with claims and could go bankrupt. Other natural or man-made disasters such as tornadoes, floods, fires, oil spills, and earthquakes can also result in huge insurance claims in short order. To avoid a financial disaster, many insurance companies transfer their risks to other insurance companies, called *reinsurance companies*. General Re Corporation is one of the largest reinsurance companies in the world, and it is owned by Berkshire Hathaway.

Size Matters: Berkshire's Acquisition of General Re

A small insurance company—for that matter, any small company—cannot take large risks even when the rewards seem attractive. For this reason, larger insurance companies are likely to be more profitable than smaller ones. For Berkshire as a whole, size is advantageous because more of the insurance and reinsurance premiums and float can be kept in-house. Furthermore, Berkshire may accept more reinsurance business from other insurance companies.

In 1998, Berkshire Hathaway acquired General Re Corporation for $22 billion. This remained Berkshire's largest acquisition until November 2009 when Berkshire announced plans to acquire Burlington Northern Santa Fe for $34 billion. Berkshire's premerger shareholder equity of $31 billion increased by 70 percent in one fell swoop. When the merger was announced, General Re was the largest professional property and casualty reinsurance group domiciled in the United States, and it conducted business in almost 150 countries. It was one of only five nongovernmental U.S.-based financial institutions with an AAA senior debt rating from Standard & Poor's.

Was $22 billion a good price to pay? At the time of the acquisition, General Re's underwriting (operating) profits were about zero and it was not expected to earn any such profits. These results had been similar in recent years. But the firm was growing fast, having expanded its insurance premiums at an annual rate of 10.7 percent in the 10-year period ending in 1997. Since General Re's underwriting profits were about zero, the value of underwriting profits per se can be assumed to be zero. However, *float*, or the amount of premiums collected in advance but claims not yet paid, was $14.9 billion. As discussed in previous chapters, float can be valued dollar for dollar or even higher owing to potential growth. Buffett has made similar arguments: "[T]hough our float is recorded on our balance sheet as a liability, it has had more economic value to us than an equal amount of net worth would have had. As long as we can continue to achieve an underwriting profit, float will continue to outrank net worth in value."[2] If float can be valued at about $14.9 billion, General Re's total value would be at least $14.9 billion. So why pay $22 billion? There may have been intangible assets such as reputation and synergy with other Berkshire units that I am unable to assess but that Buffett could have. Overall, it does not appear to be a cheap acquisition that a pure value investor would endorse. In line with our discussion in Chapter 6 on Buffett-style investing, Buffett probably saw growth potential and was willing to pay a premium for that reason.

Table 8.1   General Re's Revenues, Float, and Operating Profits

Year	Revenues	Float	Operating profits before taxes	Operating profits as a percentage of revenues
1998		$14,909		
1999	$ 6,905	15,166	−$1,184	−17.1%
2000	8,696	15,525	−1,224	−14.1
2001	8,353	19,310	−3,671	−43.9
2002	8,500	22,207	−1,393	−16.4
2003	8,245	23,654	145	1.8
2004	7,245	23,120	3	0.0
2005	6,435	22,920	−334	−5.2
2006	6,075	22,827	526	8.7
2007	6,076	23,009	555	9.1
2008	6,014	21,074	342	5.7
Total	$72,544		−$6,235	−8.6

Dollar amounts in millions.

General Re: 1998–2008

Table 8.1 shows that after the acquisition, General Re's float increased from $14.9 billion in 1998 to $21.1 billion in 2008, which represents an annual growth rate of about 3.5 percent over the 10-year period. Revenues (premiums) grew from 1998 until 2002 but have since declined. Over the past 10 years, the growth in premium revenues is close to zero. The operating profits have been volatile, and there have been some large losses. We can learn several things from this.

The huge loss of $3,671 million in 2001 reflects the effect of the 9/11 terrorist attacks. Underwriting losses from 1999 to 2002 were also large, much greater than in the years before being acquired by Berkshire. Why did this happen? In 2002, Buffett mentioned that the culture at General Re was such that premiums were not being written with as much discipline as they should have been. Once Buffett realized this cultural problem, General Re reduced the amount of insurance being written. In 2008, revenues were only 71 percent of what they were in 2002. Since the float-to-revenues ratio is about 4 to 1, float is not expected to decline at the same rate. In 2008, float was 95 percent of what it had been in 2002. Operating profits were positive during 2006 to 2008, which is a good sign. Based on the first nine months of results, 2009 was likely to be even a stronger year. However, to really evaluate the quality of underwriting, it will take us another 10 years or more because losses from new policies do not surface immediately. When estimating an insurance company's cost of float, you should take a long-term view.

How has the General Re acquisition turned out so far? From 1999 to 2008, float increased by $6.2 billion, an increase from $14.9 billion to $21.1 billion. However, the company incurred large operating losses during this period, also amounting to $6.2 billion. Valuing float dollar for dollar, the increase in the value of float is nullified by operating losses. There are some underwriting profits now, but they are not significant. I approximate that Berkshire has earned just about nothing from its investment in General Re over the past 10 years. The good news is that the cumulative 10-year return on the S&P 500 index from year-end 1998 to 2008 was about −13 percent. Thus, if Berkshire had invested the same amount in the S&P 500 index, the results would have been even worse. Buffett is optimistic about the future: "General Re, our large international reinsurer, also had an outstanding year in 2008. . . . Today General Re has regained its luster. . . . Charlie and I are . . . certain that, with Tad [Montross, CEO], General Re's future is in the best of hands."[3]

Was buying General Re a mistake on Buffett's part, or is there something systemic that we can learn? This episode is a good reminder that reported profitability may not reflect reality. Before the acquisition, General Re had a stellar record. I studied the preacquisition 1997 General Re annual report carefully. The results looked very good, and even in hindsight I could not see any prevailing culture at General Re that would lead to subpar underwriting. General Re's growth in revenues was slowing, but it had recently acquired other insurance companies. Its profits had increased steadily. In general, when a public company is acquired, there is some probability of hidden problems. Many of Buffett's acquisitions have been family-controlled companies. My guess is that if General Re were a family-controlled firm, the cultural problem might not have occurred or would have been discovered in time to prevent the acquisition.

GEICO *versus* General Re Strategies on Capturing Market Share

Why does General Re not focus on market share the way GEICO does? It seems that the two insurance companies under the same Berkshire umbrella follow different if not opposite strategies. General Re's revenues have declined for several years, starting in 2003. Its policy is not to write unprofitable policies. On the other hand, GEICO makes a serious effort to increase its market share and spends large sums on advertising. Thus, unlike General Re, GEICO probably incurs a loss in acquiring new customers. This difference, once again, shows that no two companies are alike and they need not follow the same strategies. The reasons for the two different approaches are the nature of the customers and the amount of the premiums.

In the case of GEICO, once a customer buys automobile insurance, he is likely to remain a customer for a long time because of inertia and low absolute premium amounts. So, it makes sense to work hard to attract a customer even if the initial cost of doing so is high. However, General Re writes reinsurance policies to other insurance companies. Since reinsurance premium amounts are large, it is likely that General Re's customers do not suffer from inertia and shop around when a reinsurance policy is up for renewal. Hence, repeat business will not materialize as it does in the case of GEICO. Overall, it is not highly beneficial for General Re to write unprofitable policies to grab market share. Berkshire has another large reinsurance unit that is worth discussing because its profitability is substantially different from that of General Re.

Berkshire Hathaway Reinsurance Group

Berkshire's third major and probably the most profitable insurance group, Berkshire Hathaway Reinsurance Group, is managed by Ajit Jain with a staff of only 31 employees. Buffett has praised Ajit Jain lavishly almost every year in the annual letter to the shareholders. In the most recent annual report, he writes, "This [B.H. Reinsurance Group] may be one of the most remarkable businesses in the world, hard to characterize but easy to admire. ... It features very large transactions, incredible speed of execution and a willingness to quote on policies that leave others scratching their heads."[4] Once again, no two businesses are alike,

Table 8.2 Berkshire Hathaway Reinsurance Group's Revenues, Float, and Operating Profits

Year	Revenues	Float	Operating profits before taxes	Operating profits as a percentage of revenues
1998		$ 4,305		
1999	$ 2,382	6,286	−$256	−10.7%
2000	4,712	7,805	−162	−3.4
2001	2,991	11,262	−647	−21.6
2002	3,300	13,396	534	16.2
2003	4,330	13,948	1,047	24.2
2004	3,714	15,278	417	11.2
2005	3,968	16,233	−1,069	−26.9
2006	4,976	16,860	1,658	33.3
2007	11,902	23,692	1,427	12.0
2008	5,082	24,221	1,324	26.1
Total	$47,357		$4,273	9.0

Dollar amounts in millions.

even if they are in the same industry. This is one of the many reasons why a simple comparison of financial ratios alone is not enough to find good stocks. You need to think about the company-specific business, acquire the most knowledge that you can about the business and its high-level managers, then compute its intrinsic value to make buy or sell decisions.

Table 8.2 highlights the financial performance of Berkshire Hathaway Reinsurance Group from 1998 to 2008 and can be juxtaposed against the General Re data in the previous table. B.H. Reinsurance Group's earnings are also volatile with losses in 4 out of 10 years. However, over the past 10 years, B.H. Reinsurance Group has produced pretax profits of $4,273 million (9.0 percent of revenues) in contrast to General Re's losses of $6,235 million (−8.6 percent of revenues). GEICO's corresponding profitability number is 7.5 percent.

To further illustrate the argument that no two businesses even in the insurance industry are alike, I compute float-to-revenues for each of the three major Berkshire insurance businesses. GEICO's float is only about

70 percent of the revenues, or the float is about eight months of revenues. This reflects the fact that most of GEICO insurance policies are related to automobiles and are renewed every six months or thereabouts. On the other hand, a similar analysis of Tables 8.1 and 8.2 shows that General Re's and B.H. Reinsurance Group's floats are equivalent to 3 and 3.4 years of premiums, respectively. This example illustrates the point that financial ratios often characterize the nature of the underlying businesses.

As we previously did, assuming that the value of float is basically dollar for dollar, B.H. Reinsurance Group's float has increased in value from $4.3 billion at the end of 1998 to $24.2 billion at the end of 2008. In addition, the company has generated operating profits of $4.3 billion whose after-tax value without discounting is about $2.8 billion. Adding $2.8 to the current value of float of $24.2 produces a value of $27.0 billion, which is a conservative approximation to study the growth rate from the value of $4.3 billion in 1998. In 10 years, B.H. Reinsurance Group's value has increased at the annual rate of about 20 percent. This is remarkable for a large company in a low-growth industry. While Berkshire's insurance and reinsurance businesses as a whole have done very well, you should not generalize this to other firms in the industry unless you view their CEOs to be outstanding. With that in mind, I present two interesting examples of large reinsurance companies on the verge of going bankrupt.

Failure of Reliance Insurance Company

A reinsurance business is not necessarily safer than an insurance business. You must look at the kinds of reinsurance risks a company may be taking. Here is an example worth keeping in mind if you are planning to invest in a reinsurance company stock. Reliance Group Holdings Inc., a 183-year-old insurer, suffered such huge losses in its reinsurance business that its stock price dropped from $19 per share in 1998 to $0.25 in 2000—a loss of $2 billion in market value. In this case, workers' compensation liability was passed from the primary insurers to several reinsurers, including Reliance. The reinsurers got stuck with low premiums and potentially large claims. A simple lesson from this is that a single large mistake can lead an established reinsurance company into bankruptcy.

Berkshire Hathaway, operating through its subsidiary Cologne Re, also wrote some of the reinsurance contracts and took a $275 million pretax charge in 1999. Fortunately, Berkshire's share of this reinsurance pool was not large. Whereas $275 million is a large sum in absolute terms, it was only about one-fourth of 1 percent of Berkshire's market value. If you plan to invest in reinsurance companies, you should try to find out if the company is making conscious efforts to avoid large losses. Buffett has clarified that given the diversified portfolio of insurance policies and the nature of risks taken, Berkshire is unlikely to face a large one-time claim from any of its policies. And Berkshire can easily absorb a claim worth several billion dollars as it did following the 9/11 terrorist attacks. Buffett aptly captures Berkshire's advantages:

> [W]e sell policies that insurance and reinsurance companies purchase in order to limit their losses when mega-catastrophes strike. . . . What you must understand, however, is that a truly terrible year in the super-cat business is not a possibility—it's a certainty. The only question is when it will come.[5]

Berkshire's advantages include its size and conservative financing policy. Let these attributes always be your guides for investing in general.

The 2008–2009 Market Crash and AIG

American International Group (AIG) wrote about $84 billion of insurance premiums in 2008, compared with $26 billion written by Berkshire. With a stock price of about $100 per share in 2000, its market value was $260 billion, much larger than Berkshire. But in early 2009, AIG was almost bankrupt, its share price around $1. What happened to such a great company? Can that happen to any company?

First, consider how it happened. There are many parts to this puzzle, but one aspect stands out. AIG got into an insurance business that it thought it knew well. AIG thought it was in its circle of competence—insurance. The insurance it provided, called *credit default swaps*, was against corporations defaulting (usually as a group) on their debt. While credit default swaps are essentially insurance policies, they require posting of immediate collateral when losses occur. AIG failed to consider the effect of a recession on many companies simultaneously and the maximum amount of loss it can face. As the economy slowed significantly in 2008, policyholders (called *counterparties* in credit default swaps) demanded many billions of additional collateral that AIG did not have. The federal government had to step in with an emergency loan to AIG as it became clear that AIG may have to declare bankruptcy. By May 2009, AIG had received $180 billion from the government in one form or another, about the value of all the gold held in Fort Knox. It appears that AIG did not know what it was doing or that the employees responsible knew but gambled with other people's money anyway.

Disasters can strike any insurance company, of course, because unforeseen circumstances occur. For example, the September 11, 2001, attack on the World Trade Center could have been fatal to General Re. Buffett writes, "[H]ad Gen Re remained independent, the World Trade Center attack alone would have threatened the company's existence."[6] Even if large insurance companies are bailed out by the government, their business can dry up and shareholders can suffer huge losses. In 2009, large bond insurers MBIA and Amback, among many others, fell into this category.

Graham and Buffett advocate conservative financing because when companies have the ability to borrow a lot, they sometimes do. In bad times, highly levered companies suffer and can even go bankrupt. Similarly, when insurance companies become aggressive, they write economically unsound insurance policies (because they collect float, which is similar to borrowing), and in bad times, they suffer and can go bankrupt. How do you know if a company is becoming aggressive? It is difficult to know for sure. But here is a hint. Risk-taking behavior of individuals is likely to be reflected in the risk-taking behavior of the companies. In investing in insurance and other companies where computation of earnings requires significant estimates, you will be better off with managers who are financially conservative in their personal lives.

Conclusions

At the end of 2008, out of Berkshire's total insurance float of $58.5 billion, General Re and Berkshire Hathaway Reinsurance contributed

$21.1 billion and $24.2 billion, respectively. These large sums are virtually cost free, but they truly belong to the insurance holders or are other people's money. When using other people's money, a company has the added responsibility of using that money effectively. In situations when other people's (your) money is being managed, one should look for extraordinary managers with the highest level of integrity. It is easy to stray when money is cheap and it is not your own, but it can be very destructive to the company.

Chapter 9

Tax Deferment: Interest-Free Loans from the Government

So long as Wesco [a Berkshire subsidiary] does not liquidate, and does not sell any appreciated securities, it has, in effect, an interest-free "loan" from the government equal to its deferred incomes taxes on the unrealized gains, subtracted in determining its net worth.[1]

—*Charlie Munger*

You may find it difficult to believe that at the end of 2008, Berkshire Hathaway had a $10 billion interest-free loan from the U.S. Internal Revenue Service and other tax authorities. According to most tax rules, neither you nor anyone else has to pay taxes on paper gains on stocks until those paper gains are converted into real gains. For example, Berkshire's Coca-Cola investment, purchased about 20 years ago, has increased from the initial $1.3 billion to $9.1 billion, but Berkshire has not yet paid any taxes on the paper gains of $7.8 billion. The nonpayment of taxes is indirectly an interest-free loan that Berkshire enjoys. The longer you wait to capture your paper gains, the longer you don't have to pay taxes.

Value of Berkshire's $10 Billion Interest-Free Loan from the Government

What is the value to Berkshire of the interest-free loan? We can understand this using a simple example. Assume that your mother gives you $100 interest free and says that you can keep it forever. Since you need not pay any interest and need not ever pay the money back, it is essentially a gift. If an interest-free loan is held forever, its value is the same as the amount of the loan. So, if Berkshire can keep the securities forever, the value of the tax deferment is $10 billion. If the holding period is more than 10 years, the value will be close to $10 billion, say, $8 billion. Another way to think about this is that if Berkshire earns a 10 percent annual return on this interest-free loan, Berkshire makes about $1 billion a year that it would otherwise not make.

An interesting and somewhat dramatic discussion appears in Berkshire's 1989 annual report. Buffett writes[2]:

> Imagine that Berkshire had only $1, which we put in a security that doubled by year-end and was then sold. Imagine further that we used the after-tax proceeds to repeat this process in each of the next 19 years, scoring a double each time. At the end of 20 years, the 34% capital gains tax that we would have paid on the profits from each sale would have delivered about $13,000 to the government and we would be left with about $25,250. Not bad. If, however, we made a single fantastic investment that itself doubled 20 times during the 20 years, our dollar would grow to $1,048,576. Were we then to cash out, we would pay a 34% tax of roughly $356,500 and be left with about $692,000.

Unlike most mutual funds that buy and sell frequently, Buffett does not engage in frequent trading. Buffett's example shows that mutual funds that trade often cause investors to pay more in taxes than investors who trade less often. Most discussions in the popular press on mutual fund investing do not mention the advantages from tax deferment. If tax deferment were discussed, most mutual funds would be unattractive to tax-paying individuals.

Returns on a $10,000 Investment in 25 Years with and without Tax Deferment

Let's assume that you invest $10,000 in a mutual fund that is expected to earn the same return as the S&P 500 index. Also assume that all your taxes can be deferred until you sell your investment. If you had invested on January 1, 1984, and held this investment for 25 years until the end of 2008, your investment would have increased to about $103,500. This equals a rate of return of about 9.8 percent per year. You have to pay taxes when you take the money out at the end of the 25-year period. Assuming the long-term tax rate of 20 percent, you will pay $18,700 in taxes and your initial investment would grow to $84,800 net of taxes.

Figure 9.1 shows this amount, $84,800, and compares it with a second amount that your investment would grow up to if you paid taxes on your income every year. For comparison, assume that your marginal tax rate is 35 percent including state and local taxes. Then, you would have earned only 6.37 percent (0.65 ×9.8 percent) per year, and your final amount would have been about $46,800. In the first case, your money would have grown about 8.48 times ($10,000 to $84,800) and in the second case 4.68 times ($10,000 to $46,800). It seems to be a very large difference to me, and I did not even consider the fact that mutual funds also charge a management fee. It is reasonable to assume that in 25 years, you would earn only half of what you would otherwise earn if you can save on frequent taxes and money management fees.

Why do people trade so often or have so much money invested in mutual funds that trade often? Many people who invest in mutual funds do so because they do not feel confident enough in their stock-picking abilities to make their own investments and give in to advice from mutual fund salespeople. They do not think in terms of compounding and

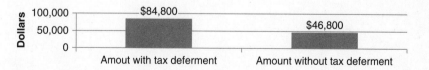

Figure 9.1   Final Amount with and without Tax Deferment from Initial $10,000 Investment in S&P 500 from 1984 to 2008

long-term returns often enough and are too quick to sell to try to make a quick buck (greed) or avoid losses (fear). Also, the fact that putting your money into a mutual fund that trades frequently results in a much higher tax rate is not the first point mutual fund salespeople emphasize in their pitch.

The lesson here is that you should search for stocks that are good long-term investments. If you do not have time to search for stocks or if you do not believe in investing in individual stocks, invest in index funds, not in actively traded mutual funds.

Conclusions

The lesson on tax deferment and compounding teaches two things. First, it implicitly suggests that you should start investing early. If you are going to be leaving your money alone for long periods, you will want to make your initial investment as early as possible to allow for the maximum growth before you need to pull your money back out. Second, do not buy and sell your investments frequently. This will cause a substantial percentage of your taxes to be deferred and your returns to be higher. Buffett practices tax deferment for Berkshire shareholders. Instead of constantly making trades, buy good stocks and go to the beach. If you do not know what to buy, buy the Vanguard 500 Index Fund and hold it for as long as you can.

Part Four

SUCCESS IN RETAILING, MANUFACTURING, AND UTILITIES

Berkshire Hathaway owns several companies in the retailing, manufacturing, and utility sectors. Chapters 10 to 13 explore why Buffett purchased these companies and what he does to create their subsequent profitable growth.

Chapter 10

If You Don't Know Jewelry, Know Your Jeweler

[T]here was never any question in my mind that, first, Helzberg's was the kind of business that we wanted to own and, second, Jeff was our kind of manager.[1]

—*Warren Buffett*

In 1989, Berkshire purchased Borsheim's, a jewelry store in Omaha. When I read about the announcement in the newspaper, I was puzzled. Why is the well-known value investor buying a dazzling business? Where is the value? Later, Buffett explained the cost advantage of Borsheim's: "We attract business nationwide because we have several advantages that competitors can't match. The most important item in the equation is our operating costs. ... Just as Wal-Mart sells at prices that high-cost competitors can't touch and thereby constantly increases its market share, so does Borsheim's. What works with diapers works with diamonds."[2]

Comparison with Wal-Mart: Cost Advantage

Buffett's analogy is worth repeating because it is not conventional wisdom: "What works with diapers works with diamonds." His point is that in almost any industry, cost advantage is important.

Cost advantage in the jewelry business may come from various sources. First, there is an advantage in location: Omaha is a less expensive place to operate a business than New York, and this can be especially relevant during economic downturns. Overheads are smaller, period. Keeping this philosophy in mind, most Wal-Mart stores are located in the suburbs, not in expensive city centers. Consequently, Wal-Mart has slowly built a reputation of reliably low prices. Second, once a company or a store has built a good reputation, its costs go down even more. This happens for a variety of reasons. For example, it does not have to advertise much. Spending less on advertising helps bring down the cost per unit of sales. Until recently, Wal-Mart did not advertise much in newspapers and on television. Beyond easily identifiable cost advantages such as advertising, additional cost advantages come from superior managers who built the reputation in the first place. As Buffett points out, he liked Jeff Comment, the manager, who was running Helzberg Diamonds at the time. Buffett did not just mean that he liked Jeff as a golf buddy. He liked Jeff for his abilities as a manager. Good managers know what quality items to buy and in what quantities to order. This gives them a cost advantage through purchasing and low customer returns.

For big-ticket items such as jewelry, the reputation of the store and its managers also helps generate higher revenues and, hence, higher profitability. Average consumers often find it difficult to determine the true value of diamonds and jewelry. Hence, trust plays a major role in buying decisions. The average customer would rather pay 10 percent more to ensure that the diamonds and precious metal are of the highest quality. In this regard, Berkshire's name has probably also helped increase revenues at Borsheim's. Regarding Borsheim's CEO, Buffett writes: "In the six years prior to the move, sales had doubled. Ike Friedman, Borsheim's managing genius—and I mean that—has only one speed: fast forward."[3] When you see a business managed by people like Sam Walton or Ike Friedman, the best action to take is to try to partner with them. Buffett believed in Friedman's integrity so much that he bought the business without an audit. "If you don't know jewelry, know your jeweler" makes sense for any business or stock you plan to buy. The jewelers in this maxim are the people managing the business.

Regardless of how much you research a company, you cannot learn enough about its future products, research and development (R&D) plans, new markets, alliances, corporate governance practices, and so on. However, if the company's managers are "good jewelers," you really do not need to invest a huge amount of time in investigating the business. To understand the management, you have to make a few phone calls to learn about customer service; your family and friends may tell you about their experiences, and you may try the company's products. The importance of management quality is underscored in the following Berkshire acquisitions.

Helzberg Diamonds, Ben Bridge Jeweler, and Others

Berkshire purchased Helzberg Diamonds in 1995. The inspiring story of the company's growth reveals what Buffett likes to see in a potential acquisition. This is not only about the success of the business but also, once again, about the people. Here is the story of the people behind Helzberg Diamonds.

Morris Helzberg opened the first Helzberg jewelry store in 1915. His young son Barnett often worked in the shop on Saturdays. When his father became ill, Barnett became responsible for the entire operation at the age of 14. By the time his older brother Gilbert returned from World War I to join the business, Barnett had become an exuberant businessman. An aggressive promoter, he ran large newspaper ads touting the slogans "Meet the Helzberg Boys" and "Wear Diamonds." He also offered free airplane rides with a purchase. By 1925, Helzberg had expanded significantly and quickly became known as a prominent jeweler in the Midwest.

When Berkshire purchased Helzberg, it had 134 stores scattered all over the United States. By the beginning of 2009, the number had risen to 270 stores. Buffett explains what led him to acquire Helzberg[4]:

In May 1994, a week or so after the Annual Meeting, I was crossing the street at 58th and Fifth Avenue in New York, when a woman called out my name. I listened as she told me she'd been to, and had enjoyed, the Annual Meeting. A few seconds later, a man who'd heard the woman stop me did so as well. He turned out to be Barnett Helzberg, Jr., who owned four shares of Berkshire and had also been at our meeting.

In our few minutes of conversation, Barnett said he had a business we might be interested in. When people say that, it usually turns out they have a lemonade stand—with potential, of course, to quickly grow into the next Microsoft. So I simply asked Barnett to send me particulars. That, I thought to myself, will be the end of that.

Berkshire was made to order for him. It took us awhile to get together on price, but there was never any question in my mind that, first, Helzberg was the kind of business that we wanted to own and, second, Jeff was our kind of manager. In fact, we would not have bought the business if Jeff had not been there to run it. Buying a retailer without good management is like buying the Eiffel Tower without an elevator.

You may notice that even though Buffett liked the business and the management, he did not want to overpay for it. As he said, it took them a while to get together on price. However, as Barnett Helzberg said, "Buffett didn't change a hair in the leadership of Helzberg."[5] This statement by Helzberg is a hallmark of Buffett's management style. After Buffett invests in a company or acquires a company, he does not try to influence the management. He looks for a company that has an excellent long-standing reputation and superior management already in place. Helzberg's thinking about developing a successful business is similar to Buffett's: "Business *is* People."[6] This sounds simple, but it is not necessarily easy for every manager to implement. If you find a company with a Sam Walton, don't worry about whether he sells diapers or diamonds. You have found a good jeweler, and you should think of becoming his partner.

Berkshire's jewelry business has grown steadily, adding more businesses with excellent reputations. In 2000, Berkshire acquired Ben Bridge Jeweler, a chain of 65 stores. The number of stores had risen to 77 by early 2009. Ed Bridge and Jon Bridge were the fourth-generation owner-managers of a highly reputed jewelry business that had grown steadily under their leadership. Ed Bridge called Buffett on a recommendation from Barnett Helzberg. He was especially impressed by Buffett's preference to let the current management of his acquisitions operate with little interference. In 2007, Berkshire acquired two gold jewelry manufacturers: Bel-Oro International and Aurafin LLC. One additional point to draw from Berkshire's initial purchase of Borsheim's and subsequent expansions is that the various companies are kept independent of one another in terms of management. He made no effort to merge his jewelry companies into a single entity. Overall, Buffett seems to emphasize the long-term reputation of the business and its management quality.

Profitability: Berkshire's Jewelry Businesses versus Tiffany & Co.

In any business, what ultimately matters is profitability. Under Berkshire, acquired companies are able to do even better than what they would have done independently because risks are reduced and expansion plans can be implemented, possibly through Berkshire's financial support. In Table 10.1, I present an analysis of Berkshire's jewelry businesses for 1996 to 1999. (More recent data are not available.) Sales revenues of Berkshire's jewelry businesses grew from $392 million to $486 million, a 24 percent increase. This translates into a growth rate of about 7 percent per year, a good growth rate for mature businesses. However, operating profits went up substantially more, from $28 million to $51 million, which translates into 82 percent, or about 22 percent per year. Similarly, profitability of the assets employed—that is, the return on assets—increased from 10 percent to 20 percent. The increase in return on assets shows that Berkshire's jewelry businesses did not need the same level of inventories and other assets per unit of sales in 1999 that they did in 1996. Given that Buffett emphasizes profitability, I think that Buffett influenced their focus on the efficiency of the assets employed.

I use Tiffany & Co. as a yardstick for comparison because it is the premier jewelry business in the United States. It has been operating since 1837 and commands the greatest respect in the jewelry industry. It is also highly profitable and successful in maintaining its leadership position. If we compare the profitability of Berkshire's jewelry businesses with that

Table 10.1 Profitability of Berkshire's Jewelry Businesses Compared with Tiffany & Co.'s

Berkshire's Jewelry Business				
	1999	1998	1997	1996
Revenues	$486	$420	$398	$392
Identifiable assets at year end	$258	$234	$219	$267
Operating profits before taxes	$51	$39	$32	$28
Operating profits as a percentage of revenues	11%	9%	11%	7%
Operating profits as a percentage of identifiable assets	20%	17%	15%	10%

Tiffany & Co.				
	1999	1998	1997	1996
Revenues	$1,461	$1,169	$1,018	$922
Total assets	$1,343	$1,057	$827	$739
Operating profits	$257	$161	$133	$109
Operating profits as a percentage of revenues	18%	14%	13%	12%
Operating profits as a percentage of identifiable assets	19%	15%	16%	15%

Dollar amounts in millions.

of Tiffany's, we will be putting Berkshire's jewelry businesses up against the best in the industry. Table 10.1 shows the two sets of data.

Tiffany's revenues are about three times those of Berkshire's jewelry businesses. In the four years from 1996 to 1999, Tiffany's also increased its revenues substantially, from $922 million to $1.46 billion, a 58 percent rise. Ultimately, it is not the dollar amount of revenues or the dollar amount of operating profits that matters the most. What matters is profitability. We should always ask: "What is the return on assets employed?" The last row of data in the table is the most useful for comparing Berkshire's jewelry businesses with Tiffany's. In 1996, Berkshire's jewelry businesses lagged behind Tiffany's in terms of operating profit as a percentage of total assets: 10 percent versus 15 percent for Tiffany's. However, by 1999, Berkshire's jewelry businesses had achieved parity: 20 percent versus Tiffany's 19 percent. The main reason for this success seems to be that Buffett picks high-quality managers to run reputed businesses and then allows those managers to run those businesses as if they owned them.

Conclusions

While they are all retail jewelry stores, Borsheim's, Helzberg Diamonds, and Ben Bridge Jeweler are run as separate businesses under the Berkshire umbrella. The principal reason is *managers* who made those businesses successful in the first place by keeping costs low and customers satisfied. Hence, their successes are likely to continue under the existing management. Remember, "What works for diapers works for diamonds and for other businesses." When Berkshire acquires a business, it maintains the business's original organizational structure to suit the management, rather than requiring the management to conform to a common organization structure.

Chapter 11

Compete Like Mrs. B

There's no operation in the furniture retailing business remotely like the one assembled by Berkshire. It's fun for me and profitable for you.[1]

—*Warren Buffett*

I have often asked my friends and colleagues about their thoughts on investing in furniture retailers. Not surprisingly, most of them consider the business mundane and have never thought of investing in one. In 1983, Berkshire acquired a 90 percent interest in Nebraska Furniture Mart, which was run by its then-owner Rose Blumkin, popularly known as Mrs. B. Why did Buffett purchase this business? The answers we get further strengthen our conclusions in the previous chapter.

Know When Not to Compete:
Nebraska Furniture Mart

Regarding the Nebraska Furniture Mart acquisition, Buffett wrote:

One question I always ask myself in appraising a business is how I would like, assuming I had ample capital and skilled personnel, to compete with it. I'd wrestle grizzlies rather than compete with Mrs. B and her

progeny. They buy brilliantly, they operate at expense ratios competitors don't even dream about, and they then pass on to their customers
much of the savings. It's the ideal business—one built upon exceptional value to the customer that in turn translates into exceptional
economics for its owners.[2]

Clearly, the main reason for the success of Nebraska Furniture Mart
is that it is run by incredible managers who remain focused on customers
and cost. Their philosophy is not very different from Wal-Mart's philosophy of "We sell for less." Mrs. B summarized her philosophy as "Sell
cheap and tell the truth."[3]

Nebraska Furniture Mart continued to do well after its acquisition by
Berkshire and is still doing well under the management of Mrs. B's children and grandchildren. Revenues increased steadily from $100 million
in 1983 to more than $300 million in 1999. Since then, the company's
sales data have not been publicly available. Nebraska Furniture Mart
now has stores in Des Moines, Iowa, and Kansas City, Kansas. Nebraska
Furniture Mart was not acquired because it had wonderful products. It
was acquired because it had wonderful managers. In 1996, Buffett wrote
of Mrs. B: "She's 103 now and sometimes operates with an oxygen
mask that is attached to a tank on her cart. But if you try to keep pace
with her, it will be you who needs oxygen."[4] One Berkshire practice
that may play a role in the continuity of excellent management is to
offer desirable incentives to managers. In the case of Nebraska Furniture Mart, 10 percent of the store's ownership was kept in the Blumkin
family.

In a walk around your town, you will no doubt see some incredible businesses that have been operating there for many years. Besides
furniture stores, you may find a few restaurants, grocery stores, bars,
bakeries, cafes, dry-cleaning stores, and pizza parlors. Some of them
may be large enough to be publicly traded. Most people ignore small
businesses—they are too boring to be discussed in the *Wall Street Journal*
or on CNBC. Peter Lynch discusses the importance of buying boring but
well-run companies: "If a company with terrific earnings and a strong
balance sheet also does dull things, it gives you a lot of time to purchase
the stock at a discount."[5] You should not hesitate to partner with such
businesses.

R.C. Willey Home Furnishings

The acquisition of Nebraska Furniture Mart led Buffett to another successful furniture acquisition. Berkshire acquired the five-store R.C. Willey Home Furnishings in 1995. The number of stores has since grown steadily and reached 15 by 2008. Nebraska Furniture Mart's Irv Blumkin was the main person behind this acquisition. Buffett writes, "It was Nebraska Furniture Mart's Irv Blumkin who did the walking around in the case of R.C. Willey, long the leading home furnishings business in Utah. Over the years, Irv had told me about the strengths of that company. And he had also told Bill Child, CEO of R.C. Willey, how pleased the Blumkin family had been with its Berkshire relationship."[6] R.C. Willey's history also tells us something about its likely future success. From a small business with sales of $250,000 in 1954, CEO Bill Child built it into a $257 million revenue establishment.

As I discussed in the previous chapter, Buffett respects independence. In the case of Nebraska Furniture Mart and R.C. Willey, he said that, like the CEOs of other businesses, the managers of these two businesses would operate autonomously. The philosophy behind this—worth repeating many times over—is that it is easier to handle a large number of competent managers if they are given independence. If competent managers are not given independence, they are likely to leave. Buffett writes, "If I have one person reporting to me and he is a lemon, that's one too many, and if I have managers like those we now have, the number can be almost unlimited."[7]

Star Furniture and Jordan's Furniture

The Nebraska Furniture Mart and R.C. Willey stories continued to unfold as Berkshire Hathaway acquired Star Furniture in 1997. When Buffett asked R.C. Willey's CEO about furniture industry standouts, one of the names he gave was Star Furniture, a five-store retailer. Several years later, Star Furniture became available, and Buffett appeared happy to acquire it. "As was the case with Blumkins and Bill Child, I had no need to check leases, work out employment contracts, etc. I knew I was dealing with a man of integrity and that's what counted."[8] Of course, in addition to excellent management, Buffett saw opportunity for growth. And the company has grown steadily ever since. In 2009, there were 10 Star Furniture stores.

Excellent managers contribute not only through the superior profitability of their businesses but also through their ideas. They become extra voices who can advise you on how to do business within their field. And Buffett listens to them. The idea to purchase Jordan's Furniture also came from the managers of other furniture stores that Berkshire already owned. Buffett explains how he came across Jordan's Furniture: "I have persistently asked the Blumkins, Bill Child, and Melvyn Wolff whether there are any more out there like you. Their invariable answer was the Tatelman brothers of New England and their remarkable furniture business, Jordan's."[9]

In the case of Jordan's, the company not only sells furniture; it also presents customers with a dazzling entertainment experience called *shoppertainment*. Parents can go to Jordan's and simultaneously find a new ottoman and take their kids out for an afternoon of fun. Are we likely to see innovations from one unit, say, Jordan's, transferred to the other units? As we know, Buffett does not interfere in the day-to-day management of the various subsidiaries, but he does provide all possible opportunities for interaction. As long as managers have incentives to improve profitability, they will adopt the innovations that are suitable to them but avoid the ones that are not. This is more efficient than requiring all the furniture stores to adopt practices that have been successful for one of them.

CORT Business Services

Here is another twist to Berkshire's furniture business. CORT is not a furniture store in the same manner as Nebraska Furniture Mart. CORT is a leading national provider of rental furniture, accessories, and related services. CORT was acquired in 2000 by Berkshire's subsidiary Wesco for $385 million. In January 2008, CORT agreed to acquire Roomservice Group, a similar smaller firm in the United Kingdom. In November 2008, it acquired a business division of Aaron Rents and expanded to several new markets. CORT has grown minimally in the past eight years (revenues of $395 million in 2001 to $410 million in 2008), probably because of market conditions.

However, CORT has promise, as Charlie Munger writes:

> CORT has continued to make several selective acquisitions since it was purchased by Wesco, and it is believed that CORT is now better positioned to benefit from job growth and any corresponding economic expansion.... CORT is well positioned ... due not only to its national presence and liquidity, but also because the business reputation of Berkshire Hathaway gives it entrée to the offices of many prospective customers, and thus a competitive advantage.[10]

The story of CORT tells us that not all of Berkshire's acquisitions grow fast. However, they are all managed with a long-term point of view. This approach to slow and steady growth resembles the one we saw for GEICO. CORT is building its reputation now and will probably become aggressive in capturing market share and acquiring weaker competitors when the economy is down because it does not have to worry about quarter-over-quarter profits. Low cost, reputation, and financial strength are keys to long-term success in furniture and similar businesses.

Conclusions

You might think that other than a few businesses like jewelry that we discussed in the previous chapter, consumers do not care much about the *reputation* of a business. That is not so. There is at least one important reason to care about the reputation of a furniture store. How often do you see ads for furniture stores' going-out-of-business sales? They seem omnipresent. When a furniture store goes out of business, customers often lose their deposits, warranties, and return privileges. It is difficult to rebuild a reputation once it is destroyed by such events. Levitz Furniture, for example, has filed for Chapter 11 bankruptcy three times: 1997, 2005, and 2007. Businesses run by reputable firms or managers rarely, if ever, go out of business. Instead they continue to grow. Whenever possible, invest with reputable managers running reputable businesses.

Chapter 12

Why Invest in Utility Companies?

Though there are many regulatory constraints in the utility industry, it's possible that we will make additional commitments in the field. If we do, the amounts involved could be large.[1]

—*Warren Buffett*

In 2000, Berkshire Hathaway invested $1.7 billion to acquire MidAmerican Energy (MEC) with Walter Scott as its partner. MEC is an electric utility based in Iowa with operations in the United States and the United Kingdom. With this acquisition, Berkshire came to own a major utility company and entered into a new industry. Investments in the utility sector are generally regarded as low risk, which is something Buffett always looks for in a potential acquisition. But what else could have prompted Buffett to break into the utility industry?

Similarity between the MEC and Other Acquisitions

The MEC acquisition has several features in common with Buffett's prior acquisitions in the furniture and jewelry retailing businesses. First, customers buy most of their furniture and jewelry locally, just as they do electricity. Second, these industries are all likely to continue to grow because of increases in population and standards of living. Third, Buffett once again emphasizes the importance of management in this acquisition. Talking about Walter Scott, MEC's then largest shareholder, and David Sokol, the CEO, Buffett writes: "If I only had two draft picks out of American business, Walter Scott and David Sokol are the ones I would choose for this industry."[2]

Why does Buffett focus on management? Going back to Berkshire's investment in Nebraska Furniture Mart, not many people would have predicted that Berkshire would acquire furniture businesses all over the country. The subsequent acquisitions were made with the help of Nebraska Furniture's management. Similarly, several jewelry businesses were acquired after the initial acquisition of Borsheim's. Likewise, Berkshire hoped to benefit by using the MEC management select follow-up acquisitions.

Buffett was not buying a cheap company as a pure value investor would like to do. Berkshire paid $35.05 per share for MEC, which itself at the time was growing fast through acquisitions. Over the prior 10 years, its total assets had grown from less than $500 million to above $10 billion, a twentyfold increase. Revenues had grown along the same lines. The average earnings per share for two years before the acquisition was $1.74, giving MEC an acquisition price-to-earnings (P/E) of 20, compared with the long-run S&P 500 P/E average of about 16. Other metrics such as market-to-book (M/B) ratio similarly did not suggest that the company fit the profile of a traditional value investment.

Most state regulators allow utilities to earn a return on equity of about 10 percent. MidAmerican was earning about the same rate of return at the time it was acquired by Berkshire. Utilities, regulated or otherwise, do not earn a high rate of return on equity, but most of them earn a steady rate of return. Thus, they are usually considered to be low-risk investments, but their long-run stock market returns are only a tad below the corresponding returns from industrials. From data available for 1993 to 2008, compounded annual returns on the Dow Jones Utilities index including dividends are 7.8 percent (233 percent over 16 years) in comparison with 8.6 percent (276 percent over 16 years) for the Dow Jones Industrial Average. (Prior data on Utilities index with dividends factored in are not available.) Overall, it seems to me that Buffett invested in the utility industry to earn a reasonable rate of return, somewhat better than the rate he could earn by investing in medium- or long-term bonds. In the long run, there may also be profitable growth opportunities because of outstanding managers Berkshire picked up with the MEC acquisition. Finally, utilities would allow Buffett to invest a large sum of money over time, a much-needed outlet for Berkshire's ever-growing insurance float. Let's consider Buffett's acquisition criteria in connection with MEC.

Four Nonprice Acquisition Criteria

"We buy good companies with outstanding management and good growth potential at a fair price, and we're willing to wait longer than some investors for that potential to be realized. This [MEC] investment is right in our sweet spot," writes Buffett.[3] Note the four criteria, in addition to price, mentioned by Buffett:

1. Outstanding management
2. Good company
3. Good growth potential
4. Patience

The MEC acquisition provides a good example to discuss these criteria.

Outstanding Management

Buffett recalls how he started thinking about the MEC deal: "Walter casually asked me whether Berkshire might be interested in making a large investment in MidAmerican, and from the start the idea of being in partnership with Walter struck me as a good one.... Walter characteristically backed up his convictions with real money: He and his family will buy more MidAmerican stock.... Walter will also be the controlling shareholder of the company, and I can't think of a better person to hold that post."[4] Given these statements, the key element for the postacquisition success of a merger is the quality of management. In the case of

MEC's acquisition, Walter Scott participated by investing $300 million of his own funds that also signaled his confidence in the future of the company.

It is not easy to identify outstanding management. Buffett emphasizes a long track record of success, at times a very long track record. He has mentioned that there should be no mandatory retirement age for CEOs because experience only makes them better. Mrs. B at Nebraska Furniture remained active well past the age of 100. Other Berkshire managers older than 80 years of age include A. L. Ueltschi, chairman of FlightSafety, and Charlie Munger, vice chairman of Berkshire. As I discussed earlier, high-quality managers also fuel growth through acquisitions, as they know what to buy in their industry. Their human capital is not reflected on the company balance sheet, and hence Buffett is willing to pay a reasonable price-to-earnings (P/E) ratio when he buys a company that comes with excellent management.

Good Company

Buffett does not say "great company"; he says "good company." The definition of a good company is also not easy to pin down. In my mind, a good company is one that has given satisfactory returns on investment and is likely to give satisfactory returns for the foreseeable future. This condition is clearly met by MEC as the company for most part is regulated. Buffett has also said that significant barriers to entry are desirable company characteristics, and in the case of MEC, that condition is met because utilities require large sums of money for power plants. But his main focus in acquisitions seems to be to place a good company in the hands of excellent management with full support from Berkshire. That management may transform a good company into a great company. If it does not become a great company, the returns will still be satisfactory. If the company is already recognized as a great company, the stock price may be too high for it to be a Buffett investment. On the other hand, the potential increase in the value from transferring a good company into a great company is enormous.[5]

As shown in Table 12.1, MidAmerican's return on assets (earnings before interest and taxes/total assets [EBIT/TA]) in 2008 and 2007 is 5.4 percent and 5.5 percent, respectively, or an average of 5.45 percent.

The overall conclusions are similar if we use all the available data. If we include only tangible assets (in other words, if we exclude accounting Goodwill), the average return is 6.35 percent. I also estimated return on equity, which turns out to be about 8 percent.[6] Ignoring accounting Goodwill, the return on equity is about 13 percent. Since detailed data on replacement costs of property, plant, and equipment are not available, my guess is that the return on equity is somewhere between 8 percent and 13 percent, or an average of 10.5 percent. This return is close to what the regulators often grant the utilities. Consistent good returns are a tell-tale sign of a good company.

Like most utilities, MidAmerican has a large amount of debt. At the end of 2008, MidAmerican's debt was $20.1 billion against $41.6 billion of total assets, or about half of total assets. Does it go against Buffett's philosophy of maintaining a low financial leverage and make MidAmerican a bad company? The main reason for a preference toward low financial leverage in general is to avoid financial stress. However, well-managed utilities generate steady cash flows and have large amounts of plant assets. Such companies can avoid financial distress by remaining focused on their business. Utilities sometimes get into trouble primarily because of inept management as Enron did when it entered into huge derivative contracts. Also, debt issued by MidAmerican is not guaranteed by Berkshire. Overall, a high level of debt at MEC does not seem to be a concern.

Good Growth Potential and Patience

You might have noticed that Buffett does not cite "excellent growth potential." Once again, if a company has excellent growth potential, the market price is likely to already be too high for the investment to be a Buffett investment. On the other hand, when a company has no growth potential, small changes in technology or demand for its products may create significant diseconomies requiring the company to shut down. Nor do such companies attract talented employees. Buffett refers to investing in a company with little to no growth potential as a "cigar butt" approach to investing. Such investments do not offer high long-term gains just as cigar butts do not offer much long-term smoke. Thus, good growth potential is a healthy acquisition criterion.

In the utility sector, the growth potential for good companies appears promising, but an investor may have to wait for a long time to realize any actual growth. Specifically, new laws will ultimately allow unbundling of the generation, transmission, and distribution functions traditionally performed by utilities in one unit. This unbundling in the United States will be similar to that in the United Kingdom, and MEC should benefit greatly from its experience in the United Kingdom. But it will not happen quickly because it is a political process. In the interim, Berkshire will continue to earn a reasonable rate of return.

Table 12.1 shows that MidAmerican's total assets have more than tripled to $41.57 billion in eight years. How did this growth occur? It appears that the presumed low-risk characteristic of the utility industry applies only to the regulated sector. The unregulated sector, dominated by firms selling electricity and natural gas in the open market, is not as low risk as the regulated sector, owing to the high level of financial leverage. Therefore, acquisition opportunities arise when companies get into trouble because utility companies are highly levered. Opportunities for Berkshire to invest in the energy sector appeared in 2001 and 2002 in the wake of Enron's bankruptcy and problems at other energy companies. Berkshire purchased Northern Natural Gas pipeline from Dynegy for $1.9 billion and another gas pipeline, Kern River, from the Williams Companies for $950 million. In 2006, Berkshire invested $5.2 billion in PacifiCorp. MidAmerican is also growing organically. From 2006 to 2008, MidAmerican's capital expenditure in excess of depreciation was $6.7 billion. Overall, there are good growth potentials.

You are not likely to earn high rates of return by investing in a utility. The best time to invest in a utility is probably when a utility's book return on its equity goes down, affecting the stock prices negatively. This can occur when input prices of coal, gas, and the like go up, when customer demand goes down (perhaps resulting from economic slowdown), or when interest rates go up. A utility would be a good value investment then. Of course, you should invest in only healthy companies lest you lose your investment completely when a company is not able to survive the slump. Since utilities generate a reasonable rate of return on equity over the long run, a low return in one period is likely to bounce back to a higher return in subsequent periods.

Table 12.1 Berkshire Hathaway Energy Sector (MidAmerican Energy Holdings)

	2008	2007	2006	2005	2004	2003	2002	2001	2000
Property, plant, equipment, and other assets, net	$36,290	$33,917	$30,942	$16,037	$15,597	$14,862	$14,177	$ 8,987	$ 8,008
Goodwill	$ 5,280	$ 5,591	$ 5,548	$ 4,156	$ 4,307	$ 4,306	$ 4,258	$ 3,639	$ 3,673
Total assets	$41,570	$39,508	$36,490	$20,193	$19,904	$19,168	$18,435	$12,626	$11,681
Total revenues	$13,971	$12,628	$10,644	$ 7,279	$ 6,727	$ 6,145	$ 4,968	$ 4,973	$ 4,013
Earnings before interest and taxes (EBIT)	$ 2,203	$ 2,086	$ 1,737	$ 1,698	$ 1,331	$ 1,591	$ 1,253	$ 1,004	$ 616
EBIT/Total Assets (%)	5.4%	5.5%	6.1%	8.5%	6.8%	8.5%	8.1%	8.3%	5.3%

Dollar amounts in millions.

Conclusions

Berkshire's acquisitions have been for the most part successful, probably because of Buffett's emphasis on the quality of management and keeping the current management in place after the merger. Unless you are in a position to clearly foresee the success of the merged company, you should avoid investing in companies that are acquiring other companies. Other than price, you should ask at least four questions when evaluating an acquisition situation: Is the quality of management excellent? Is it a good company? Is the growth potential good? And does the acquirer have patience?

Chapter 13

High Profits in Honest-to-Goodness Manufacturing Companies

The company's [Scott Fetzer's] success comes from the managerial expertise of CEO Ralph Schey—The reasons for Ralph's success are not complicated.[1]

—*Warren Buffett*

S cott Fetzer has been a Berkshire Hathaway subsidiary since 1986 and manufactures or sells such wide-ranging items as utility tree vehicles, brushless DC (direct current) and universal motors, Ginsu knives, World Book encyclopedias, Kirby vacuum cleaners, and professional cleaning products, among other small industrial and consumer items.

Ralph E. Schey's leadership in salesmanship and management was instrumental in Scott Fetzer's success before it was acquired by Berkshire. When Schey joined Scott Fetzer in 1974, Scott Fetzer's stock price was $8 per share. Ten years later, it sold for $62 a share. At one time, Ivan

Boesky, a corporate buyout expert, offered to buy the company; and at another time, the company's management tried to take it private. Both those attempts failed, and Berkshire Hathaway purchased the company in 1986 for $61 per share, or about $315 million. It was acquired after its significant growth in prior years under Ralph Schey's management. Until his retirement in 2000, Schey managed the company and produced high returns for Berkshire.

Scott Fetzer's Success

Table 13.1 shows that for the first nine years after Berkshire acquired the company, Scott Fetzer earned a total of $555 million and paid dividends of $635 million to Berkshire. The rate of dividend payments, on average, was 22 percent per year on Berkshire's initial investment. Earnings grew steadily during this period. While revenues grew at the rate of

Table 13.1   Scott Fetzer's Earnings and Dividends

Year	Earnings	Dividends	Return to Berkshire as a Percentage of Initial Investment	
			Earnings	Dividends
1986	$40.3	$125.0	13%	40%
1987	48.6	41.0	15	13
1988	58.0	35.0	18	11
1989	58.5	71.5	19	23
1990	61.3	33.5	19	11
1991	61.4	75.0	19	24
1992	70.5	80.0	22	25
1993	77.5	98.0	25	31
1994	79.3	76.0	25	24
Total	555.4	635.0		
Average			20	22

Dollar amounts in millions.

about 4 percent per year, reaching $1 billion in 1994, earnings grew at about 8 percent per year—a rate that seems remarkable given that all the companies in the Scott Fetzer group were from seemingly old-fashioned industries.

Although detailed data on earnings and dividends are not available after 1994, data on operating earnings before taxes are available from 1996 until 2002. An analysis of those data shows that the group of Scott Fetzer companies continued to do well, although growth seems to have slowed since 1996. Based on numbers from operating earnings, net earnings seem to be about $78 million per year, which translates into a rate of 25 percent per year on Berkshire's initial investment. Overall, Scott Fetzer has been a remarkable investment and continues to generate high returns.

How did Scott Fetzer do so well when many companies from traditional industries did not survive the competition or faced declining profitability? Your understanding of Scott Fetzer will help you find other companies that are publicly traded and follow similar principles.

Companies in traditional or old-fashioned industries typically face declining profitability—so it is important for management to avoid the temptation to plow back earnings into the company. Essentially, managers need to remember not to throw good money after bad. From 1986 to 1994, total earnings were $555.4 million, but most were not plowed back into Scott Fetzer. Instead, they were paid to Berkshire in the form of dividends. In the so-called old-fashioned industries, high growth is not the norm; growing either internally or through good acquisitions is not easy. So credit goes to Schey and Buffett for not expanding simply for the sake of expanding. If you notice a company that has good cash flows but whose managers expand the company by acquiring other companies or by internal growth of assets, you need to investigate it carefully.

How does Buffett accomplish exemplary behavior from his managers? Beyond picking the right type of people, the key to success may be carefully designed CEO compensation contracts. The focus should be on profitability and not on total profits, which disregards the capital base. In the case of Scott Fetzer, Schey could have easily generated even higher levels of earnings if cash flows had been plowed back into the company. However, the rate of return on investment would have gone down and would not be optimum for Berkshire as a whole.

Lest we think that Scott Fetzer's growth has been inappropriately deemphasized, we should not forget that Buffett can use the dividends received in any way he wants. The capital allocation job for Berkshire as a whole is in Buffett's hands. In that sense, growth from the dividends received from Scott Fetzer can occur in another company, giving higher rates of return to Berkshire shareholders, who are the ultimate owners of Scott Fetzer. A brief examination of other similar Berkshire subsidiaries is presented next.

Shaw Industries, Marmon, and McLane

Several other Berkshire subsidiaries are also from honest-to-goodness traditional industries. We get like insights from the way Buffett manages these subsidiaries. In Table 13.2, I present the profitability numbers of one subsidiary because it is a relatively recent acquisition, and its major numbers are available from various Berkshire annual reports. Shaw Industries is a leading manufacturer and distributor of carpets and rugs for residential and commercial use. Berkshire acquired 87.3 percent of the company in 2001 and the remaining 12.7 percent in 2002. In total, Berkshire paid $2.4 billion.[2]

Shaw's revenues and earnings climbed steadily from 2001 to 2006 but declined in 2007 and 2008 as the housing market collapsed. (Dividend numbers are not available.) Identifiable assets also increased as the demand for Shaw's products rose during the booming housing market. In terms of return on Berkshire's investment of $2.4 billion, the average level of annual return from 2002 to 2008 is about 15 percent after accounting for taxes. This is certainly a very healthy return because the investment in Shaw should be considered relatively safe from a long-term perspective. It is difficult to imagine that the market for carpets will go away and that a well-managed, dominant company will not remain profitable for a long time.

In the cases of both Scott Fetzer and Shaw, the CEOs in charge at the time of the acquisitions were not replaced. Ralph Schey at Scott Fetzer continued as the CEO for 14 more years, and Robert E. Shaw continued as the CEO for six more years. Neither of them left the companies they managed for another position, but retired.

Table 13.2 Shaw Industries: Profitability and Growth after Berkshire's Acquisition of Shaw

Year	Revenues	Earnings before taxes	Earnings before taxes as a percentage of revenues	Identifiable assets at year-end	Earnings before taxes as a percentage of identifiable assets at year-end
2001	$4,090	$298	7.3%	$1,619	18.4%
2002	4,334	424	9.8	1,932	21.9
2003	4,660	436	9.4	1,999	21.8
2004	5,274	466	8.8	2,153	21.6
2005	5,723	485	8.5	2,718	17.8
2006	5,834	594	10.2	2,776	21.4
Average			9.0		20.5

Dollars amounts in millions.

In 2008, Berkshire acquired 60 percent of Marmon Holdings, which consists of 130 manufacturing and service businesses that operate independently within 11 diverse business sectors. The products range from nuts and bolts, wire, and cable to shopping carts and railroad tank cars. The remaining 40 percent will be acquired in future years for consideration to be based on the future earnings of Marmon. From limited data that are available, I surmise that profitability is highly satisfactory at about 10 percent operating income on tangible assets.

I also examined similar numbers for McLane Company, which was acquired by Berkshire in May 2003. McLane is one of the nation's largest wholesale distributors of groceries and nonfood items to convenience and discount stores. The after-tax return on the initial Berkshire investment of $1.5 billion has been about 10 percent per year, on average. For 2008, earnings before taxes were $276 million, which is about 18 percent before taxes or about 11 percent after taxes. Chances are its earnings will grow with time even without additional Berkshire investment. One reason for its growth potential is that, when McLane was a Wal-Mart subsidiary, it was not viewed as an independent distributor by Wal-Mart's competitors. Many of the potential customers would then not buy from

McLane. However, as a Berkshire unit, it will not have that impediment to growth. Overall, when a company is run well, the profitability in businesses from traditional industries does not have to be low. As a matter of fact, Buffett's success may come partly from the fact that his managers do an outstanding job in managing seemingly old-fashioned companies.

Conclusions

The main ingredient behind the success of companies in traditional industries is the presence of competent CEOs who might have made them successful in the first place. To praise the CEO of Shaw Industries, Buffett writes: "Any man who can start from absolute scratch in a tough, competitive industry and build a $5 billion business is someone I want to be partnered with."[3] As an investor looking to invest in companies that have been around for a while, you should give considerable importance to the quality of management. To judge the quality of management, Shaw CEO Robert Shaw says, "Investors can look at our track record and get on the train or get off. It's that simple."[4] So it all boils down to track record; find CEOs who have a good—and long—track record.

Part Five

RISK, DIVERSIFICATION, AND WHEN TO SELL

Warren Buffett's concept of risk from investing in common stocks is different from what is taught in business schools. His ideas on diversification and when to sell are also very insightful and worth spending some time thinking about, even if you have studied these topics from other perspectives before. Chapters 14 to 17 are devoted to these issues.

Chapter 14

Risk and Volatility: How to Think Profitably about Them

[W]e define risk, using dictionary terms, as "the possibility of loss or injury."[1]

—*Warren Buffett*

hat does the word *risk* mean? Think about it. Because of the U.S. government guarantees, U.S. Treasury bills and bonds are considered to be the least risky securities around the world. In this context, risk implies default risk or downside risk. Following this line of thinking, corporate bonds are riskier than U.S. bonds, common stocks are riskier than corporate bonds, and options are riskier than common stocks. However, when academics mention that common stocks are riskier than corporate bonds, they invariably imply that common stocks have a higher "beta." In simple terms, *beta* measures how stock returns are correlated with market returns: The higher the correlation, the higher the beta, with the average beta of all stocks being normalized to 1.0. However, in most research studies, beta has *not* been found to be a useful definition for predicting common stock returns, especially for individual stocks.[2] So, academics are still trying to develop better measures of risk. In the meantime, as an individual investor, you are better off ignoring beta for picking individual stocks. You should instead carefully differentiate between the downside risk and the upside potential. At the very least, you should know what you mean by the word *risk*.

A vague understanding of risk is a dangerous thing. Consider the well-known case of the Orange County bankruptcy. In 1994, Orange County, California, lost more than $1.5 billion. State and local governments are generally considered to be some of the most conservative investors. How did Orange County lose such a huge amount? In this case, the answer lay in a misunderstanding of the risk embedded in derivative securities: call and put options and futures contracts. In the minds of some administrators, these derivative securities were supposed to have reduced risk and enhanced returns. However, they did just the opposite. A clearer understanding of risk would have helped Orange County avoid this huge loss. If Orange County's administrators had asked about the probability and potential magnitude of loss (downside risk), they probably would have made better decisions.[3] In your investing, you should always ask those questions.

Risk and Return: Holding Period

Warren Buffett suggests that returns from quarter to quarter, or even year to year, are not very important if the returns in the long run are predictable. Volatility of returns in the short run should not be the main criterion for assessing risk. What matters is the return at the end of the investment period. Assume that you invest $1,000 in a 30-year Treasury bond yielding 5 percent. If your investment horizon is 30 years, you will earn $50 in interest per year, plus the principal of $1,000 at the end of 30 years. However, the market price of the 30-year bond will change from month to month depending on the market interest rate, which could create significant short-term volatility. If you have a 30-year investment horizon, should you define the monthly volatility of bond prices as risk? No. The investment is risk-free so far as the payments are concerned in nominal dollars. Consider the same 30-year bond investment from the perspective of a person with a one-year investment horizon. This investor can lose a significant amount if interest rates rise because the prices of long-term bonds fall as interest rates rise. In early 2009, the 30-year Treasury bonds declined in price by 20 percent when the interest rates went up by about 1.5 percent.

Let's move on to stocks and return volatility. Assume that an insurance company has underwritten a large number of hurricane insurance policies in Florida. You are probably already thinking of Berkshire's insurance business. The insurance company will show high profits in the years Florida is not hit by a major hurricane. Since the stock market usually focuses on the short term, you should not be surprised if the company's stock enjoys high returns in those years. But during a year in which a major hurricane hits the state, profits will go down and the stock price could be bid down substantially. "However, Berkshire's management is willing to accept volatility in reported results, provided there is a reasonable prospect of long-term profitability," writes Buffett.[4] An investor who recognizes that a one-time event may not affect the underlying long-run risk profile of the company is likely to invest more in a good insurance company when the stock price goes down.

The main lesson to take away from this discussion is that there is an interaction between the length of the holding period and risk, especially if you think of risk as downside risk. This applies to both bonds and stocks. If stock returns from one period to another were statistically independent, the length of the horizon would not be important. However, there is ample empirical evidence that stock volatility in the long run is lower than volatility in the short run. Thus, the length of the investment horizon should be an important consideration for an investor.

Volatility Offers Opportunities

An investor who views volatility as risk will be tempted to avoid volatile stocks, which may not be the right investment approach. Indeed, Buffett suggests just the opposite: "In fact, a true investor *welcomes* volatility."[5] As an example, consider volatility and firm size. Smaller companies are usually more volatile than larger companies, probably because a small number of buy and sell orders can dramatically change the stock prices of smaller companies. But small companies need not be fundamentally risky, especially when you know a lot about the specific companies you plan to invest in. Opportunities are more likely to arise in smaller companies than in larger companies. Buffett has expressly said that if he had a smaller amount of money to manage, he would be able to generate higher returns. Since the Berkshire investment portfolio is huge, Buffett restricts himself to investing in large companies. However, if you follow an industry closely enough, you should not ignore smaller companies.

Increased volatility does not imply increased risk because there are many factors that can cause volatility that have nothing to do with risk. Professor Robert Shiller of Yale University has often argued that the stock market is too volatile to be easily explained by rationality alone. He concludes, "Prices change in substantial measure because the investing public en masse capriciously changes its mind."[6] Usually, after an earnings announcement, a company's stock price becomes more volatile. The stock price is also more volatile after a stock split because the price per share decreases. Such a rise in volatility does not necessarily mean that the stock has become more risky. Volatility also increases when the Federal Reserve announces interest rates or when other macroeconomic data are released. Most company fundamentals are not affected by these news items, and you should buy more of your favorite stocks whenever "Mr. Market" is willing to sell them to you at a lower price because of market volatility. In October 1974, the Dow Jones Industrial Average (DJIA) was below 600 after having declined 40 percent, and when *Forbes* asked Buffett how he contemplated the stock market, he shot back, "Like an oversexed guy in a harem. This is the time to start investing."[7]

Opportunities from the Sharp Decline of 1987

There are many potential reasons for sharp declines in stock prices, and unless you are fairly certain about the reason for the decline, you should not increase your investment in stocks simply because their prices have declined. A careful search for a reason will keep you from catching a falling knife. The decline of about 20 percent on October 19, 1987, is usually attributed to the so-called *portfolio insurance effect*, which required many institutional investors to sell part of their holdings as prices fell, which in turn pushed prices down further. Was this justified? A detailed examination of the fundamentals may provide a satisfactory answer.

Prices had been going up steadily since the middle of 1982, when the DJIA soared from below 800 to a high of 2,722 in August 1987, an increase of 240 percent in five years. While predicting the market is next to impossible, many investors were feeling uncertain because interest rates on long-term bonds had increased from around 7.5 percent to 10 percent in a matter of months. At the same time, the market P/E ratio was hovering around 22 from a low of around 10 in 1982. Generally, the relationship between interest rates and the P/E ratio is inverse—the two move in opposite directions—yet this time around, the P/E ratio was increasing as interest rates were going up. Until prices suddenly came crashing down.

Even if you could not predict the downfall of October 1987, you were probably tempted to start investing aggressively when prices became reasonable after the downfall. In recognizing that the market was ready for reinvesting, we have the benefit of hindsight. But history teaches us that when prices rapidly go down, the probability of finding good businesses or stocks at lower prices goes up. Buffett invested heavily in Coca-Cola stock in 1988 in the wake of the 1987 market correction. Although the stock market in this case recovered in less than two years, it could have easily taken longer. Just as we cannot foresee a coming crash, we should not feel comfortable predicting a quick recovery.

A Slow Decline in 1973–1974 and 2008–2009

During 1973–1974, prices declined slowly, from the Dow's high of 1,057 in 1973 to a low of 577 in 1974—a drop of about 45 percent. In percentage terms, the decline in 1973–1974 was more severe than the decline in 1987. Why did this occur, and was it possible to know at various stages if an opportune time to invest had arrived? Buffett noted in October 1974 that it was time to start investing. Once again, with hindsight, we can all conclude that late 1974 certainly was a good time to start investing. However, it seems that most investors had begun to invest earlier than that. The market P/E ratio at the end of 1973 was already around a reasonable 12. How could you have known that you should wait almost another full year for the P/E ratio to fall to a low of around 7? There is no way to time the market perfectly. It is extremely difficult to know when prices have bottomed out. The main lesson that we can learn from the various bear markets is that it is impossible to develop a general theory about the causes of bear markets because there are different causes for every decline. The market in 1973–1974 declined primarily because of the simultaneous recession and increase in the inflation rate. The Arab oil embargo in late 1973 did not help matters. Although prices had declined substantially in 1973, no end to the recession was in sight for a while.

When the rest of the world was fearful of investing in the stock market, Buffett invested $10.6 million in Washington Post in the wake of the market decline. At the time, this amounted to 21 percent all of Berkshire's common stock investments in unaffiliated companies. He writes, "We bought all of our holdings in mid-1973 at a price of not more than one-fourth of the then per-share business value of the enterprise."[8] Washington Post price continued to decline for another year. It illustrates the point that it is not possible to pick the price bottom perfectly. By mid-1974, as the recession was finally giving way to optimism, the oil embargo was lifted, and the Federal Reserve lowered the federal funds rate from 8 percent to 7.75 percent, and additional rate cuts followed. The prices finally bounced back.

In 2009, the year of this writing, the Dow has been as low as 7,500, down from a peak of over 14,000 just 18 months earlier. The United States, Europe, and Japan have been in serious recessions and growth in China and India has slowed considerably. The main difference between the 1973–1974 decline and the current recession is that there is no increase in inflation and interest rates are low. The Dow rebounded to about 10,000 by November 2009. Is this a good buying opportunity? No one can be sure. I personally bought some earlier and am still buying a little bit, but it is no sure thing that we will see a quick turnaround to 14,000 again. However, if you have a 10-year investment horizon, it seems like a good time to buy stocks in your favorite companies, with the Dow 10,000. Between the third quarter of 2008 and the second quarter of 2009, Berkshire invested a large sum of about $18 billion in various preferred stocks and notes of Goldman Sachs, General Electric, Wrigley, Dow Chemical, and Swiss Re. In addition, in November 2009, Berkshire announced plans to acquire Burlington Northern Santa Fe which will constitute its largest acquisition ever. These investments seem to have been influenced, in part, by the market decline.

More on Downside Risk

The best way to avoid financial catastrophe is to understand downside risk well. If possible, you should completely avoid stocks that have a large downside risk. Downside risk is not just a default risk for bonds or bankruptcy risk for stocks; you should also incorporate the risk of a large decline in a company's market value owing to adverse developments. For example, a company investing in mortgage-backed securities may see a large negative effect on its stock prices if housing prices fall. When housing prices are going up, stock prices of such companies may also go up. They may appear to be good buying opportunities, but note that downside risk is also going up at the same time. As another example, consider buying stocks on margin. A decline in the stock market may result in a margin call that may require selling off the securities at a time when buying is more desirable. An investor who has thought about the downside risk carefully is more likely to avoid investing on margin and avoid ruin in the long run.

Large public corporations do not default often, but sometimes they do. Some large companies have suddenly gone bankrupt (for example, Enron and WorldCom), and their stockholders have lost their investments completely. In early 2007, Bear Stearns' stock price was $150 per share, but the company was sold to J.P. Morgan for just $10 per share a year later. As an investor, you should take this into account. In general, you should be especially careful in investing in highly leveraged companies. At least compare their financial leverage with the corresponding industry leverage, and avoid investing a large percentage of your net worth into highly leveraged companies.

Earlier, we talked about the risk of inflation that can be serious even in countries like the United States. The problem with inflation is not inflation itself. The problems arise from the unforeseen hardships for those who are not prepared for a substantial fall in the purchasing power of their savings or for the economy shedding jobs. Buffett says, "In our opinion, the real risk an investor must assess is whether his aggregate after-tax receipts from an investment (including those he receives on sale) will, over his prospective holding period, give him at least as much purchasing power as he had to begin with, plus a modest rate of interest on that initial stake."[9]

To avoid inflation risk, you can invest in inflation-adjusted Treasury securities or the so-called TIPs. After all, you are probably not investing in Treasuries for high returns. You can also avoid some inflation risk by owning real assets. For example, it makes a lot of sense to own your own house. If you have a mortgage, a fixed-rate mortgage is better because it allows you to avoid the large surprises that can result from a variable rate. In my opinion, you should pay off your mortgage as soon as possible so that you have the security of owning your own home (and your monthly expenses do not include a mortgage payment) in the event you lose your job. If possible, you should try to acquire some other real estate; maybe some farmland so that you can live there and grow your own food if things really go south! Finally, you should not ignore short-term investments in money markets because they are liquid, and the rates usually adjust as inflation rises. Overall, safety first and liquidity are good rules that people often forget when the going is good. Berkshire has always maintained high liquidity and low financial leverage. Shouldn't you?

Another downside risk is the decline in the value of the dollar. The value of the U.S. dollar against other currencies may decline, which may affect your consumption if you travel abroad. To some extent, you can avoid this risk by holding some other currencies; Chinese and European money are logical choices in this situation. It is worth summarizing Buffett's outline on how to think about risk. He writes[10]:

Though this risk [in owning stocks] cannot be calculated with engineering precision, it can in some cases be judged with a degree of accuracy that is useful. The primary factors bearing upon this evaluation are:

1. The certainty with which the long-term economic characteristics of the business can be evaluated;

2. The certainty with which management can be evaluated, both as to its ability to realize the full potential of the business and to wisely employ its cash flows;

3. The certainty with which management can be counted on to channel the reward from the business to the shareholders rather than to itself;

4. The purchase price of the business;

5. The level of taxation and inflation that will be experienced and that will determine the degree by which an investor's purchasing-power return is reduced from his gross return.

These factors will probably strike many analysts as unbearably fuzzy because they cannot be extracted from a database. But the difficulty of precisely quantifying these matters is not insuperable and does not negate their importance. Just as Supreme Court Justice Potter Stewart found it impossible to formulate a test for obscenity but nevertheless asserted, "I know it when I see it," investors—in an inexact but useful way—can "see" the risks inherent in certain investments without reference to complex equations or price histories.

Conclusions

When you think that there is a large downside risk in investing in a company, you should be especially vigilant even if expected returns are high. A highly leveraged balance sheet is one indicator of high downside risk in a company. Even countries that borrow large amounts of money are not safe: Russia defaulted on its loans in 1998. If you had invested in Russian bonds, you would have lost heavily. In particular, Long Term Capital Management, the largest hedge fund at the time, lost billions of dollars as a result of the Russian default and almost went bankrupt. Since even a country the size of Russia can get into trouble, clearly you should never think of any company as "too large to fail." By eliminating or severely limiting your investments in companies with large downside risks, you should be able to avoid the huge losses emanating from market volatility. On the other hand, market volatility may cause good companies' stock prices to go down in the short run, giving you good buying opportunities.

Chapter 15

Why Hold Cash: Liquidity Brings Opportunities

[K]eep in mind that most of the value of our convertible preferreds is derived from their fixed-income characteristics. That
means the securities cannot be worth less than the value they
would possess as non-convertible preferreds and may be worth
more because of their conversion options.[1]

—*Warren Buffett*

To preserve principal and possibly invest in more profitable opportunities later, Buffett keeps a significant portion of Berkshire's
total assets in cash, short-term government securities, and preferred stock. Even in adverse situations, these investments generally
safeguard the value of the principal amount. At the end of 2008, Berkshire had $24 billion in cash or cash equivalents, or 12 percent of
total assets, in its insurance businesses. It had an additional $27 bil-
lion in fixed-maturity securities, about half of which are in government
securities.

Liquidity and Opportunities

Beyond safety, there are at least two reasons why Berkshire maintains a large amount of cash and short-term securities. First, Berkshire can invest large sums of money quickly whenever a good investment opportunity arises. An opportunity arose in 2002 when Dynegy needed to sell its 16,600-mile pipeline—the Northern Natural Gas Company—to Berkshire for $928 million, a steep discount on the $1.5 billion that Dynegy had paid only a few months earlier. In many other cases, such as buying an 80 percent stake in Iscar for $4 billion in 2006, Berkshire made the deal quickly without going to any banks. Obviously, a high level of cash is not maintained because it is a good investment per se. It is maintained and allowed to build up because of paucity of good investment opportunities. You should not feel tempted to invest your cash unless you have good investment opportunities.

During 2008, Berkshire's cash and cash equivalent decreased from $37 billion to $24 billion mainly because Berkshire invested in Wrigley, Goldman Sachs, and General Electric preferred stocks. Berkshire could not have made these investments without liquid assets that it could access quickly. Yet another opportunity arose in 2008 when Constellation Energy was about to go bankrupt. Berkshire was able to invest $1 billion immediately and made an offer within the day to acquire the entire company for $4.7 billion. The deal was struck with a break-up clause, as such deals are. Subsequently, Constellation received a higher bid and Berkshire did not compete to acquire the company. However, the original investment and the break-up fee led to a $1.1 billion profit to Berkshire.

The second reason for maintaining liquidity is to attract better-paying—or more profitable—customers. Berkshire can charge higher premiums than other insurers because it can fulfill large insurance claims more easily. In the world of insurance, Buffett compares Berkshire with Fort Knox. No one even thinks about the possibility of a liquidity problem at Berkshire resulting from large claims. Berkshire was able to pay $1.5 billion in claims arising from the 2001 terrorist attacks on the World Trade Center and $3.5 billion in claims from Hurricane Katrina and other losses in 2005. Indeed, Berkshire probably became a preferred insurer in the wake of these incidents. Berkshire most likely did not lose anything in this event. Morgan Stanley estimated that insurance premium increases alone would cover the losses from the World Trade Center attack.[2] This is the power of liquidity.

These reasons for keeping liquid assets also apply to the average investor. First, what should you do if the stock market goes down substantially and you find some wonderful investing opportunities? Of course, you should buy stocks. However, you will miss this opportunity if you are fully invested in the stock market and do not have cash or cash equivalents ready to invest. Second, what should you do if you need some cash for an emergency? Once again, it is good to have some cash on hand so that you do not have to sell your investments at unfavorable prices to cover unexpected costs.

Berkshire's Investments in Convertibles

Convertible bonds and preferred stocks are similar to rent-to-own stores, where you can rent furniture or appliances and then, if you want, purchase the items. Because of convertibility into common stocks, investing in convertible bonds or preferred stocks may work wonderfully when the stock price goes up. If the stock price goes down, the capital and interest payment is generally still safe. Put simply, it is like eating your cake and, sometimes, having another one later.

The best examples of convertible preferred stock investments by Berkshire Hathaway include $600 million in Gillette, $700 million in Salomon, $300 million in Champion International, and $358 million in U.S. Airways. Clearly, if Buffett had been absolutely convinced that the common stock prices would increase substantially, he would have invested in common stocks rather than in convertible preferred stocks. The investment in Gillette has produced excellent returns, but the others have been sort of a mixed bag.

A *convertible preferred stock* pays a dividend at a prespecified rate in a manner similar to that of a bond. For example, the Gillette convertible preferred stock purchased by Berkshire in 1989 carried a dividend rate of 8.75 percent. One advantage of receiving dividends instead of interest is that about half of the dividends received by one corporation from another corporation are not taxable. So, it makes sense to invest in preferred stocks rather than in bonds when the issuer is of sufficiently high quality.

Soon after Berkshire invested $358 million in 1989, U.S. Airways got into trouble and, over the next five years, incurred significant losses. Finally, in 1994, the airline announced that it was deferring the dividend payment. Based on this and other information, Berkshire decided that the fair value of the initial investment had declined by 75 percent, and therefore, the $358 million investment was worth only $89.5 million. Fortunately, U.S. Air's operations improved significantly, and Berkshire recovered its investment.

In the case of Berkshire's investment in Salomon, Berkshire could either have taken cash payments of $140 million or received common shares at $38 per share. In 1995, Berkshire decided to take the $140 million in cash because the Solomon share price was below $38 per share at the time of maturity of part of the preferred share investment. If the initial investment had been made in common stocks, the dividend amount would have been smaller, and Berkshire would have been stuck with the lower-priced common stock.

Berkshire acquired preferred stock in Gillette in 1989 when Berkshire came in as a white knight in response to a takeover bid by Ronald O. Perelman. Such opportunities to be a white knight and ensuing profits avail only to those who have liquidity. The preferred stock was converted into common stock in 1991, and the common stock continued to perform well. Without including dividends, Gillette generated a rate of return of about 14 percent per year from 1991 until it was acquired by Procter & Gamble in 2005, whereas the S&P 500 index generated a little over 7 percent per year.

Recent Berkshire Investments: Wrigley, Goldman Sachs, General Electric, Swiss Re, and Dow Chemical

During 2008, Berkshire acquired $4.4 billion par amount of 11.45 percent subordinated notes due 2018 of Wrigley. This is straight debt, but the rate was high because of the turmoil in the credit markets at the time. Berkshire also acquired $2.1 billion of preferred stock with a dividend rate of 5 percent per year and the redemption amount based on future Wrigley earnings. Thus, if Wrigley does well, Berkshire will share in the upside while the principal is protected. Buffett continues to follow his principles as he says, "When you think of a business that's easy to understand, with favorable long-term economics, and able and trustworthy management—you think of Wrigley."[3]

Berkshire also acquired 10 percent cumulative preferred stock of Goldman Sachs for $5 billion and preferred stock of General Electric for $3 billion. Once again, there are convertible features attached to these investments, which are available until 2013. In the case of Goldman Sachs, if the stock price goes above $115 per share, Berkshire will exercise its options—in which case, for each dollar beyond $115 per share, Berkshire will earn $43 million. In the case of General Electric, for each dollar beyond $22.25 per share, Berkshire will earn $135 million. In March and April 2009, Berkshire also invested about $6 billion in convertible preferred shares of Swiss Re and Dow Chemical.

The main lesson we learn from recent Berkshire transactions is that when there is substantial volatility in a company's stock or when you are less confident in the company's future growth, it may be worth thinking about forms of investments in which the capital is preserved. You may not be able to do exactly what Buffett does, but if you have liquidity, lots of patience, and vigilance, opportunities will find their way to you.

Conclusions

Do not rush to invest in stocks as soon as you have additional cash available for investing. Be patient and wait for good investment opportunities. Holding cash or cash equivalents is not just for safety; it can help you earn more on your investments by enabling you to take advantage of opportunities that arise with brief windows in which to strike. From this perspective, keeping some cash or investments in liquid, low-risk securities may prove to be a high-return proposition in the long run. In some cases, it might be helpful to invest in convertible preferred stocks or convertible bonds, as long as you stay with established firms the way Buffett does.

Chapter 16

Diversification: How Many Baskets Should You Hold?

Don't put all your eggs in one basket.

—*Proverb*

B ut how many baskets should you hold? *Diversification* is one of the most talked about investment concepts. The concept is simple: "Don't put all your eggs in one basket." Perhaps a more interesting question is, "How many baskets should you possess, and how do you decide the number of eggs to be placed in different baskets?" We use the basics of diversification all the time throughout our day-to-day lives. When we travel, we usually pack a variety of clothing suited to different weather conditions because we cannot predict the weather perfectly. We learn to speak different languages so we can communicate with others who do not speak our own language. We acquire a variety of skills to prepare ourselves to earn a living. A person with a diverse knowledge base finds it easier to deal with the unavoidable ups and downs of life.

A diverse knowledge base enhances our understanding of others' viewpoints and helps us make better decisions. The more different things we have in our repertoires, the more prepared we are for the unexpected. Thus, we diversify to protect ourselves from uncertainties and unpleasant situations. You should do the same to protect your wealth.

Diversification

Consider a company that owns two stores, one that sells expensive clothes and one that sells discounted merchandise. Profit margins are usually higher for expensive clothes. When the economy is doing well, the expensive clothing store will yield higher profits, not only because of profit margins but also because of sales volume. However, when the economy is in a recession, the upscale clothing store may become a burden. But remember that the company also owns the discount store, which does well in a recession. The profits from the discount store act as a cushion during the recession. Without diversification, the company can incur enough large losses to cause permanent damage to the business.

Investing in stocks is investing in businesses. If you owned shares of Abercrombie & Fitch stock, your fortunes would be tied to the successes of that store's fashionable goods. However, if you also owned Wal-Mart stock, you would be somewhat protected from the idiosyncratic habits of the high-fashion teenagers who shop at Abercrombie & Fitch. Owning more than one stock is the first step toward diversification. Beyond holding Abercrombie & Fitch and Wal-Mart, if you also owned Intel or IBM, you would be even more diversified.

The basic goal of diversification is to protect your investments from unpredictable events. Diversification is an insurance policy. When you do not diversify and put all your funds into the stocks of one or two outstanding companies, you can easily end up losing a lot of money if one company faces unforeseen difficulties. If you diversify by investing in 10 outstanding companies, you are likely to see good results even if a few of those companies do not do well. On the other hand, if you diversify a lot, you may end up with approximately the same returns as the market. So, how many stocks should you invest in? Before we can answer this question, let's examine what Buffett has done at Berkshire Hathaway.

How Diversified Is Berkshire Hathaway?

At the end of 2008, out of Berkshire's total assets of $267 billion, $55 billion was invested in common stocks of various companies. The largest investment—$9.1 billion—was in Coca-Cola. Other large equity investments included Well Fargo ($9 billion), Procter & Gamble ($5.8 billion), ConocoPhillips ($4.4 billion), and American Express ($2.8 billion). Berkshire's equity investments are concentrated in only a few companies.

We should think of diversification on at least two levels—at the level of the company's total assets and then at lower levels such as the company's equity portfolio. Out of Berkshire's total assets of $267 billion, only $55 billion or 21 percent are invested in common stocks. This implies that the company can have a reasonably high level of concentration in its equity holdings and still be well diversified. In particular, the five largest holdings mentioned here made up more than 50 percent of Berkshire's equity portfolio but only 11 percent of its total assets. These seemingly concentrated equity holdings are actually not very concentrated, as Berkshire as a whole is well diversified.

Buffett invested heavily in Coca-Cola in 1989–1999. At the end of 1999, the market value of the Coca-Cola investment alone at $1.7 billion was 18 percent of Berkshire's total assets of $9.5 billion. Buffett invested heavily in Coca-Cola because he was confident in its future. Ten years later, at the end of 1999, the Coca-Cola investment was worth $11.7 billion. Berkshire made a much smaller investment of $244 million in 2008 in two Irish banks, which went down by 89 percent within the year. Buffett invested a very large sum in Coca-Cola but only a small amount in Irish banks. The main lesson is that the lower your confidence in the future performance of a stock, the less you invest in that stock.

How Many Stocks Should You Hold?

First, if you own assets such as a house and bonds, you shouldn't worry much about diversification in your equity portfolio. In my opinion, if your common stock portfolio consists of less than half of your net worth, it does not make much sense to hold more than 15 stocks in your equity portfolio because it is difficult to stay informed about too many companies if you have a day job. Second, the more you know about certain stocks and feel good about them, the more weight you should give them. In other words, you can concentrate your holdings in the stocks you have the most reason to be confident about.

Buffett studies a large number of companies or stocks, but there are only 16 major holdings reported in the 2008 Berkshire annual report. This is probably because it is so difficult to find any outstanding businesses, much less a great many of them. If Buffett cannot find a large number of outstanding businesses, it is unlikely that an average investor could either. The Dow Jones Industrial Average (DJIA) is based on 30 stocks, but its returns, especially over many years, are generally similar to those of the S&P 500 index, which includes 500 stocks. For several decades, academic research has shown that most benefits of diversification are achieved through holding 20 to 30 stocks in a portfolio. This evidence has been well known for a few decades and is now widely discussed in textbooks.[1] Figure 16.1 shows that once you have 20 to 30 stocks in your portfolio, adding more stocks does very little to reduce the volatility of the portfolio.[2]

Benjamin Graham has been explicit on the number of stocks that a defensive investor should invest in. In outlining various rules for investors, he says, "There should be adequate though not excessive diversification.

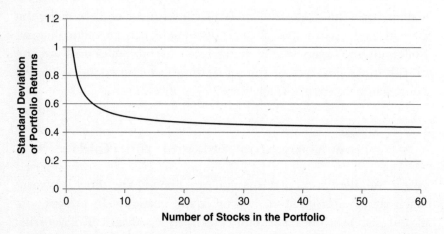

Figure 16.1   Standard Deviation of Portfolio Returns with Number of Stocks in the Portfolio

This might mean a minimum of 10 different issues and about a maximum of 30."[3] Note his mention of a maximum as well as a minimum. Buffett has clearly avoided excessive diversification. Similarly, John Neff, the legendary mutual fund manager, places heavy bets on stocks. When he retired in 1995 after 31 years at the helm of the highly successful Vanguard Windsor Fund, his four largest positions accounted for 23 percent of the portfolio.

Philip Fisher Warns against Too Much Diversification

Phil Fisher, the acclaimed growth investor, warns that the principles of diversification are so simple and widely accepted that most investors embrace diversification to the point of excess. "There is very little chance of the average investor being influenced to practice insufficient diversification," he writes. "Investors have been so oversold on diversification that fear of having too many eggs in one basket has caused them to put far too little into companies they thoroughly know and far too much in others about which they know nothing at all. It never seems to occur to them, much less to their advisors, that buying a company without having sufficient knowledge of it may be even more dangerous than having inadequate diversification."[4]

One reason that diversification may not be as important as it initially seems is that many companies are already diversified internally. General Electric has 12 large divisions that are entirely different businesses ranging from aircraft engines to refrigerators. Thus, if you own General Electric stock, it is almost like owning 12 different stocks. Essentially, you need to hold only a few large stocks (such as Microsoft, IBM, and Wal-Mart) to become well diversified.

Sometimes, experienced investors recommend international diversification. This recommendation should not be overemphasized because many U.S. companies, including Coca-Cola and McDonald's, earn a large percentage of their income from their international operations. Also, it may be more advantageous to invest in global U.S. companies than to invest in companies outside the United States. Because many countries have less stringent regulations to protect shareholders, they do not offer the same protection as U.S. companies do, creating a riskier investment portfolio that would defeat the purpose of diversifying in the first place. Furthermore, by investing in companies in developed economies, shareholders are more likely to be partnering with a well-educated, well-trained, superior management team than if they invested in companies in the developing world. Before you invest in companies abroad, you should familiarize yourself with the country and its financial regulations, and not just the companies themselves.

Diversification and "Diworsification"

"If the one basket I owned was Wal-Mart stock, I'd have been delighted to put all my eggs into it," argues Peter Lynch, who usually had hundreds of stocks in his Magellan Fund.[5] How do you reconcile his argument that you should own a limited number of stocks with his documented practice of owning a large number of stocks? The best answer is provided by Lynch himself, who says, "In my view, it's best to own as many stocks as there are situations in which: (a) you've got an edge; and (b) you've uncovered an exciting prospect that passes all the tests of research. Maybe that's a single stock, or maybe it's a dozen stocks."[6]

In a related context, Lynch explains how some profitable companies often waste money on foolish acquisitions. For example, General Mills owned Chinese restaurants, Italian restaurants, steak houses, Parker Brothers toys, Izod shirts, coins, stamps, travel companies, Eddie Bauer retail outlets, and FootJoy products, many of which it acquired in the 1960s. While each acquisition may have been justified in some way, General Mills could not manage all the subsidiaries effectively and suffered financially. Individuals are equally capable of wasting money on foolish investments. Most people are unlikely to invest efficiently in a large number of stocks from several industries. In such cases, diversification can become "diworsification," a situation in which diversification can hurt your returns, rather than protect them. Of course there are always exceptions. As Lynch himself admits, "Buffett's Berkshire has bought everything from candy stores to furniture stores to newspapers, with spectacular results. Then again, Buffett's company is devoted to acquisitions."[7]

Conclusions

By studying the teachings of Graham and Fisher, and taking into account analyses in modern financial literature and the practices of Buffett, we can conclude that a prudent investment strategy involves investing in 10 to 30 stocks. The less emphasized, but more important, point demonstrated by Buffett's practices is that the more you know about certain stocks that you have deemed desirable, the more of them you should own. I hold about 40 percent of my equity portfolio in Berkshire Hathaway common stock.

Chapter 17

When to Sell

If you aren't willing to own a stock for ten years, don't even think about owning it for ten minutes.[1]

—*Warren Buffett*

A typical mutual fund portfolio holds a stock for one to two years; a turnover of 100 percent is not uncommon. Not Berkshire Hathaway's portfolio, though. By examining Berkshire's turnover of stocks and the stocks sold, we can learn what Buffett would recommend about the length of time you should hold a stock in your portfolio and when you should sell.

Turnover of Berkshire's Equity Portfolio: Why Buffett Holds Almost Forever

I started analyzing Berkshire's buying and selling of stocks in about 1994. At the end of 1994, Berkshire's investment portfolio of $70 billion consisted of $15.2 billion in common stocks. During 1995, Berkshire sold $1.35 billion in common stocks from its portfolio. In other words, it turned over about 9 percent of its portfolio. Purchases were $1.46 billion, slightly in excess of sales. Berkshire's common stock portfolio grew to $39.8 billion in 1999, and the turnover from 1994 to 1999 averaged about 10 percent per year. In recent years, Berkshire's turnover has declined to about 5 percent, implying an average holding period of about 20 years.

This analysis does not fully capture Buffett's strong belief in long-term investing. Since some of Berkshire's investments are for short-term arbitrage, this computation is conservative in reporting the average holding period. Nevertheless, 10 to 20 years is still a very long holding period. I can only imagine how few investors have such lengthy holding periods.

Part of the reason Buffett holds his stocks for such a long time must be that he acquires a considerable amount of knowledge about the company before he acquires stock in the company. Long-term investments best serve those who, like Buffett, buy because they know a lot about the company and have confidence in its long-term prospects. You could divide your portfolio into permanent, or core, holdings and an "other" category consisting of stocks you would like to learn more about. With time and further examination, you eventually decide whether to purchase more of the stocks in the second category or to sell off the shares you have, depending on your more educated opinion of the companies' potential. Buffett writes, "[W]hen we own portions of outstanding businesses with outstanding managements, our favorite holding period is forever."[2]

Why is it a good thing to hold stocks forever? It is only preferable when the business is expected to give a satisfactory return forever. Such stocks, on average, do not come from high-tech or hot industries. This may sound counterintuitive, but most high-tech businesses do not survive for a long time. If you invest in high-tech companies, you are likely to lose more often than when you invest in low-tech. If you invest with an intention to preserve your capital, you should not invest in high-tech companies unless you are extremely knowledgeable about the company. High-tech stocks are extremely volatile and fraught with risk. How about returns?

People often argue that businesses from everyday, low-tech industries cannot earn high returns. Buffett has repeatedly proved them wrong. Businesses perform well even if they are from traditional industries when they are leaders in their industries and when they are run by owner-oriented managers. Owner orientation is especially important in this case because managers must know when not to throw good money after bad. They must make difficult decisions. If Berkshire Hathaway had not been in such good hands in the 1960s, management probably would have tried to survive in the dying textile business rather than taking money out of it. Berkshire pulled out of the textile business, while several other companies stayed in and went bankrupt. In 2009, most people would agree that one reason General Motors faces such trouble is that the management never made the right call on hard decisions. If General Motors had not expanded by buying companies around the world and starting new brands, it would have given satisfactory returns to its shareholders. Overall, Buffett's principles of investing in easy-to-understand (low-tech) companies with excellent management and then holding them forever go hand and hand. Together, they produce high rates of return.

Of course, Buffett does not hold every stock forever. To get a better idea of Buffett's thoughts on when to sell, let's examine some of Berkshire's major sales.

Two Main Reasons to Sell

Buffett has periodically sold Berkshire's major holdings, including McDonald's in 1998, Travelers in 1998, Disney in 1999, Freddie Mac in 2000, and PetroChina in 2007. The latest reported market values of these stocks were $1.4 billion, $1.3 billion, $1.5 billion, $3.9 billion, and $4.0 billion, respectively.

First and foremost, investors should sell when they conclude that they have made a mistake. Sometimes, tax losses can be balanced against gains to reduce the overall tax bite. One major mistake, which Buffett admitted, was the purchase of ConocoPhillips stock from 2006 to 2008 for $7.0 billion. By the end of 2008, the market value of the $7 billion investment had declined to $4.4 billion, a slide of 33 percent, which was in line with the drop in the stock market. In 2009, Berkshire sold 16 percent of its ConocoPhillips holdings and reported plans to sell more in the near future. What remains a mystery to me is the reason for this purchase. The simple explanation that he was betting that oil prices would rise is not convincing because oil prices had already gone up several hundred percent in the prior few years. And Buffett could have simply bet on oil in the futures market.

You should sell when the stock price is high in relation to its intrinsic value. In other words, you should sell when there are better alternatives, including investing in short-term securities or holding cash. Buffett sold PetroChina stock in the second half of 2007 for about $4 billion after its price had gone up eight times since the stock's acquisition in 2002 and 2003 for $488 million. Some in the press speculated that he sold PetroChina because he was criticized for investing in it in the first place: It is alleged that PetroChina supported the Sudanese government's involvement in genocide against people in the Darfur region. Buffett, denying this speculation, has said that his decision was based only on price considerations. Both PetroChina and the S&P 500 index declined by about 40 percent over the next 18 months. Buffett's timing on this sale was correct from the price point of view.

In 1997, Berkshire sold about 5 percent of its portfolio to increase bond holdings in relation to stocks. Buffett writes, "Some of the sales we made during 1997 were aimed at changing our bond-stock ratio moderately in response to the relative values that we saw in each market, a realignment we have continued in 1998."[3] In 2008, Buffett sold partial holdings in several stocks, including Johnson & Johnson and Procter & Gamble. I estimate the dollar amount of these sales to be about $5 billion. Berkshire sold these stocks to fund large purchases in bonds and preferred stock in Wrigley, Goldman Sachs, and General Electric. Buffett must have thought that the alternatives were better. Because of psychological reasons, investors sometimes do not sell when they have to take a loss. They should think about the sunk-cost fallacy and sell. Overall, if you know you have made a mistake, or if there are better alternatives, you should sell.

Why Were McDonald's and Disney Stocks Sold?

Buffett confessed that he should not have sold McDonald's stock. Just as with purchases, it is not possible to time sales perfectly. This is one additional reason to plan for the long run when buying in the first place. He wrote in Berkshire's 1998 annual report, "I need to make a confession (ugh): The portfolio actions I took in 1998 actually *decreased* our gain for the year. In particular, my decision to sell McDonald's was a very big mistake. Overall, you would have been better off last year if I had regularly snuck off to the movies during market hours."[4] He sold McDonald's soon after the Dairy Queen acquisition, which was announced in October 1997 and consummated in January 1998. It is possible that he did not want to hold both Dairy Queen and a major holding in McDonald's because the two compete directly with one another. A critic could argue that Berkshire was trying to monopolize the fast-food market. Buffett would like to avoid those speculations to protect his reputation. Similarly, when Berkshire announced its acquisition of Burlington Northern Santa Fe in November 2009, he sold Berkshire's $900 million investment in Union Pacific (2 percent stake in the company) and the company's roughly $100 million investment in Norfolk Southern (1 percent stake in the company). Even if there is no impropriety of any sort, impressions matter, and, if so, why risk reputation at all by holding competitors' shares? Buffett probably also sold Disney shares for reasons of reputation.

Berkshire sold Disney stock in 1999. There are two potential explanations for this decision. First, he did not seem to like the management at Disney at the time. Until 1995, Buffett's longtime friend Tom Murphy was the chairman of the board and CEO of Capital Cities/ABC Inc. However, Murphy retired when Disney acquired Capital Cities/ABC. Berkshire received Disney stock in exchange for its holdings in Capital Cities/ABC. Buffett has spoken highly of Murphy but has never been as complimentary of Disney's follow-up management.

Second, Disney's executive compensation had been subject to unfavorable publicity on at least two counts. Michael Eisner, Disney's chairman of the board, exercised stock options at a profit of about $565 million in 1993, following a profit of $202 million in 1992. Even without the stock options, Eisner was among the highest-paid executives in the United States. Furthermore, he had been granted an additional 10-year contract that would have kept him as chairman and chief executive of the company through 2006. The compensation issues were hotly debated in several Disney annual shareholders' meetings.

Buffett does not believe in extremely high compensation. Hence, it is likely that he was unhappy with the controversy surrounding Eisner's compensation package. Another controversial issue had been the departure of the company president, Michael Ovitz, who received a $57 million severance package. Overall, it is not a complete surprise that Buffett decided to sever his association with Disney.

Why Was Freddie Mac Stock Sold?

In Berkshire's 2000 annual report, Buffett noted that nearly all Freddie Mac shares had been sold during the year. Why? He did not elaborate then. However, with time, we have learned something very interesting and useful.[5] In October 2007, Buffett testified for the government in its case against Freddie Mac's former CEO. Buffett disclosed that he was troubled in part by a Freddie Mac investment that had nothing to do with its business. "I follow the old dictum: There's never just one cockroach in the kitchen," Buffett said. He made two observations in his testimony. First, when executives offer earnings projections and cannot make the numbers, they start making up numbers. Second, when companies engage in other activities that seem to be motivated by a need to make the numbers, investors need to be careful. Freddie Mac was forecasting earnings growth in the mid-teens; and it appears that Buffett thought that the company, unable to make the numbers, would engage in nonproductive activities to make up the numbers. Overall, Buffett was able to read early warnings of trouble at Freddie Mac. In 2000, Freddie Mac's stock price was around $60 per share. It remained between $50 and $70 per share between 2001 and 2006, but in 2009, it was trading at around $1 per share.

Conclusions

Buffett sells his stock holdings infrequently because he buys only after he is convinced of their long-term value. One reason to sell is the price of the stock in relation to alternatives available, including holding cash. Buffett sold PetroChina for this reason. He sold the Disney holding because he did not seem to have as much confidence in the new management as he had in the old management. Once again, this shows that quality of management is very important to him. Finally, I like the cockroach theory of earnings manipulation or management behavior that Buffett described. When you see any signs of improper management behavior or questionable numbers that make you uncomfortable with the company, you should sell the stock because if you are picking up on one problem from the outside, there is likely more wrong with the company on the inside. There is rarely just one cockroach in the kitchen.

Part Six

MARKET EFFICIENCY

B uffett doesn't think you need to have a high IQ to be successful in the stock market. Markets are not always efficient. In Chapter 18, I discuss some of the less commonly covered aspects of the market efficiency paradigm, and in Chapter 19, I extend the discussion to the related field of arbitrage and hedge funds.

Chapter 18

How Efficient Is the Stock Market?

Essentially, it [Efficient Market Theory] said that analyzing stocks was useless because all public information about them was appropriately reflected in their stock prices. In other words, the market always knew everything.[1]

—*Warren Buffett*

F ew people consistently make money betting on horse races. In finance terms, the horse racing market is efficient. But is the stock market efficient?

Some people argue that the stock market is efficient and that you should not spend any time trying to beat the market averages. On the other hand, others, including Buffett, argue that the market is not efficient. It is not productive to debate whether the market is efficient; the important point is to think about the extent to which it is efficient. We come across many questions in our lives when a simple yes-or-no answer is not very meaningful. When someone asks, "Am I going to be able to make a living if I study engineering?" or "Am I going to get a job if I have a degree in mathematics?" the correct answer is generally "Yes, of course." However, it is more important to know how good a living you can expect to make if you become an engineer or what kind of job you can land if you get a degree in mathematics. In the same manner, a simple yes or no to the market efficiency question is not worth getting agitated about. It is more important to know how, when, why, and to what extent the market is efficient and, especially, how, when, why, and to what extent it is not efficient.

Can I Make Money in the Stock Market?

Instead of thinking about market efficiency, you should ask, "Can I make money in the stock market?" Making money in this case means generating above-average returns. My answer to this all-important question is "Yes, of course." If I thought otherwise, I would not be writing this book, I would not be investing in individual stocks, and I would not be teaching Buffett's ideas. But it is also important to recognize that making money is not effortless. There may be bargains out there, but there is no free lunch.

As a starting point, consider these two simple questions. They should help you start thinking about making money in the stock market and whether you should try to beat the market or whether you are better off investing your money in an index fund.

1. Do most professional money managers generate above-average returns in the stock market?
2. Do most individual investors generate above-average returns in the stock market?

The answer to both questions is no. It has puzzled me for a long time that most professional money managers can't beat the S&P 500 index. Among those who can, few do it consistently. Roughly speaking, this evidence supports market efficiency. You then need to ask, "If most money managers cannot beat the S&P 500 index, how can I?"

First of all, since most money managers do not beat the market averages, it should be clear that you should not listen to most money managers. What does it imply about reading the *Wall Street Journal* and *Barron's* and watching CNBC? You should read the financial press and watch TV for facts, for events, for news, for analysis, but *not* for opinions. You should listen to only a select few, such as Warren Buffett, John

Templeton, and Peter Lynch, who have built a preeminent record over many years. Otherwise, you should tune out when unsolicited advice from talking heads comes your way.[2]

Most Academics Favor Market Efficiency

Most academics promote the efficient market theory as the mantra for investing in the stock market. It does *not* suggest that intelligent investors can never beat the market. The main reason academics have internalized the efficient market theory is that it builds on appealing assumptions of rationality. But people are often irrational. So, at the very least, be careful in taking academic advice to heart: Use a pinch of salt. Once again, the research findings may be interesting to look at, but you do not have to agree with interpretations that can sometimes be a bit of a stretch, given the evidence. And the academics do not always agree with one another; some new academic research now casts doubt on earlier evidence that the stock market is efficient.[3] In academia, new ideas are always welcome and debated vigorously. In a well-known book, Professors Andrew Lo and A. Craig MacKinlay explain several developments and argue that financial markets are predictable to some degree but far from being specimens of inefficiency or irrationality.[4] It takes convincing evidence from a variety of research findings before new ideas are widely accepted.

Even if the market were efficient, there is still no harm in buying individual stocks using your own knowledge. In an efficient market, you *cannot* lose money even if you want to. For example, consider a game in which your friend tosses a fair coin, and you randomly call heads or tails. In this game, you will win half the time and lose half the time regardless of what you call. In other words, in a fair game of chance, even if you try to lose your money, you cannot do so consistently. If the stock market is efficient, you cannot, on average, lose money even if you want to. You will incur the cost of trading in terms of brokerage commissions, but as long as you do not trade often, you will do as well as, or better than, most money managers. On the other hand, if the market is not efficient, you can learn from your trades and you may develop the skills necessary to beat the market.

Other evidence in the academic literature suggests that academics still know little about the workings of the stock market. For example, they have not yet come up with a good definition of risk that works well in predicting individual stock returns. One problem with reported beta is that it is only an estimate. True beta could be substantially different from the estimated beta in various publications such as *Value Line*. In academic parlance, the standard deviation around the estimated beta is very large. For example, when the reported beta is 1.0, true beta could easily fall anywhere between 0.5 and 1.5. And, there is generally no way to tell if an error has been made.

Most evidence in support of market efficiency comes from research that falls into the category of so-called *event studies*, which are carefully done and present some fascinating findings. They often examine performance of a portfolio of stocks *after* selected events, such as announcements of earnings and mergers. Many of these studies conclude that after such an announcement is made, it is generally too late for an average investor to invest in that stock. Therein lies the rub. These studies should not be interpreted to imply that you cannot identify stocks that are likely to be good long-term investments in the first place.

Why do prices deviate from fundamentals? This happens when an unusual number of buyers or sellers come to the market in a short time, creating an imbalance. This is a classic example of the effect of supply and demand on prices. For example, consider a situation when you come across many houses for sale in your neighborhood. This can happen by chance alone, with no long-term effect on the housing prices in the neighborhood. Prices will then temporarily fall and will remain low until the number of houses on the market reverts back to normal. The main point here is that there are frequent imbalances in demand and supply that cause prices to deviate from their intrinsic values.

In the stock market, demand and supply seem to fall out of balance frequently. If an influential financial analyst advises his clients to sell a particular stock, the supply of sellers may outpace the supply of buyers. Prices can then fall quickly and may go well below what the fundamentals would suggest. This example can be generalized to include the effect of any news or disclosure of financial information. Some investors react to such disclosures optimistically while others react pessimistically. When one group or the other dominates any particular situation, prices can deviate from the fundamentals.[5] This can also happen for the entire market. In 1987, the so-called *portfolio insurance scheme* practiced by mutual fund managers required them to sell more and more stocks as prices fell. On October 19, 1987, an initial decline of a few percentage points in the market indexes in the previous few weeks made portfolio managers sell additional stocks, leading the market to decline by 23 percent in one day. Investors who understood the circumstances benefited from the buying opportunity. In general, individual stocks, rather than the market as a whole, are more likely to afford good investment opportunities because a smaller dollar amount can affect their prices considerably.

Recent Evidence on Market *In*efficiency

Many recent academic studies have begun to provide evidence that even within the simple research framework of event studies, the market may not be efficient. Academic researchers are at a loss to explain why, after a good earnings report, a company's stock price continues to move up—and similarly, after a bad earnings report, why the stock price continues to move down. This evidence on momentum in prices has also been documented for other events, such as spin-offs and stock splits.[6] The results from other studies show that stocks that have done well in the recent 6 to 12 months continue to do well during the following 6 to 12 months. Similarly, the evidence suggests that you should avoid stocks that have been performing poorly in the recent 6 to 12 months.[7] Evidence also shows that stocks that underperform over a 5-year period do well in the following 5-year period and vice versa.[8] After a rigorous examination of the data, Professors Louis Chan, Narasimhan Jegadeesh, and Josef Lakonishok rule out the possibility that market risk, size, and book-to-market effects can explain momentum in stock prices.[9] They conclude that the results suggest a market that responds only gradually to new information. These results are disturbing to market efficiency advocates but may give you opportunities to earn superior returns in the stock market.

For a critical thinker, it is easy to criticize any evidence, including the evidence on market *in*efficiency. Some studies find that the market reacts slowly (underreacts) to earnings and other announcements. However, other studies show that the market overreacts to some other types of announcements. This leads to the conjecture that researchers look for patterns in historical data, and given enough computer time, they may conclude that there are patterns where there are none. Essentially, we should be aware that we use hindsight when we conclude something from our research findings. Often, we can conclude things about the past: that the market was undervalued in 1974 or overvalued in 1972, for instance. Without the benefit of hindsight, can we really tell when the market is over- or undervalued? Not really. Putting it another way, there are always enough pundits with bullish and bearish sentiments, and some of them inevitably end up being correct. Overall, inside academia, there is an ongoing lively and healthy debate on the extent to which the markets are efficient and how to measure risk.

Warren Buffett does not say that beating the market is easy. In his discourse on market efficiency, he concludes, "An investor cannot obtain superior profits from stocks by simply committing to a specific investment category or style. He can earn them only by carefully evaluating facts and continuously exercising discipline."[10] Buffett makes three main points about choosing stocks and trying to beat the market.

1. To beat the market, you must invest only in companies about which you are likely to know more than most participants in the market. It is a basic principle of most games. If you are not better than your opponent, you are probably not going to win very often. Like Buffett, you should focus on one or more industries that appeal to you.

2. Buffett has proposed that investors think of making only a limited number of stock market decisions in their lifetime. Once they have made those decisions, they should not be allowed to make any more decisions. If you keep this in mind, you are unlikely to make many mistakes. To cement this thought, think about the effort you expended before you bought a house or a computer, before you decided to attend a particular college or accept a job offer. Because these decisions are not easy to reverse, most people make good decisions. If you think of buying a stock as a similarly long-term commitment, you will make better decisions.

3. To beat the market, you must learn to ignore its volatility. It is common for investors to become anxious and sell when stock prices go down or buy when stock prices go up. But when an investor buys a stock for the long run after learning about the company, market volatility will have less of a psychological impact on the investor. Ignorance may make volatility your enemy, but knowledge makes it your friend.

Conclusions

Overall, the stock market can help you make money if you are willing to put in the time and effort to develop the winning mind-set to learn to play the game well. Since most people do not put much effort into it, it is not surprising that most of them do not beat the market averages. For these people, the markets are efficient. For those who are willing to do what is necessary to master the game, even if only in small corners of a single industry, it should be possible to beat the opponent: the market averages.

Chapter 19

Arbitrage and Hedge Funds

We will engage in arbitrage from time to time—sometimes on a large scale—but only when we like the odds.[1]
—*Warren Buffett*

The fancy word *arbitrage* is nothing to be afraid of. An arbitrage is nothing more than the simultaneous buying and selling of one or more securities that are either identical or similar to each other. Think about stock brokerage firms such as Charles Schwab. Beyond the brokerage fee, brokers often make a small profit from a transaction when buying a stock from one client and selling the same stock to another client because the buying and selling prices are slightly different. Essentially, the broker plays a little game of arbitraging the profit between the buyer and the seller.

An arbitrage is not risk-free, because the brokerage firm, like a wholesaler, carries inventory. Some of the deals that such middlemen or arbitrageurs put together are more sophisticated than simply holding inventory. Many hedge funds specialize in similar deals, and from time to time, Buffett has also engaged in arbitrage deals. There is no reason for you to be completely averse to them if you understand the risks involved.

185

Arbitrage in Merger Deals

One common form of arbitrage that many can take advantage of is mergers. Consider the merger between General Re and Berkshire Hathaway in 1998 (discussed in Chapter 8). According to the deal, 200 shares of General Re would be transferred into 21 shares of Berkshire Hathaway, class B. If there was no uncertainty surrounding the merger, the price for 200 shares of General Re should be the same as the price of 21 shares of Berkshire Hathaway, class B. For many months while the merger was pending, you could have bought 200 shares of General Re for about 5 percent less than the price you would have paid for 21 shares of Berkshire Hathaway, class B.

Consider another example. In December 1998, Exxon announced its intention to buy Mobil. The terms of the deal called for Mobil shareholders to receive 1.32015 Exxon shares for each Mobil share. As late as May 1999, Mobil shares were trading at around $105, and Exxon shares were trading at $84. It was about 6 percent cheaper to buy Mobil shares than to buy Exxon shares. Thus, the way to play that arbitrage was to buy Mobil shares and simultaneously sell short the Exxon shares. Since the merger was to take about four months to complete, the investor would have earned an annualized return of about 18 percent. This is about twice the average return on the stock market.

Not all announced merger deals are completed, and when a deal is not completed, the arbitrageur may lose a large percentage of the investment. Therefore, you should not gamble a large amount in these transactions, and when a deal seems risky, it is best to avoid it. It appears that immediately after a failed deal, investors looking for arbitrage opportunities become more risk-averse, and the expected percentage returns from such deals increase. This is similar to the situation in the insurance industry in which insurance premiums tend to go up after a hurricane or a natural disaster. Not only are the arbitrageurs less willing to invest their money in such deals, but it also appears that only the more-likely-to-succeed mergers are brought to the market.

So, a savvy investor should increase, rather than decrease, the money devoted to such arbitrage activities soon after a failed merger. The proposed $3.1 billion takeover of American Bankers Insurance Group by Cendant collapsed in 1998 when it was discovered that Cendant had engaged in accounting irregularities and fraud and its stock price fell 70 percent. Almost immediately after this failure, the expected returns from arbitrage deals increased substantially. Another consideration is that when a number of large mergers are taking place at the same time in the market, there is not enough money to go around, and expected arbitrage profits go up.

In some situations, companies such as Berkshire Hathaway can generate good returns for a short time at a lower risk than an average investor can. Thus, not only is Berkshire able to generate good returns on its investing activities in the stock market, but it also generates an overall superior return partly because of its arbitrage activities. For example, when a company bids for another company and needs money on short notice, Berkshire may be able to provide cash quickly in exchange for a higher-than-normal return.

An Example of a Successful Arbitrage Deal by Buffett

The following example illustrates that the better you understand the financial markets, the more likely you are to find arbitrage opportunities. Here is what Warren Buffett wrote in the 1988 Berkshire annual report:

> Some offbeat opportunities occasionally arise in the arbitrage field. I participated in one of these when I was 24 and working in New York for Graham-Newman Corp. Rockwood & Co., a Brooklyn-based chocolate products company of limited profitability, had adopted LIFO inventory valuation in 1941 when cocoa was selling for 5 cents per pound. In 1954 a temporary shortage of cocoa caused the price to soar to over 60 cents. Consequently Rockwood wished to unload its valuable inventory—quickly, before the price dropped. But if cocoa had simply been sold off, the company would have owed tax of close to 50% on the proceeds.

> The 1954 Tax Code came to the rescue. It contained an arcane provision that eliminated the tax otherwise due on LIFO profits if inventory was distributed to shareholders as part of a plan reducing the scope of a corporation's business. Rockwood decided to terminate one of the businesses, the sale of cocoa butter, and said 13 million pounds of its

cocoa bean inventory was attributable to that activity. Accordingly, the company offered to repurchase its stock in exchange for the cocoa beans it no longer needed, paying 80 pounds of beans for each share.

For several weeks I busily bought shares, sold beans, and made periodic stops at Schrodder Trust to exchange stock certificates for warehouse receipts. The profits were good and my only expense was subway tokens.[2]

Long-Term Capital Management: The Story of a Hedge Fund and Berkshire Hathaway

Consider a famous case that explains why Buffett wanted to purchase a hedge fund and liquidate it. In September 1998, Berkshire Hathaway proposed acquiring Long-Term Capital Management (LTCM), through a $4 billion limited partnership comprising Berkshire Hathaway, Goldman Sachs, and American International Group. Many individual investors think that hedge funds take large positions but are somehow hedged against losing money and produce consistently high returns. As the near bankruptcy of LTCM hedge funds suggests, investing in hedge funds is not as hedged as you may believe. So what are the important lessons for an individual investor?

The one distinguishing feature of LTCM was the extent of its leverage: about 25 to 1. The fund reportedly had 60,000 trades on its books, including long securities positions of over $50 billion and short positions of an equivalent magnitude. The gross notional amounts (total value of leveraged positions) of the fund's contracts on futures exchanges exceeded $500 billion, swap contracts more than $760 billion, and options and others over $150 billion.

LTCM's size and leverage, as well as its trading strategies, made it vulnerable to the extraordinary financial market conditions that emerged following Russia's devaluation of the ruble and declaration of a debt moratorium in August 1998. Russia's actions sparked a flight to quality in which investors avoided risk and sought liquidity. As a result, risk spreads and liquidity premiums rose sharply in markets around the world. During the single month of August, LTCM suffered losses of $1.8 billion, bringing the loss of equity for the year to more than 50 percent.

By September 21, LTCM's liquidity situation was bleak, and further unfavorable market movements could have caused it to default in a few days.[3]

On the morning of September 23, Berkshire and partners proposed purchasing LTCM's portfolio. However, at the same time, a consortium of 15 firms that were themselves significantly exposed in a default scenario proposed investing in LTCM. While Berkshire's proposal was to take over 100 percent of the fund's equity, the counterproposal allowed the current principals and investors to keep 10 percent of the equity. Berkshire's proposal was rejected. Buffett's interest in LTCM was not an isolated event considering his ongoing interest in arbitrage. In July 1998, Berkshire contributed 90 percent of the capital ($270 million) for the West End Capital fund (essentially a hedge fund) managed by Mark Byrne. Overall, to a knowledgeable person, hedge funds may offer risky but profitable opportunities.

The main lesson from the LTCM episode is that large leverage positions even in the biggest of funds can lead to bankruptcy, because events such as the Russian default cannot be planned into any model. At the time of its near failure, LTCM was the most highly leveraged large hedge fund reporting to the Commodities Futures Trading Commission. Its assets were nearly four times the assets of the next largest hedge fund. The liquidity problems faced by LTCM were compounded by the size of its positions, as it could not unwind its positions easily.

How, then, could Berkshire benefit from acquiring LTCM? The basic point to recognize is that in such volatile situations, margin calls require the leveraged party to liquidate its portfolio at unfavorable prices. Markets become inefficient. Since Berkshire undoubtedly had enough liquidity, it would not have had to liquidate LTCM's positions in a hurry. In an orderly liquidation over a long time, LTCM would have been much more profitable. A firm such as Berkshire with excellent liquidity will probably come across opportunities like this from time to time.

This is also likely to be true for individual investors. When major exogenous shocks in the market create volatility, prices generally fall temporarily because investors prefer less risky investments such as investing in Treasury securities. If you have invested in the stock market, you will suffer paper losses, but you are less likely to panic if you are not highly leveraged. If possible, you should take an additional position in stocks. When the LTCM saga was in full swing, equity markets also declined. As an investor, you could have benefited if you had invested in your favorite companies. We know that Berkshire's equity holding in American Express was increased by about 1 million shares during that period.

Buffett's interest in LTCM might have come from the fact that the financial markets were down heavily when the Russian government defaulted on its debt. Although Berkshire's bid to acquire the assets of LTCM was denied, Buffett's conjecture proved to be correct: LTCM earned high returns in the months following the crisis. This episode, once again, shows the importance of investing when others are fearful. Furthermore, anyone interested in investing in positions that are risky in the short run had better have a large capital base in case there is sudden demand for additional capital.

Should You Invest in Hedge Funds or Private Equity Funds?

It is difficult to create reliable hedge fund indices because hedge funds are not required to release their performance data publicly. Several indices are frequently reported in the media, the most popular of which is CSFB/Tremont Hedge Fund Index and includes data since 1993. If you ever plan to use them, you should know that there are two serious problems with most hedge fund indices. First, some of the indices backfill the data as funds report their historical performance. Funds have incentives to report only favorable historical data. Second, most analyses suffer from what is known as *survivorship bias*: Returns of indices may include only the currently existing funds, omitting the data from funds that have gone bankrupt. Burton Malkiel and Atanu Saha examined a reasonably comprehensive database of hedge fund returns and estimated the effects of these two biases.[4] After correcting for biases, they find that hedge funds have returns lower than commonly supposed. From 1995 to 2003, the hedge fund universe as a whole earned annualized returns of 8.82 percent, versus 12.38 percent for the S&P 500. With additional analysis, they conclude that hedge funds are extremely risky, as the range of individual hedge fund returns are far greater than they are for traditional asset classes. Professor Andrew Lo—one of the world's most respected financial economists—comes to similar conclusions.[5] He also presents a detailed analysis of risk, returns, and liquidity of hedge funds.

Private equity and venture capital funds are usually regarded as the most sophisticated investment vehicles. The funds are generally run by creative, experienced, and articulate managers who have proven track records in managing money. They are also very secretive and do not readily share their performance results. Hence, there is less research on returns from investing in private equity funds. However, the conclusions from the best available research suggest that outside investors (those who do not participate in management) do not earn above-average returns. Based on voluntary data for the period from 1980 to 2003 provided by about 2,000 large private equity investors, Ludovic Phalippou and Oliver Gottschalg found that, on average, net-of-fees annualized performance is 3 percent below that of the S&P 500 index.[6] An earlier study by Steve Kaplan and Antoinette Schoar concluded that the returns are about the same as those on the S&P 500 index. In addition, the cross-sectional variation across managers is high.[7]

On average, there seems to be no advantage in investing in hedge funds because the returns are not larger than the market indices. A higher volatility of returns also results in a bigger bite in taxes because taxes are paid when returns are high but may not be recouped when returns are low. Finally, the fee structure of hedge funds is not friendly to investors. In the hedge fund industry, it is common to charge a fee of 2 percent of the assets under management and 20 percent more of the returns beyond a certain level. If a fund return is 8 percent per year and the expenses are about 2 percent, you effectively lose 25 percent of your earnings, and that does not include the additional amount you would lose when the hedge funds do well. This management fee structure borders on highway robbery.

Conclusions

The hedge fund industry is made up of investors who manage highly leveraged positions and generally either earn extremely high returns or earn poor returns that often lead them to face bankruptcy. It is not true that hedge funds consistently earn high returns and that capital is hedged from large losses. High leverage does what it is supposed to do: increase volatility. When losses occur, they are fierce, as illustrated by the LTCM example. Hedge fund managers do well because of high fees. Investors in hedge funds do not. There may be some good hedge funds, but it is close to impossible to identify them. My suggestion is to avoid investing in hedge funds altogether.

Part Seven

PROFITABILITY AND ACCOUNTING

Buffett has often mentioned that studying accounting and understanding financial statements are necessary to become a successful investor. In Chapters 20 to 24, I discuss some ideas essential to understanding Berkshire's impressive profitability and learning to become a better investor.

Chapter 20

M = Monopoly = Money

A *monopoly* exists when a company controls the entire market for a specified product or service and when there are significant barriers to entry in that market. We can debate whether Microsoft or Google have monopolies in their respective markets, but we will certainly agree that they have large market shares in personal computer operating systems and Web-based search, respectively. Much has been written about monopolies and near-monopolies, but one thing is clear: Almost all of them make good money. There have been large monopolies such as Standard Oil and Microsoft and small monopolies such as tollbooths across bridges. In the minds of investors, the letter *M* should stand not only for "money" but also for "monopoly." So, start searching for near-monopolies or companies with what Buffett refers to as wide moats around them.

Widen the Moat

Buffett has often discussed the idea of a moat around a company, which means an enduring competitive advantage for the company, or a means of protection to maintain the company's profitability for a long time. He fully understands the power of earning superior returns through such businesses. This is evident in a memo he wrote shortly after September 11, 2001, urging Berkshire managers to remain focused: "What should you be doing running your businesses? Just what you always do: Widen the moat, build enduring competitive advantage."[1]

You don't have to identify and invest in a monopoly in its early stages of development. For example, Microsoft went public in 1986. You could have waited five years and bought Microsoft shares in 1991, or you could have waited another five years and bought in 1996. Only if you had waited until about 1999—when Microsoft stock was already overvalued, the company was being scrutinized by the government, and growth was slowing—would you have been too late to the game to make money.

Profitability of Monopolies

Monopolies make above-average returns—which appeals to common sense and can easily be supported by data. There is no better contemporary example of a near-monopoly than that of Microsoft. Microsoft has considerable power to set the prices it charges for several of its products. The number of people buying a computer is not likely to change much whether Microsoft charges $199 or $299 for the operating system that must reside inside most personal computers. Most buyers, whether new or repeat, prefer the Microsoft operating system because so many consumers already have a compatible system. The same is true for some of Microsoft's other products.

How profitable is Microsoft? One way to judge is to compare Microsoft's profitability with that of another large computer company. For illustration purposes, IBM is a reasonable benchmark. Although IBM has a stake in both the software and hardware segments of the computer industry, the profitability of its sales revenue and that of assets employed can still be compared because both companies are in an industry that requires significant research and development.

Table 20.1 presents the financial highlights for Microsoft and IBM. The basic metric for comparing the two companies is operating income as a percentage of revenues or as a percentage of total assets. Over the past six years for which data are available, Microsoft's operating income as a proportion of revenues, or operating margin, on average, was 34 percent. In comparison, IBM's operating margin in the same period was only 14 percent. Comparing operating income to total assets ratio across the

Table 20.1 Profitability Comparisons of IBM and Microsoft

	Financial Highlights—IBM					
	2008	**2007**	**2006**	**2005**	**2004**	**2003**
Revenues	$103.6	$ 98.8	$ 91.4	$ 91.1	$ 96.3	$ 89.1
Total assets	$120.4	$109.5	$103.2	$105.8	$111.0	$106.0
Operating income	$ 15.9	$ 13.5	$ 13.3	$ 12.2	$ 12.0	$ 10.9
Operating income as a percentage of revenues	15.3%	13.7%	14.6%	13.4%	12.5%	12.2%
Operating income as a percentage of total assets	13.2%	12.3%	12.9%	11.6%	10.8%	10.3%

	Financial Highlights—Microsoft					
	2008	**2007**	**2006**	**2005**	**2004**	**2003**
Revenues	$60.4	$51.1	$44.3	$39.8	$36.8	$32.2
Total assets	$72.7	$63.2	$69.6	$70.8	$94.4	$81.7
Operating income	$24.3	$18.5	$16.5	$14.6	$ 9.0	$ 9.6
Operating income as a percentage of revenues	40.2%	36.2%	37.2%	36.6%	24.5%	29.7%
Operating income as a percentage of total assets	33.4%	29.3%	23.7%	20.6%	9.6%	11.7%

Dollar amounts in billions.

two companies also suggests that Microsoft (21 percent over six years) is much more profitable than IBM (12 percent over six years).[2]

Whenever a company creates a near-monopoly or an enduring competitive advantage, it offers a good investment opportunity. In many situations, it may not be possible to invest in those companies because they are not traded publicly. For example, De Beers is considered a monopoly in diamond mining and distribution, especially in the high-quality diamond market. However, you cannot invest in De Beers because it is a privately held company.

A monopoly still needs to be managed well to protect its profitability. Because of their high profitability, monopolies attract competition, and unless the monopolist can maintain its monopoly, profitability will decline over time. In the drug industry, a company may have a monopoly on a drug for a particular disease. Whenever a drug is a huge success, other drug companies start researching in the same area to discover a similar chemical that is equally or more effective in treating the disease. Drug prices remain high as long as the company has a monopoly over the product but decline when competition emerges. Conversely, consider the example (discussed next) of a Berkshire-owned newspaper that went from losing money in a competitive environment to becoming highly profitable when the major competitor folded. However, monopolies do not last forever. For example, unless newspapers react efficiently to Internet-based news and advertising, they are likely to face a decline in their profitability and may even become extinct.

Buffalo News: *How Profitability Changed Dramatically*

Berkshire Hathaway owns the *Buffalo News,* a daily newspaper in Buffalo, New York, a city known for its blue-collar workers and traditional industries. When Berkshire bought it for $32.5 million in early 1977, the *Buffalo News* was a distant second to the local *Courier-Express* and was losing money.[3] But since October 1982, it has been the only daily major newspaper serving the Buffalo area. The monopoly came about because of events that included a long legal battle emanating from action by the *Courier-Express.* In early 1982, Charlie Munger wrote, "If the litigation continues and if the competing paper succeeds in somehow changing the law as enunciated by the Federal Court of Appeals and in obtaining the kinds of injunctions it is seeking, or if any extended strike shuts down the *Buffalo News*, it will probably be forced to cease operations and liquidate."[4] However, the *Buffalo News* persevered, and its victory was indeed sweet. In 1983, the first full year after the competitor closed, the $19 million the company earned in operating profits covered the losses from the previous years with some profit left over.

Figure 20.1 illustrates the advantage of a monopolistic environment. Using the available data from 1979 to 1999, I report the profitability (operating profits as a percentage of total sales) of the *Buffalo News* in relation to the profitability of all other non-insurance Berkshire subsidiaries, including See's Candies, Nebraska Furniture Mart, and Borsheim's. The *Buffalo News*'s profits jumped significantly in 1983 when it became the only newspaper in town—when it became close to a monopoly. In the subsequent five years, profits more than doubled to $41.8 million. In 1999, the *Buffalo News* earned more than $55 million on revenues of $160 million. In general, if you find a company that is likely to increase its monopolistic stance—or widen its moat—growth in profits will follow, and you will probably earn a high return on your initial investment.

Dominance Does Not Mean High Profits

When you look for a monopoly, be careful to investigate whether the company is likely to remain profitable for the foreseeable future. A large or even dominant company is not always a monopoly or near-monopoly. General Motors (GM) has been the world's largest car manufacturer and currently has annual revenues of about $200 billion, yet it generates almost no earnings for its shareholders and went bankrupt in 2009. It has not been earning monopolistic profits for at least 20 years. GM's decline illustrates the inevitable: Monopolies do not last forever. Their allure from an investment point of view diminishes as competition sets in or growth potential diminishes. Microsoft had lost its appeal as an investment by 1999 once it was no longer able to expand its business and profits easily. IBM, once the largest computer company in the world, was essentially a monopoly from the 1950s to the 1970s, but it appears to be an average company at best today.

Facing stiff competition from the Internet, the *New York Times* and many other newspapers in 2009 remain dominant and monopolistic so far as newspaper circulation is concerned in their region, but most of them are no longer profitable. Their stock prices have gone down with their declining profitability. In a span of seven years starting in 2002, the stock prices of the New York Times Company and Gannett (publisher of *USA Today*) have declined by about 90 percent. The *Washington Post*

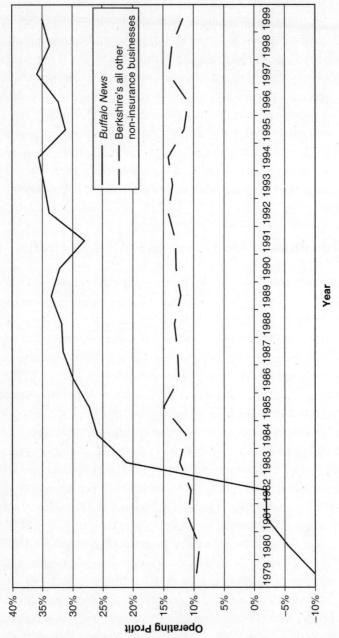

Figure 20.1 *Buffalo News* Profitability from 1979 to 1999

200

has also suffered, and its stock price trades at about half of its peak price of a few years back. Some newspapers will transform into profitable businesses by shrinking in size or investing judiciously, while others will make bad decisions by throwing good money after bad. For an investor, it is a time to watch and not to invest in these companies.

In most cases, utilities dominate their local markets and are near-monopolies. However, these companies' profitability is often regulated because they are considered to be natural monopolies; and their returns to shareholders, while adequate, are not high. *Duopolies*, or market domination by two companies, are more frequent than monopolies. Probably, Coke and Pepsi, Boeing and Airbus, and FedEx and UPS fall in this category. Often they are highly profitable, but their stock prices are also high. Hence, returns to investors may not be high. However, in economic slowdowns, their prices decline along with the rest of the market. Then, they offer good opportunities to buy because their profits almost surely revert back to normal when economies recover.

How to Look for Monopolies

The best way to identify a monopoly is to look around. Generally, smaller companies in regional markets are somewhat monopolistic. While the banking sector is slowly becoming competitive, some regional banks have very little competition. Some resorts, cruise lines, and theme parks have long-established, well-managed monopolies in their regions. Disney is likely to earn monopolistic profits in Florida. Carnival Cruise Lines also has long-established dominance that makes it a near-monopoly. You can investigate companies that operate toll roads, as many states look to privatize their toll roads. Monopolies or near-monopolies that are as large, well-known, or dominant as Microsoft, Intel, and Cisco are not common. Many other opportunities may be found in less glamorous industries, such as exporters or regional suppliers for other firms. Every so often, you may stumble upon a monopoly, and when you do, do not let it go without a thorough investigation.

Simply because a firm appears to be a monopoly does not necessarily mean that it is a good investment opportunity. You should confirm your initial impressions by examining the company's return on assets and on equity and, of course, compute its intrinsic value and margin of safety. You should try to estimate the sustainability of its profitability for a number of years in the future. Some sports franchises, such as the Boston Celtics basketball team, used to be publicly traded. There may be others. Sports franchises often appear to be monopolies in their markets, although it is not obvious that profitability is sustainable in the same way that Microsoft's profitability is sustainable. Sports fans don't have to go to the games. When the market punishes the team's share price because opponents are punishing the team, you might start thinking of buying some shares in the company if you think that the team will recover.

Beyond profitability, the price you pay is even more important. The stock of a monopoly, such as Microsoft, Intel, or Cisco, generally trades at a high P/E ratio. Even at a high P/E ratio, shares of a monopoly are usually not expensive for a long-term investor. Although no definitive rule exists for choosing a cutoff P/E, I have developed a working rule after 30 years of watching the market. If the P/E multiple is about 200 percent of the average multiple for the S&P 500, I wait for a decline in the stock price. In absolute terms, a P/E multiple of 35 is high for me, even for a firm that seems to be widening its moat or is a near-monopoly. Stock prices decline periodically for a variety of reasons, including not meeting analysts' sales or earnings expectations, bearish reports on an industry, or fears of interest rate hikes or a recession. For a long-term investor, these price declines, such as those in early 2009, signal good opportunities for investing.

Do Not Sell a Monopoly in a Hurry

I have met many people who bought Microsoft stock when it was a young company or its price had dipped for one reason or another. However, they were quick to take profits when the stock price went up 50 percent to 100 percent even when there was no competitor on the horizon. More often than not, it is a mistake to sell your shares in a near-monopoly or even a growing company once you have become knowledgeable about the company and its products. Peter Lynch shared his experiences with owning Philip Morris and Subaru stock, explaining that if the growth story is still good, one should not sell.[5] When you think that there is a high probability of a competitor's success, you should sell. The stock may appear expensive from time to time, and it may not be a good time to add more shares to your portfolio. But selling is often a mistake because the price may not come down for a while for you to buy it again, and by the time it does, you might have lost interest in the stock or no longer have the funds to reinvest in it.

Periodically, stock prices of a monopoly or a near-monopoly company go up substantially. If the price does become excessive—say, a price-to-earnings (P/E) ratio of 50—does it make sense to sell the stock? The main tool in your arsenal, once again, is your estimate of the company's intrinsic value. The P/E ratio is just a shortcut to computing intrinsic value. You should always compute a stock's intrinsic value before making a decision. Usually, there comes a time when a company's monopolistic edge erodes, which should show up in your estimated intrinsic value. If you find yourself in that situation, you should sell your shares. In recent years, I sold my shares in *Washington Post* and Whole Foods when the P/E was very high or I saw that the profitability was declining. In both these cases, it appeared that company dominance was slipping. It became too difficult to predict the future, indicating that it was time to sell.

Conclusions

Standard Oil was a monopoly in the early part of the twentieth century. Currently, Microsoft seems to be a near-monopoly, although it is losing market share. For a long time, all these companies rewarded their shareholders well until, ultimately and inevitably, competition set in. Although large and powerful monopolies are not easy to find, many well-run companies with enduring competitive advantages are excellent long-run investments if their stock prices are not excessive. Among the stocks owned by Berkshire, such companies include American Express, Procter & Gamble, Wal-Mart, Coca-Cola, and Wells Fargo.

Chapter 21

Who Wins in Highly Competitive Industries?

[W]e believe that [GEICO's] cost of new business, though definitely rising, is well below that of the industry. Of even greater importance, our operating costs for renewal business are the lowest among broad-based national auto insurers. Both of these competitive advantages are sustainable. Others may copy our model, but they will be unable to replicate our economies.[1]

—*Warren Buffett*

Insurance is a highly competitive industry, but GEICO is far more profitable than its competitors. Retailing is also considered highly competitive, but Wal-Mart is more profitable than others. What characteristics are helpful for a company to remain a leader in an industry that may be classified as a commodity business or a highly competitive business? Let's try to find some answers by looking at GEICO, Wal-Mart, and other cutthroat commodity businesses.

Insurance Is a Commodity Business Like Retailing

Wal-Mart clearly dominates the discount retail industry. It is so far ahead of its competition that it is difficult to tell who is second. Kmart and

Sears together are under one corporate umbrella known as Sears Holdings, considered to be Wal-Mart's main competitor. Wal-Mart's annual revenues are about $400 billion, whereas Sears Holdings' annual revenues are about $50 billion, only one-eighth of Wal-Mart's. But it was not always that way. Both Kmart and Wal-Mart were major retailers until Wal-Mart pulled into the lead and eventually won the race. Before Kmart and Wal-Mart became the industry leaders, other dominant retailers included J.C. Penney, Sears, and W.T. Grant. You may not recall W.T. Grant, which went bankrupt in 1975 because it could not compete with Kmart effectively. Then Kmart went bankrupt in 2002 because it could not compete effectively with Wal-Mart. Clearly, other companies are now trying to take market share away from Wal-Mart. While Sears Holdings is now considered to be Wal-Mart's main competitor, Target and Costco also compete with Wal-Mart effectively in clothing and wholesale markets, respectively. And, internationally, Carrefour and Tesco do very well against Wal-Mart in some countries. If you are watching Wal-Mart, you should also watch its competitors.

In many other industries, such as grain processing, gold coin minting, high-end retailing, long-distance telephone service, home-building materials, and cars and motorcycles, a few leaders emerge over time as businesses become commodity businesses. Similar to Wal-Mart's success in retailing, the success of McDonald's in fast-food restaurants and GEICO's success in auto insurance have the same underlying reasons.

Two Main Characteristics of a Leader: Low Cost and Customer Satisfaction

"We sell for less" and "Satisfaction guaranteed" are two of Wal-Mart's slogans that effectively capture two important principles: low cost and customer satisfaction. To answer a question in Berkshire's annual shareholder meeting in April 2000, Buffett essentially echoed Wal-Mart's slogans. He said that GEICO's sustainable advantages were low operating costs and high-quality service. Like Wal-Mart's, the McDonald's operating model has been a case study in business schools for a long time. So far, Burger King, Wendy's, and many others have been unable to replace McDonald's. As long as you know that McDonald's sells for less and its customers are happy, you are likely to earn respectable, if not high, returns over an extended period by investing in McDonald's. In November 2009, Berkshire announced the acquisition of Burlington Northern Santa Fe for $34 billion. The acquisition seems to have been motivated, at least in part, by the fact that railroads are a more cost-efficient method of transporting goods than truckers.[2]

A race for dominance can last a long time, and there is no unique path to success. In the automobile sector, there were many manufacturers for decades before General Motors, Ford, and Chrysler became the Big Three. But even in the 1920s and 1930s, it was probably not difficult to discern which one was emerging as the leader: General Motors was becoming larger and larger by successfully combining Oldsmobile, Chevrolet, Cadillac, and other manufacturers. In the 1980s, Wal-Mart's strategy was different. Wal-Mart did not emphasize buying local retailers. Instead, it built stores and drove the competition out of the market. Lest we forget, outstanding managers are invariably the real jewelers behind developing these jewels. Alfred P. Sloan and Sam Walton were to General Motors and Wal-Mart, respectively, just as Warren Buffett is to Berkshire Hathaway.

GEICO, under the leadership of Tony Nicely, focuses on direct marketing to keep costs low. Slowly and surely, it has increased its presence in the market by advertising and, if necessary, reducing insurance premiums. Typically, as a commodity business adds to its market share, its per-capita cost to keep its sustainable advantage goes down. Consider, for instance, advertising costs. A full-page advertisement in the *New York Times* does not depend on the size of the insurance company. So, the cost per customer is smaller for a larger company. A 30-second TV spot on a Super Bowl Sunday will be cheaper for Wal-Mart for each dollar in sales than for Kmart. In addition, given its smaller sales revenue, Kmart may not have as much of a budget for advertising as Wal-Mart. Once a competitive advantage is established, it is difficult to unseat the leader.

However, watch out for the potential of old dominant players to become dinosaurs. The main reason Kmart failed was that it started expanding in unrelated businesses such as do-it-yourself stores (Builders Square) and drugstores (Payless Drug Stores). Technological changes also affect the competitive field, especially when a dominant player takes its competitive advantage for granted. A case in point is IBM, which was a leader in the computer industry for years. In the 1980s, when the personal computer market started to bloom, IBM took it for granted that it would maintain its leadership position. But that was not to be.

The development of the Internet has taken a toll on Barnes and Noble's leadership in the book industry. Amazon.com has emerged as the leader in revenues from book sales over the Internet. With time, Amazon.com is increasing its dominance and, hence, its cost advantage. It is also taking some market share from Wal-Mart. Somehow, someday, Wal-Mart's dominance will erode, but I can't predict which competitor will emerge to challenge Wal-Mart. If retailing is in your circle of competence, you may spot such a candidate early and invest in that company.

The second important ingredient for success in the commodity business is customer service or customer satisfaction. American Express was not the first credit card company; Diners Club was. But American Express came from behind, established its name on the strength of its customer service, and captured market share. Interestingly, VISA then came from behind and, using a low-cost strategy, became the market leader. At least for now, VISA, MasterCard, and American Express seem to be surviving well in this market by differentiating their products. The main advantage for American Express is its excellent customer service. Overall, it earns about one percentage point more on charges than VISA and MasterCard. But it is expensive to provide good customer service. For this reason, you may notice that companies often decide to service one segment of the market or the other. In credit cards, American Express prefers to service high-end customers by charging a higher annual fee and a higher fee to book airline tickets.

Good customer service is one important reason for Berkshire's success in traditional industries. Buffett explains Berkshire's emphasis on customer service through the following example: "Our two pipelines, Kern River and Northern Natural, were both acquired in 2002. A firm called Mastio ranks pipelines for customer satisfaction. Among the 44 rated, Kern River came in 9th when we purchased it and Northern ranked 39th. There was work to do. In Mastio's 2009 report, Kern River ranked 1st and Natural 3rd. Charlie and I couldn't be more proud of this performance."[3] In the 2008 American Customer Satisfaction Index survey conducted by the University of Michigan, GEICO ranks higher than it major competitors Allstate, Progressive, and State Farm. It seems that it is neither low cost nor customer service but a combination of the two that results in the winning strategy for companies in highly competitive industries.

Just as a company's cost advantage grows with market share, the same is true of customer satisfaction. As the number of retail customers increased, many Wal-Mart stores started to remain open 24 hours a day. In my neighborhood, Wal-Mart is open 24 hours, whereas Kmart is not. Longer store hours often reduce costs and leave customers more satisfied.

How Do Companies Keep Costs Low?

Companies keep costs low in a variety of ways. Wal-Mart has kept the company headquarters in the small town of Bentonville, Arkansas. Its executives share hotel rooms and do not dine at fancy restaurants while traveling. Even though the largest cost for companies is the cost of goods sold, cost advantage seems to emanate more from indirect or overhead costs. For example, have you ever wondered why lunch prices are a fraction of dinner prices at many fancy restaurants? Restaurants pay a fixed monthly rent, so if they can serve extra meals, their cost per meal goes down. Also, even if there are plenty of customers available to nice restaurants during regular dinner hours, a reduced price can help attract additional diners earlier in the day. At one of my favorite restaurants in New Orleans, a fixed-price dinner before 6:30 p.m. is only $19, whereas the same meal after 6:30 p.m. costs twice as much. Extending hours of operation also reduces overhead costs and attracts a different set of customers—a mechanism known as *price discrimination*, in economic terms. Airlines that offer reduced prices on afternoon flights or on nonbusiness days also use this principle to boost their profits.

You may be surprised to know that it is not the high gross margin that is the driving force behind Wal-Mart's profitability. Gross margins at Wal-Mart and Kmart have been similar for years. But Wal-Mart, whose inventory turnover is much higher than Kmart's, is known for maintaining a highly sophisticated and technologically advanced system to keep inventory moving. This system considerably reduces overhead costs per item sold, which brings about higher profitability.

Proper use of technology can cut overhead costs substantially. Before the telephone became ubiquitous, GEICO could not possibly have sold insurance policies directly to customers. Today, many companies exploit the Internet and other technologies to operate their businesses in dramatically new ways. As an investor, keep your eyes on how technology is being used to improve a company's cost structure. You don't need to buy the stock of the company that invents a new technology; it may be easier to find a company that uses that technology effectively.

There is at least one additional example of a low-cost company among Berkshire's subsidiaries. After buying an airplane, Buffett must have recognized that the plane was sitting idle most of the time. If a mechanism could be developed to make greater use of the airplane, overhead costs could be reduced. In 1998, Berkshire bought NetJets, a company that sells and manages fractionally owned airplanes. In NetJets, Buffett found a business that adheres to the same cost-reducing principles that GEICO and Wal-Mart follow even though NetJets caters to the rich. While there are differences across businesses, it is highly likely that NetJets will grow in time as GEICO did. Most businesses finally face fierce competition. Survivors follow Wal-Mart's strategy of low cost and customer satisfaction.

Conclusions

The next time you visit Wal-Mart, think about other companies that may be similar. They need not be in the same industry. You should ask, "Who is like Wal-Mart? Who sells for less than their competitors and provides customer satisfaction like Wal-Mart?" For example, when the airline industry was deregulated, Southwest Airlines, under the leadership of Herb Kelleher, emerged as a low-cost provider with good customer service. It has rewarded its shareholders handsomely.

Chapter 22

Property, Plant, and Equipment: Good or Bad?

Warren and I have hated railroads our entire life. They are capital intensive. .... [They] have long been a terrible business and have been lousy for investors.[1]

—*Charlie Munger*

Despite what Charlie Munger claimed, from 2006 to 2008, Berkshire acquired 70.1 million shares of a U.S. railroad, Burlington Northern Santa Fe. It is currently one of the largest Berkshire holdings, with a market value of $5.3 billion at the end of 2008. With the November 3, 2009, Berkshire announcement of a plan to acquire the remaining shares, Burlington Northern will become a wholly owned subsidiary in 2010. So, have Buffett and Munger changed their opinion on investing in capital-intensive companies, or is there more to it? Even before the Burlington investment, Berkshire often invested in capital-intensive companies. Buffett had invested in U.S. Airways, PetroChina, and POSCO (a Korean steel company), all of which are relatively capital-intensive.

Capital Intensity

Let's examine Berkshire's 10 largest common stock holdings to understand whether Buffett prefers low-capital-intensity companies. In
Table 22.1, I present an analysis of Berkshire's 10 largest holdings to
understand their levels of capital intensity.

There are only three companies that could easily be classified as
highly capital intensive, with property, plant, and equipment (PPE) as a
share of total assets above 50 percent. These three are Burlington Northern Santa Fe, ConocoPhilips, and Tesco. Three out of the 10 (American
Express, U.S. Bancorp, and Wells Fargo) need almost no property, plant,
and equipment, and are clearly on the other extreme. It appears that
Buffett does not prefer to invest in highly capital-intensive companies.
Should we conclude that an average investor should not invest or should

Table 22.1 Berkshire's Holdings and Their Capital Intensities

Company	Berkshire's common stock investments, market value*	Total assets (TA) of the company	Property, plant, and equipment (PPE)	PPE as a percentage of TA (capital intensity)
American Express	$2.8	$ 126.1	$ 2.9	2.3%
Burlington Northern Santa Fe	5.3	36.4	30.8	84.6
Coca-Cola	9.1	40.5	8.3	20.5
ConocoPhillips	4.4	142.9	83.9	58.7
Johnson & Johnson	1.8	84.9	14.4	17.0
Kraft	3.5	63.1	9.9	15.7
Procter & Gamble Company	5.7	138.2	19.0	13.7
Tesco	1.2	45.0	31.8	70.7
U.S. Bancorp	1.9	265.9	1.8	0.7
Wells Fargo & Co	9.0	1309.6	13.5	1.0

Dollar amounts in billions.
*As of December 31, 2008.

invest very little in common stocks of high-capital-intensity companies? The question merits discussion.

Because of their large investments in property, plant, and equipment, high-capital-intensity companies are usually slow in responding to market forces or changes in the economy. For example, it is very difficult for an automobile manufacturer to change its current product when a competitor's product sets a new trend in the market. High-capital-intensity companies have low variable costs and high fixed costs, which equals high operational risk. When times are good, profits go up faster than sales. When times are bad, profits also go down faster than sales. This cyclicality is further accentuated by financial leverage, which also tends to be high for high-capital-intensity companies because it is easy to borrow against property, plant, and equipment.

The combination of operational and financial risks suggests that high-capital-intensity companies have a higher probability of facing a severe financial hardship that could threaten their existence. In other words, the downside risk from investing in their stocks is high—and that is one good reason to avoid investing in them. If markets viewed risk this way, stock returns for high-capital-intensity companies would also be high. But this does not appear to be the case. We can use the Dow Jones Transportation Index as a proxy for high-capital-intensity companies because most companies in the index are highly capital intensive. Data from Dow Jones with dividends included are available only from 1993. From 1993 until 2008, annualized returns including dividends on the Dow Jones Transportation Index are 7.1 percent (201 percent over 16 years) versus 8.6 percent (276 percent over 16 years) for the Dow Jones Industrial Average.

One reason that high-capital-intensity companies do not do well in the long run may be that they face problems in restructuring themselves when it may be necessary to do so. Consider an airline. When demand falls and airplanes are only half full, it is difficult to reduce the number of pilots and the number of airplanes. On the other hand, a low-capital-intensity company such as American Express can trim the number of employees rather easily.

Beyond common stock investments, which trade independently, Berkshire owns several businesses that are in high-capital-intensity industries, and their common stocks do not trade independently. The utilities and energy segment employs $41.6 billion in total assets, of which $28.5 billion or 69 percent is in property, plant, and equipment. FlightSafety, Iscar, and Marmon are also in high-capital-intensity industries, in which I estimate that Berkshire has invested more than $10 billion. So, Buffett doesn't avoid all high-capital-intensity businesses, and these businesses seem to have increased in the Berkshire portfolio over the years.

Capital Intensity and Management Quality

When do Buffett and Munger think that a high-capital-intensity business is worth investing in? Let's go back to airlines because Berkshire was not very successful with its investment in U.S. Airways. An equally capital-intensive Southwest Airlines, on the other hand, generated outstanding returns to its shareholders. What is the difference between Southwest and other airlines?

The main difference is that an excellent CEO, Herb Kelleher, was running Southwest Airlines. Not only did he start the company; he also maintained a large personal stake in it. In 2009, the company had a market value of about $8.0 billion, and Kelleher owned about 12 percent of the common stock, which he has owned since the airline was started in 1971. He ran Southwest as a low-cost airline during his tenure as CEO and did not diversify into other businesses. At age 76, Kelleher is still the chairman of the board, although he has relinquished his CEO position. When it comes to management, ownership stake, and dedication to the company, Kelleher is similar to Warren Buffett.

For a high-capital-intensity company to be successful, the quality of its management is far more important than it is for a low-capital-intensity company. When times are tough, management of high-capital-intensity companies needs to hang on and not give in to change for the sake of change. During recessionary periods, if a high-capital-intensity company makes a serious mistake, it may find itself in financial straits and may even face bankruptcy. Many airlines have gone bankrupt over the years, and some have done so twice. Several railroads and U.S. Steel have gone bankrupt, at least once. In general, it is easy for high-capital-intensity companies to invest large sums of money, borrow a lot from creditors, and compound their chances of getting into trouble during downturns or recessions. One solution to this problem is to hold a large stake in the company, as Berkshire often does.

In 1963, just before Buffett invested heavily in Berkshire Hathaway, the company's capital intensity was high, with its net PPE constituting about 32.5 percent of its total assets.[2] Ten years later, by the end of 1973, net PPE was only 1 percent of total assets. In discussing his mistakes over the prior 25 years, Buffett said, "My first mistake, of course, was in buying control of Berkshire."[3] As the company lost money, it was not easy to quickly withdraw the investments from the mill. Plant assets needed to be utilized for several more years before the mill could be shut down. Not only is the process of responding to declining demand slow, and changing technology troublesome; such adjustments also consume precious managerial time.

Your temperament may also work against you when you invest in a high-capital-intensity company. Profitability of high-capital-intensity companies is highly changeable, so stock prices may periodically drop significantly. An investor may become nervous and sell the stock in the high-capital-intensity companies in a down year, when it is the absolutely wrong time to sell. Pessimism in the marketplace may actually be a good time to buy if the long-term prospects are not affected. Consider the November 2009 Berkshire announcement of the acquisition of Burlington Northern Santa Fe. While Berkshire purchased the initial 22 percent stake in Burlington Northern at $78 per share during 2006–2008, the price had gone up to $114 per share by June 2008 as the stock market as a whole went up. However, with the market crash of 2008–2009, Burlington Northern's stock price came down substantially, and Berkshire made an offer to buy the remaining shares at $100 per share when the stock was trading at $76 per share. If the market and the Burlington Northern stock price had not come down, it is unlikely that Buffett would have made an offer to buy the remainder of the company. He has reportedly said that $100 per share was the maximum he was willing to pay.

You should also consider whether the company is in its growth period. High-capital-intensity companies are even more profitable than other companies in their growth phase because the overheads are spread over a larger output. Thus, their stock prices increase rather quickly. You may recall that steel companies, infrastructure companies, and housing companies prospered in a few years leading up to 2007, when the economy was doing well. They also invested heavily in property, plant, and equipment because it was easy for them to raise capital. As the economy slowed down in 2008 and 2009, they were likely to suffer heavily.

Conclusions

For an average investor, it is best to avoid investing in stocks of high-capital-intensity companies because the downside risk appears high. This is not to suggest that you should pass on a good opportunity if you understand a high-capital-intensity company well. It appears that for such companies, quality of management is even more important than for other companies. Berkshire's large recent investment in Burlington Northern would allow Berkshire and the company management to run the company more efficiently, and that may be one additional reason that Buffett decided to invest in the company.

Chapter 23

Key to Success: ROE and Other Ratios

The best gauge of the success of an enterprise is the percentage earned on invested capital.[1]

—*Benjamin Graham, David Dodd, and Sidney Cottle*

You are likely to earn a good return on your stock in the long run only if the underlying business is earning a good return on its capital. From the shareholders' perspective, return on equity (ROE) is usually the best yardstick, as it isolates the returns that belong to the shareholders from the returns to the enterprise as a whole.

ROE: Underlying Performance of a Business

Buffett often mentions financial ratios when discussing a business's underlying performance. The most important of them all—return on equity (ROE)—is net income divided by the book value of shareholders' equity. Because Costco is a well-run business, I use it as an example to illustrate some of the notable aspects of ROE and related issues. Let's look at Costco's ROEs for the past 12 years in Table 23.1.

Year after year, Costco has produced an ROE in excess of 10 percent, averaging 12.9 percent over the most recent 12 years. Have the

Table 23.1   Costco's Consistent Return on Equity and Return of Assets

Fiscal year	Net income	Shareholders' equity	Return on equity	Total assets	Interest expense after adjusting for taxes	Return on assets
1997	$ 312	$2,468	12.6%	$ 5,476	$46	6.5%
1998	460	2,966	15.5	6,260	29	7.8
1999	397	3,532	11.2	7,505	27	5.6
2000	631	4,240	14.9	8,634	23	7.6
2001	602	4,883	12.3	10,090	19	6.2
2002	700	5,694	12.3	11,620	17	6.2
2003	721	6,555	11.0	13,192	22	5.6
2004	882	7,625	11.6	15,093	22	6.0
2005	1,063	8,881	12.0	16,514	20	6.6
2006	1,103	9,143	12.1	17,495	8	6.3
2007	1,083	8,623	12.6	19,606	38	5.7
2008	1,283	9,192	14.0	20,682	61	6.5

Dollar amounts in millions.

stock returns been about the same? Costco's fiscal year usually ends at the end of August, and earnings data are publicly known by November of the same year. For comparing the 12-year ROEs to stock returns, we should therefore use the 12 years of stock returns from the end of November 1996 until the end of November 2008. During this period, Costco's stock price (split adjusted) went up from $11.60 to $51.47, giving annualized returns of 13.2 percent without dividends. With dividends, the annualized returns are about 13.8 percent. Thus, the ROE and stock returns are close to one another. The annualized growth in earnings per share was similarly 13.6 percent. However, for various reasons, it may not be the same for other firms and even for Costco for other periods. For example, returns are affected by P/E expansion or contraction independent of ROE. Overall, an examination of ROE over an extended period of time should help an investor determine the performance of the underlying business that finally is reflected in stock returns.

Since ROE is computed from accounting data, you should use it as a starting point for inferring stock returns, but be careful not to follow the numbers blindly. As you may know, there are far too many caveats to consider when you use accounting numbers in complex settings. For example, when a company purchases its own shares in the market or pays dividends, book value of equity is reduced and the ROE may temporarily become very high. In general, you should not rely on any one financial ratio. You should study growth in earnings per share over an extended period beyond examining the levels of ROE. Any financial ratio can be meaningless or lead you to misleading inferences under certain circumstances. Here is an example to illustrate this point.

I analyzed IBM's 2004 financial data in 2005 and discovered that the average ROE for the six years that ended in 2004 was 31.5 percent. At first glance, this seemed to be very good. However, IBM's growth in earnings per share (EPS) was pitiful. EPS was $4.25 in 1999 and remained about the same, except for an increase in 2004 to $4.93. On a compounded basis, the annual growth rate was only 2.5 percent. If the ROE was 31.5 percent, why did the EPS fail to grow? Where were those earnings used? With a little more analysis of the financial statements, I discovered the main reason. The company purchased shares at market prices but issued them to employees below cost as compensation. For IBM, the net result was that shareholders' equity did not grow because some of the earnings were effectively used for employee compensation and for repurchases. As the IBM example demonstrates, if earnings are not increasing, you should determine if the shareholders are getting dividends, if the company is buying shares back, or if the funds are being used in an unproductive manner.

When you are not comfortable with the computed ROE and growth in earnings, you might still ask, "What is the value of the company's common stock?" There are usually no easy answers, but you should be able to find out what is going on by analyzing the financial statement. Unless you know the answer, avoid investing in that company. This advice is similar to Buffett's argument that investors should stay in their circles of competence. In this case, instead of focusing on the company's products, I am focusing on the company's accounting output such as earnings. In the case of IBM, dividends had grown at the rate of 6 percent in recent years. Using this growth rate and a discount rate of 10 percent, I valued

IBM at $25 per share, which seemed ridiculous given the stock price of $90 per share. I did not invest in the stock.[2]

ROA: Return on Assets

A companion ratio to ROE is return on assets (ROA). The main objective in computing ROA is to obtain a measure of performance that is independent of financing. ROA presents performance of all the assets employed by the company, not just equity. Thus, the denominator is total assets and the numerator is earnings before interest expenses, adjusted for taxes. ROA in Table 23.1 is given by net income plus after-tax interest expense divided by total assets. Also, for simplicity, I use the end-of-the-year data in both numerator and denominator. Overall conclusions are similar whether we use the averages or the end-of-the-year numbers.

A comparison of ROA to ROE tells us the extent to which the company may be using implicit or explicit leverage. Many of the items in the liabilities section of the balance sheet are non-interest-bearing, so an examination of interest expense or the balance sheet analysis would not tell you the extent of financial leverage. For example, there is usually no explicit interest expense for accounts payable or for float in insurance companies. For Costco, the important point to note is that because of implicit use of low-cost liabilities, the average ROE of 12.9 percent is about twice the average ROA of 6.4 percent. It appears that Costco has also been able to use non-interest-bearing liabilities such as accounts payable to accomplish a high ROE from a low ROA.

This discussion on ROE and ROA should make you realize that knowledge of accounting is your friend in understanding the underlying profitability of the company. The analysis would also help you assess the quality of management. If management quality is good, the financial statements are generally easier to understand. You should view the financial ratios to help you assess the performance of the management rather than lifeless assets and equity. Ultimately, there are people behind performance metrics. I have discussed only two of the important ratios, but that does not mean that these are the most important ratios for each company. It depends on the business model of the company and what aspect of the underlying performance you want to better understand.

You should think about financial ratios carefully in deciding what ratios to use and how to interpret them. In particular, the main purpose of digging deeper into financial statements is to finally develop better forecasts of future earnings and better estimates of intrinsic value.

Buffett and Accounting

Buffett encourages investors to develop a good knowledge of accounting. In a Berkshire shareholders' annual meeting, a New York University MBA student asked Buffett for his advice on how to develop Buffett-like skills. In his response, Buffett mentioned that the student should take as many accounting courses as possible. Remember that you are a consumer and not a preparer of financial information. Act like a detective trying to understand the company's business from reading financial statements. Buffett reads a lot of financial reports; and for him, perhaps, that is like reading detective novels. As a reader of financial statements, you could have fun discovering behind-the-curtain stories.

Accounting numbers are based on a large number of estimates, and hence, they are not really hard numbers. Yet, academic research shows that long-short investing strategies can often be developed by using accounting knowledge.[3] When you study financial statements, be a skeptic. Buffett writes, "Managers thinking about accounting issues should never forget one of Abraham Lincoln's favorite riddles: 'How many legs does a dog have if you call his tail a leg?' The answer: 'Four, because calling a tail a leg does not make it a leg.' It behooves managers to remember that Abe's right even if an auditor is willing to certify that the tail is a leg."[4] Most accounting numbers are reliable, but you must remain vigilant. Here are some aspects of accounting that you should keep in mind:

1. **Accountants make many assumptions.** Every reported number is based on assumptions that are different across companies and on accounting rules that change over time. Here are two examples. First, if a company owns a building, its reported depreciation expense is based on assumptions. Second, expected future expenses such as promised health care benefits to retirees are based on assumptions about life expectancies and future costs.

2. **Most accounting numbers are historical in nature.** When someone asks you the value of your house, you are likely to give its current market value. In contrast, most accounting valuations of property, plant, and equipment are made at their depreciated amounts. In the case of land, it is never depreciated. Assume that a company such as General Electric purchased some land for $5 million 100 years ago. Even 100 years later, the reported value of the land on financial statements will be $5 million.

3. **Accountants may or may not use market prices for liquid assets.** This practice is confusing because companies have a choice in selecting accounting methods depending on the declared purpose and the amounts of stocks and bonds held as investments. Some assets and liabilities are marked to market while others are not.

4. **Accountants are supposed to be conservative.** Often they are indeed conservative, but in many cases they are aggressive. Don't forget that WorldCom accountants were too aggressive to report high earnings. The approach they used is not difficult to discern. From 1999 to 2002, WorldCom misclassified $8.1 billion in expenses as assets.[5] The amount was so large that when it was detected, the company went bankrupt. So you should not assume that accountants are always conservative.

Buffett has often discussed accounting issues in Berkshire's annual reports. In general, the better you are at accounting, the better you will be at understanding financial statements and, by extension, understanding and valuing companies.

Conclusions

Ultimately, the return on your investments in common stocks will depend on the underlying return on the capital used in the business, which can be measured by return on equity and return on assets. Those returns, when used properly, give rise to growth in earnings per share that engenders increases in the price of the stock. Thus, it is imperative that you compute ROE, ROA, and other financial metrics such as growth in per-share earnings and book value to examine how the underlying business is performing.

Chapter 24

Accounting Goodwill: Is It Any Good?

You can live a full and rewarding life without ever thinking about [accounting] Goodwill.... But, students of investment and management should understand the nuances of the subject.[1]

—*Warren Buffett*

Here is a surprising fact: The accounting *Goodwill* amount shown in financial statements has almost nothing to do with the word *goodwill* in everyday use. However, it is often a significant percentage of total assets on a company's balance sheet. To better understand accounting Goodwill, I present data on Goodwill and other assets for several well-known companies. I also discuss its implications for you in evaluating company profitability.

Accounting Goodwill and Its Economic Value

Table 24.1 reports summary balance sheets along with the recent Goodwill amounts for several well-known companies. Goodwill as a proportion of total assets for these companies is between 3 percent for ConocoPhillips and 42 percent for Procter & Gamble. There is no

Table 24.1 Goodwill and Other Assets of a Few Large Companies, 2008.

	Berkshire Hathaway	Coca-Cola	ConocoPhillips	General Electric	Microsoft	Procter & Gamble
Cash	$ 26	$ 5	$ 1	$ 48	$ 10	$ 3
Investments	102	6	0	21	13	0
Receivables	29	3	12	365	14	7
Inventories	8	2	5	14	1	8
Property, plant, and equipment, net	45	8	84	79	6	38
Goodwill	**34**	**4**	**4**	**82**	**12**	**60**
Other assets	24	12	37	189	16	27
Total assets	$ 267	$ 40	$143	$798	$ 73	$144
Goodwill as a percentage of total assets	13%	10%	3%	10%	17%	42%

Dollar amounts in billions.

224

apparent association between these percentages and the everyday meaning of the word *goodwill*. For Microsoft, reported Goodwill of $12 billion is only 17 percent of its total assets. By contrast, Procter & Gamble's Goodwill of $60 billion is 42 percent of its total assets. How, then, should you analyze the reported Goodwill in financial statements?

Consider Berkshire Hathaway's $34 billion of reported accounting Goodwill. Where did it come from? This amount represents the value given in cash or stock by Berkshire in various acquisitions in excess of identifiable net assets. For example, Berkshire acquired General Re in 1998 for $22 billion, but General Re had only $7 billion of net assets. The additional $15 billion Berkshire paid is reported as Goodwill. Similarly, when Berkshire acquired GEICO in 1996, Berkshire added $1.6 billion of Goodwill. The total amount of Goodwill of $34 billion derives from various Berkshire acquisitions over the years. In addition to General Re and GEICO, Dairy Queen, Executive Jet Aviation, and Iscar Metal Works have contributed to Berkshire's Goodwill.

As an investor, you would like to know if the economic value of accounting Goodwill is worth more or less than the $34 billion for Berkshire. First, Berkshire did pay $34 billion in cash or stock to acquire Goodwill. Hence, from an investment point of view, reported Goodwill is similar to other assets such as property, plant, and equipment. The objective then should be to analyze the Goodwill and financial statements to the extent that this asset helps produce earnings.

Goodwill and Earnings

Why did Berkshire acquire GEICO, General Re, and Iscar with acquisition premiums? The main reason that a premium is paid is the potential growth in acquired businesses. Buffett expected these companies to grow, and he paid premiums. Consider GEICO again. GEICO's revenues increased from $3 billion in 1996 to $12 billion in 2008, a growth rate of 12 percent per year. If this growth rate is higher than what was priced in Goodwill at the time of acquisition, the economic value of Goodwill is higher than what the financial records show. We do not know what Buffett expected the growth rate to be at the time of acquisition, but 12 percent is a very good growth rate given that GEICO is in a mature industry. Thus, the economic value should be higher than the $1.6 billion Berkshire paid for the accounting Goodwill. In this case, accounting Goodwill is like real estate whose value has gone up without having that increase reflected on the balance sheet.

One should consider whether the CEO of the acquiring company wanted to increase shareholder value or had another reason for the acquisition. If there appears to be some other motive, such as the CEO's ego, it may be best to avoid that company's stock. At least the value of Goodwill would be much lower, and in many cases, it may be assumed to be close to zero. In the case of Berkshire's CEO, the answer is clear. We know a lot about Buffett's historical record in terms of owner orientation, and since Buffett and Munger effectively own a controlling interest in Berkshire, they have no incentive to undertake a merger for the sake of increasing the company's size or some other perverse reason.

Buffett discusses Goodwill regarding his acquisition of See's Candies. "In 1983, See's earned about $27 million pretax on $11 million of net operating assets; in 1995, it earned $50 million on only $5 million of net operating assets. Clearly, See's economic Goodwill has increased dramatically during the interval rather than decreased."[2] As plant assets are used, their values often decline owing to depreciation. You should not think of Goodwill in the same manner. The internally generated Goodwill is not reported on the books. So, how should one think about profitability and Goodwill?

Goodwill and Profitability of Acquired Businesses

Berkshire's businesses fall into three main categories: insurance; manufacturing, service, and retailing operations; and finance and financial products businesses. In this section, I present recent data from the second category to show how investors may look at reported accounting Goodwill to think about future profitability.

Table 24.2 gives the balance sheet of various subsidiaries in Berkshire's manufacturing, service, and retailing businesses, which includes MiTek, Shaw Industries, NetJets, McLane, and other companies. At the end of 2008, the equity in this group was $30,779 million, and net income for the year was $2,283 million. For simplicity, using the

Table 24.2 Berkshire's Manufacturing, Service, and Retailing Operations

Balance Sheet, 12/31/08			
Assets		*Liabilities and Equity*	
Cash and equivalents	$ 2,497	Notes payable	$ 2,212
Accounts and notes receivable	5,047	Other current liabilities	8,087
Inventory	7,500	Total current liabilities	8,103
Goodwill and other intangibles	16,515	Deferred taxes	2,786
Fixed assets	16,338	Term debt and other liabilities	6,033
Other assets	1,531	Equity	30,779
	$49,897		$49,897

Dollar amounts in millions.

year-end data, the return on equity (ROE) (2,283/30,779) was 7.4 percent.

Successful investing is about looking ahead. Think about what Berkshire's future incremental rate of return might be. A simple approach is to imaginatively fast-forward several years when Berkshire subsidiaries in this sector will be twice their current size and earn twice their current profits. In other words, consider the situation, maybe in 10 years, when net income will be double, or $4,566 million. To generate the additional net income, total assets need not be twice the initial amount because the Goodwill part of total assets does not have to be purchased again. Some funds may have to be spent to maintain the Goodwill, but it is hard to believe that the amount needed would be twice the initial sum. This is because expenses for advertising or research and development that are required to maintain Goodwill are subtracted from revenues in computing net income.

For this illustration, I make the reasonable assumption that no additional amount in Goodwill will be needed for growth. Ignoring Goodwill, additional assets needed are $49,898 million minus $16,515 million, or $33,383 million. If the liabilities amounts equal those in 2008 ($19,118), the new equity needed would be $14,265 million. The incremental return on equity of $14,265 million would be $2,283/$14,265, or 16 percent. This would be a very good return indeed. If you had ignored the special aspect of Goodwill, you would have incorrectly assessed ROE to be only 7.4 percent as computed earlier. I repeat that in all such predictions, we make many assumptions, and one should always keep that in mind. Overall, if a company is likely to grow and has good management, you may compute the rate of return without reported Goodwill. You may then use your projected numbers to compute the company's intrinsic value.

Conclusions

Reported Goodwill in financial statements relates only to acquisitions and is the amount paid above the net tangible assets acquired. If a company after being acquired continues to grow in revenues with the same level of profit margin, the return on equity will also grow because no additional investment in Goodwill is generally needed. Accounting Goodwill is indeed a valuable asset in well-managed companies. In computing return on equity and intrinsic value, you should, therefore, pay special attention to Goodwill.

Part Eight

PSYCHOLOGY

B uffett has often mentioned that it is difficult to predict the market in the short run because market participants are not all rational. You will be a better investor if you are able to deal with the market's ups and downs. In Chapters 25 and 26, I discuss important ideas from psychology to help you better understand the markets and yourself.

Chapter 25

How Much Psychology Should You Know?

The dumbest reason in the world to buy a stock is because it's going up.[1]

—*Warren Buffett*

Many investors make dumb decisions by chasing stock prices. Do you? If so, what can you do about it? We will get better answers by studying psychology than by boning up on finance alone. The fascinating field of psychology is no longer limited to human behavior in social settings. In recent years, behavioral finance has shed light on the psychology of stock prices and financial decisions by market participants. Essentially, two main forces affect stock prices in the market: the fundamentals of the company and human behavior. Both forces have a role to play. However, a combined knowledge of the two should make a more powerful foundation for making intelligent decisions in the stock market than relying on fundamentals alone. Since a long discussion of psychology will take us away from our main goal of becoming better investors, only issues that are important from an investing point of view will be covered here.

Herding and You

You do not need a degree in psychology to understand that in the short run, the price of a stock can deviate substantially from its basic value because market participants may betray a herd instinct in their behavior. This is probably the most important concept that you need to know about market psychology. When people do not understand a company well, they follow the crowd: They chase the winners and dump the losers indiscriminately.

Because of this herd mentality, individual stocks—and the entire market—may go up or down dramatically. Herding stems from greed or fear. When interest rates rise or when there are fears that an important country's economy will falter, world markets react substantially. It is extremely difficult to time the market or to forecast events that make markets move dramatically. The lesson to learn is that when the market does go down significantly, prime buying opportunities may surface.

Do you know whether you have the herding instinct? It's a good idea to find that out if you can. The most common phenomenon I have observed is that people feel like buying a stock when its price has recently gone up or when the market has gone up. If you do so without evaluating the company, you are probably herding. Do you evaluate the price increase in a logical manner? You are probably not herding if you compute a stock's intrinsic value before you make a buy or sell decision.

Investors often extrapolate evidence from recent trends and then decide to buy or sell. If it were easy to pick stocks based on recent price trends alone, most mutual fund managers would be able to beat the market indices. But most of them don't. For every trend that continues, there is probably another one that does not. Consider two leaders in the personal computer industry in the late 1990s: Dell and Compaq (now Hewlett Packard). By 1998, Dell's stock price had gone up by several hundred percent, a trend that continued for two more years. How about Compaq? Like Dell, Compaq had a tremendous run until 1998, but in 1999, its price went down by 50 percent. Both stocks belonged to the same industry and faced similar macroeconomic environments. If you had bought Compaq instead of Dell, you would have regretted your decision. You were more likely to have chosen the better stock if you had tried to identify the fundamental reasons behind the successes of Dell and Compaq. By 1998, Compaq, in an untested strategy, was pushing into IBM's mainframe territory by acquiring Digital. Given the uncertainty, a high price for Compaq was not justified.

Investors herd often and in some cases create market euphoria. In the late 1990s, everyone bought high-tech stocks. The tech-heavy NASDAQ index peaked at 5,048 on March 10, 2000. Investors were herding. One interesting point to note is that many investors who thought themselves to be independent of the herd mentality avoided high-tech stocks but bought other stocks. During this period, most non-high-tech stocks also became expensive. For example, Coca-Cola traded at $80 per share at a price-to-earnings (P/E) ratio of about 50. What could explain this high price other than herding? It is indeed difficult to avoid herding; even those who thought they were not herding were in fact also herding by buying non-high-tech stocks such as Coca-Cola. They all suffered later in 2000 and in following years. If you bought Berkshire Hathaway stock—for which the price went down during the same period—you were not herding. (I did buy some additional Berkshire stock.) In the early- to mid-2000s, people bought homes. They were herding. Many others who thought that they were not herding bought stocks. They did not know it, but they were also herding, as stock prices were also high. All asset prices were in a bubble. Most investors suffered in the downturn in 2008.

The best antidote to herding lies in knowledge and in focusing on the long run. Buffett's suggestion of buying only what you know may help you avoid following the herd. In addition, concentrate on fundamentals. Peter Lynch has captured this idea in the chapter "Earnings, Earnings, Earnings" in his book *One Up on Wall Street.* He explains, "What you're asking here is what makes a company valuable, and why it will be more valuable tomorrow than it is today. There are many theories, but to me, it always comes down to earnings and assets. Especially earnings."[2] Reading Peter Lynch or Warren Buffett was a good start for me, but not enough. I understood them better only after I delved into learning behavioral finance and evaluating my decisions. And it took me several years to understand that I had a herd mentality. To avoid herding, I try to zero in on the long term. Follow Plato's centuries-old wisdom: "Know thyself."

Examine Your Buying and Selling Patterns

How can you determine how you make decisions? My approach is to write down my reasons for buying and selling a stock immediately after I make a decision. If I don't do this, I find that I'm not honest with myself later. With the benefit of hindsight, I can always try to justify my choices—which prevents me from understanding myself and improving my decision-making abilities. After a few years of this practice, I came to understand many of my habits. Talking with others, I have realized that many of my weaknesses are common. I saw that I was much more influenced by price movements than I thought I was. I got excited to buy when a merger was announced, when a product was launched, when the dollar-yen exchange rate changed, or when an ineffective CEO left a company.

In the short run, whenever my decisions proved to be correct, I found myself talking about them. I paid less attention to my incorrect decisions (Kmart!). I also realized that my long-run results were usually not related to what happened to the stock price right after I bought the stock. But I was paying more attention to the stock immediately after I had purchased it, when I should have been paying more attention to the stock *before* purchasing. I do that now. Although I always believed in the importance of earnings and assets, I did not understand their full significance in my decision making until I started writing. I learned the value of looking at a long historical record of performance.

In addition to writing down your decisions and analyzing them later, you may try other techniques to learn more about your decision making. For example, you may separate all the months the market went up from the months the market went down. From your broker's statements, you can find out whether you were a net buyer or a net seller during various months. If you were a net buyer during the months the stock market declined, you are more likely to be a contrarian. But if you were a net buyer when the stock market did well, you may have a herd mentality.

If you delay your decisions when the market is going up or down, you might want to analyze your buying and selling patterns in the months following the period when the market moves up or down. A simple analysis like this can tell you a lot about yourself. You could also redesign this approach to suit your needs. For example, you can examine whether you buy low P/E stocks or high P/E stocks. The most telling information about your behavior would come from identifying the events that trigger a decision, because a decision is not something you dream up from nothing. You should know the principal variables that trigger your decision. Are you motivated by the market, the evening news, a friend's recommendation, or something else? A good investor should know who he or she is. Self-reflection can be challenging but very rewarding to an investor.

Can You Change Yourself?

To benefit from the market's gyrations, you need not only to understand the basics of market psychology and yourself but also to find out whether *you* can change. If you find it difficult to change, then understanding market psychology or yourself may not be enough. Consider the following example. Say you acknowledge that if you drive after drinking alcohol at a party, you increase your chances of having an auto accident. It is also important to know, though, whether you can change your behavior and control drinking. If you cannot change your behavior at the party by refusing to drink, are you willing to change your behavior after the party? Can you leave your car at your friend's place and take a taxi home? It is one thing to know the right thing to do; it is another to change your behavior. Benjamin Graham puts this succinctly: "It is easy for us to tell you not to speculate; the hard thing will be for you to follow this advice."[3]

Buffett has often mentioned that different people are wired differently. For example, he has jokingly said that he would have been an animal's lunch if he had been born a few hundred years ago, implying that his skills are more suited to the modern world. The main message is that it is not easy to change. After reading Buffett's partnership letters from 1958 to 1969, his annual letters to shareholders from 1970 to 2008, and many of his articles, I find that Buffett has altered very little in his approach to business and investing. The good thing about his consistent behavior and decision making is that we can learn from his investing practices. This does not mean that one can change easily and follow his principles. Even after years of scouring Buffett's writings and going to the annual shareholder meetings, I look at stock prices several times during the day. I sometimes buy or sell stocks without analyzing them as well as I should, and I occasionally trade options. But I have changed somewhat. I have certainly realized that it takes me a long time to change. This seems to be a common phenomenon.

How Psychology May Help You

In his highly celebrated book *The Alchemy of Finance*, George Soros points out that the outcomes in social sciences such as economics arrive from a different process than the processes in natural sciences.[4] In natural sciences, one set of facts follows another without interference. The scientist does not influence the process. Specifically, nothing the scientist does will turn base metals into gold.

Now, to consider the financial markets, let's use an example similar to the one Soros cites. Assume that under reasonable conditions, Widget Company's stock price should be about 20 times its earnings per share. If the company's earnings per share go up from $0.80 to $1, its stock price should go up from $16 to $20 per share. If all market participants act rationally, the price may go up to $20 and stay there. However, financial market participants do not all behave rationally. As market participants observe stock prices going up after earnings increase, more buyers may come in and the price may climb higher than $20. The final price will depend on the availability of money, participants' experiences with other investments, and perhaps even weather (because their moods may vary with the weather). The main point is that the relation between earnings and prices in the short run depends on participants' perceptions and actions, not on fundamentals alone.

But the story does not end here. Let's say that the stock price goes up to $30. The company's management may evaluate the stock price and conclude that it is, at that point, overvalued. The company may then use its stock as a currency to buy another company or to issue new shares at this higher price, which generates more cash for the company. This action may indeed push the intrinsic value of the company's stock from $20 per share to a higher price. On the other hand, if the managers pay a high price for acquisitions, there may not be any gain in intrinsic value and there may actually be a loss. The managers' behavior may determine whether the company becomes successful or wastes the newly acquired resources. The final outcome is generally not easy to predict, but it is useful to think in terms of possible outcomes and to take into account both fundamentals and psychology.

In January 2000, a relatively new but successful Internet company, America Online (AOL), announced that it was buying the established publisher and media giant Time Warner. Based on the trading prices of the two companies at the time, the combined market value would be $350 billion. In April 2009, the combined market value was only $30 billion. In this transaction, AOL used its overvalued stock as a currency to purchase Time Warner. The combined firm was not as successful as merger plans had anticipated, but had AOL not engaged in the acquisition, it might not have survived as a viable company at all.

Prices do not follow fundamentals alone, because investors often want to get rich quickly when the market is rising (greed), and they want to protect their investment value when the market is falling (fear). In a rising market, initial price changes may lead to further price changes as investors pour in, which then makes the market overvalued. On the other hand, when prices are falling, more sellers come to the market to protect their investments and the market becomes undervalued. Nobel Laureate George Akerlof and Robert Shiller describe this phenomenon as price-to-price feedback leading to a vicious circle of prices going up or going down for a while.[5]

Market trends leading to bubbles and busts do not last forever; they finally reverse. There are several implications for an average investor. First, a bubble (overvaluation) usually starts in one sector of the economy and then spreads. In the late 1990s, the bubble took shape in the high-tech industry; and in the mid-2000s, the housing industry led the charge. Second, relative valuations may often not be a good guide for investing. After the initial rise of the high-tech stock prices during the Internet bubble, most other stocks also became overvalued. As I noted earlier, even Coca-Cola was trading at a 50 P/E in the late 1990s. Third, it seems impossible (at least to me) to tell how long a bubble or bear market will last. Finally, to take advantage of these bubbles or bear markets, you should buy or sell a stock only after you have objectively computed its intrinsic value as described earlier in Chapter 5.

How to Think about Psychological Biases

Many psychological studies show that the human decision-making process is imperfect. In particular, individuals deviate from economic rationality. For example, they make different choices depending on how a given problem is presented to them. Individuals are also known to violate several principles of statistical theory (for example, Bayes' theorem) in predicting uncertain outcomes.

However, simply because some investors place a lot of weight on psychological factors and less weight on fundamentals doesn't mean we should get carried away with the idea that the financial markets are crazy. We do not know whether trading by one group of irrational investors, on average, cancels out trading by another group. In general, if both optimists and pessimists trade in the market, there may not be any destabilizing effect. It is difficult to find a smoking gun that links psychological forces in individuals to mispricing in the marketplace. While it is beyond the scope of this book to examine various models in psychology, it is appropriate to discuss some of the relevant issues. In general, when you read a psychological explanation of movements in the market, evaluate it rationally just as you would evaluate a salesperson's pitch of a product.

Let's start with the so-called overconfidence bias. Overconfident people have a tendency to overestimate their skills. Those who think that they can drive well even after drinking the whole night are simply overconfident in their abilities. I want to use overconfidence as an example to show that, in my opinion, overconfidence in stock-picking ability does not necessarily mean that a person will pick wrong stocks and lose a lot in the stock market. Take the following thought experiment as an example.

First, imagine a situation where a person thinks that he can pick undervalued stocks but does not have the ability. Even if he does not have a superior ability, he will not necessarily underperform the market. Without any ability to pick undervalued stocks, he will essentially pick stocks randomly as a monkey would. Some stocks will underperform the market, and others will outperform the market. Overall, even in the absence of superior stock-picking ability, he will do just fine—that is, his performance will match the market's performance.

Now consider another person who is also overconfident but has some ability nonetheless. Not all his picks may do well, but more than five out of ten will, because of his ability. Assume that he picks 10 stocks that he is (over)confident about. Since he has some skill, he will outperform the market on average. The result will depend on his overall ability to find undervalued stocks, not on his level of confidence in them. On average, if you are able to pinpoint undervalued stocks, it does not matter whether you are highly confident or not so confident. Thus, the overconfidence bias by itself is not a bad human characteristic in picking stocks.

In some situations, biases may indeed be destructive. One common bias that I also have is that of not selling a stock at a loss. But if you believe that the stock is overvalued, then you should sell even if the current price is below your cost and you have to take a loss. Professor Terrance Odean examined trading records for 10,000 accounts at a large discount brokerage house and found that investors are reluctant to realize their losses, which may be one reason for their underperformance relative to the market.[6] Consider another bias or misperception: comparing the stock market to a casino. If you believe that you can do well in gambling at a casino, you are more likely to be wrong than right. The stock market for you becomes a casino when you try to time the short-term price movements. In that case, your beliefs may lead you to trade excessively, and trading costs will harm your performance.[7] Similarly, if you are betting in the options or futures markets, you may lose because time is not on your side, and you are probably playing against the house. Everyone has biases. However, you need to think about how biases may affect your behavior and whether that behavior is harmful.

Where do these biases come from? While they probably have their roots in factors such as genes or geography, let's just consider one source: you and your own experiences. If you lived in Seattle and saw scores of software engineers becoming millionaires from working for Microsoft, you would have lined up at a local university to become a software engineer. You may have disregarded the possibility that you did not have suitable skills to become a good software engineer. Maybe you should have gone to law school instead. Similarly, if you lived in Fayetteville, near Wal-Mart's headquarters, you would have given your left hand to work for Wal-Mart when it was growing fast.

Why do people believe that a trend in prices will continue? Probably because of their own experiences with a wide variety of charts since childhood, they naturally see patterns even when there are none. In most charts, whether they depict per-capita income, number of cars produced each year, or consumer prices, there is a noticeable trend. In most charts that I have come across in my life, there is an upward trend. Given this vast experience, when we observe a price chart, we intuitively imagine a trend even when there is none.

Likewise, why do investors flock to investing with previously successful mutual funds when it is well known that past successes generally do not predict the future? Once again, they are probably reacting on the basis of their experiences with patterns in life in general. A successful surgeon continues to be successful, a good manager remains a good manager and may even get better with age, a good artist continues to be a good artist, and a good researcher continues to be a good researcher. But, this pattern does not apply to most mutual fund managers because the luck factor looms large.[8] Overall, most of us do not have enough knowledge of the right variety to think independently all the time. We form biases because we extrapolate knowledge from past to future or from one field to another. However, if you read widely and learn from others' experiences beyond your own, you should be able to reduce your biases.

Some Important Questions for You to Consider

The purpose of understanding psychology is to reduce the irrational component in your decision making.[9] To apply psychology in your stock buying and selling decisions, the first thing you should explore is your primary reason for making that decision. Consider a situation in which you decide to buy a stock because the stock's P/E ratio is low. Knowing the primary reason for your decision, you should ask yourself, "Is buying a low P/E stock rational?" There is plenty of evidence in the literature to suggest that in the long run, buying a low P/E stock results in higher-than-average returns. Thus, your motivation appears rational. You may have follow-up questions: "Why is the P/E low?" or "What percentage of low P/E stocks actually outperforms the market within three years?" or "How long should I hold a stock after I buy a low P/E stock?" Because you realize that you are not very patient, you may not like the answer that you should hold a stock for three to five years, and you may decide not to invest in low P/E stocks.

In any case, systematic thinking will help you determine what you know or do not know and overcome your psychological biases. When you do not know the answer, you need to make a judgment call. In the case of buying a low P/E stock, you might find that one possible reason for the low P/E is that the earnings are temporarily high. It may not always be possible to gauge the extent to which earnings are temporarily high, and you may have to make a judgment call based on your knowledge of available financial data. In estimating the intrinsic value of Burlington Northern Santa Fe earlier, I entertained this possibility because the economy was doing well until 2007. But I am unable to tell the extent to which earnings may decrease in 2010 or 2011. In computing intrinsic value, we have to make estimates or judgment calls. Ultimately, everyone has to make judgment calls, but following a systematic approach will help you know when you are making a judgment call.

Consider a company that has an excellent product line and whose stock you are thinking of buying. You will probably examine the historical sales growth or past price patterns. You will also look at the company's fundamentals and management; but finally, you will have to make a judgment call. You might conclude that you do not know enough about the company's prospects but that the price looks attractive based on what you know. In other words, you do not have enough confidence in your decision. You may decide to invest only a small amount of money in the stock and revisit the information set after a few months.

Your ultimate question should always be "Is this rational based on all that I know?" On average, if you go through a set of basic questions about the stock and psychology, you should do well in the stock market. Of course, in the process of learning about yourself, if you conclude that you are likely to make irrational choices more often than not, maybe you should stay away from the stock market. In that case, your situation may be similar to someone who knows the dangers of excessive drinking but cannot help but drink when he visits a bar. He should learn not to go near a bar. Overall, knowledge of fundamentals should help you estimate the company's long-term future, and knowledge of psychology should help you inject rationality into your decisions.

Conclusions

Everyone has opinions and psychological biases. However, people may not know their own biases. The more you know about your psychological biases, the better you can function in the volatile stock market. The entire market may be influenced by psychological reasons, not by fundamental reasons alone. From an investment perspective, the bottom line is that the market will continue to fluctuate and give you solid opportunities every so often. Value in the long run is determined by fundamentals, while short-term gyrations reflect market participants' psychological weaknesses, such as herding. Knowledge is the best antidote to making wrong decisions. If you are a long-term investor, the rational thing to do is to make decisions based on long-term fundamentals of the business.

Chapter 26

How to Learn from Mistakes

What we learn from history is that people don't learn from history.[1]

—*Warren Buffett*

Both Warren Buffett and Charlie Munger believe in learning from mistakes. During Berkshire's 1997 annual meeting, Munger said that in the past, Berkshire board members have discussed their mistakes to learn from them. Members brought up one or two important mistakes they had made in their careers. Most of us find it easy to talk about our successes but difficult to talk about our mistakes, and often we attribute our mistakes to bad luck.

Mistakes versus Bad Luck

We should differentiate mistakes from bad outcomes or bad luck. A bad outcome, for example, was the drop in the stock price of Johnson & Johnson when Tylenol was found to be laced with poison and several consumers died.[2] If you had owned Johnson & Johnson stock then, it was bad luck, not a mistake. When Salomon Brothers got into trouble in 1991, Berkshire Hathaway suffered financially, and Buffett also suffered personally when he took over as the CEO of Salomon to sort out the problems. The scandal at Salomon that led to Buffett's involvement was a rare event, and so there was very little to learn from it. It was almost impossible to predict the Salomon scandal. It was simply bad luck.

It is also not a mistake when you consciously decide not to do something that turns out to be good luck. For example, if you do not participate in your office lottery pool and the pool wins a mega-million-dollar jackpot, you have not made a mistake. Although a close friend of Bill Gates, Buffett is said to have bought only 100 shares of Microsoft. Was Buffett mistaken in not investing more in Microsoft stock? No. Buffett has consciously decided not to invest outside the circles of his competence.

Nor did Buffett buy shares in Fannie Mae in the mid-1980s before the stock did very well. In one of Berkshire's annual meetings, he said that not buying Fannie Mae was a mistake. Buffett knows a lot about financial companies and felt he should have known that, ultimately, Fannie Mae was likely to be successful. From 2006 to 2008, Berkshire invested more than $7 billion in ConocoPhillips stock when oil and gas prices were near their peak. The stock price subsequently dropped by 50 percent. In the 2009 annual meeting, Buffett mentioned that buying the ConocoPhillips stock was a major mistake.

Learning from Mistakes

In 1965, Buffett took control of Berkshire Hathaway. On different occasions, he has mentioned that it was a mistake. He knew that the prospects of textile manufacturing were unpromising, but he bought it because the stock price looked cut rate. (He may have also bought it for its cash flows.) He learned, I believe, that reasonable growth prospects are important. He also seems to avoid high-capital-intensity businesses since then unless he is in a position to influence managerial decisions by holding a large stake in the company.

We often make mistakes because we do not think systematically about our decisions. Michael Mauboussin, chief investment strategist at Legg Mason, recommends creating a list to concentrate on steps needed to make a good decision.[3] On many occasions, I have asked my friends if they had made a mistake by not investing in Berkshire. Some of them answered yes. However, when I ask them what they have learned from that mistake, they usually draw a blank. Making mistakes is not a bad thing, not learning from them is. My usual suggestion to my friends is to examine whether Berkshire is still a good stock. If Buffett has been so good in the past, should we have some confidence that he will produce at least reasonably good results in the future? This sequence of questioning led me to continue to invest in Berkshire. In early 2009, I bought more of Berkshire stock when the class B shares were trading at around $2,500 per share.

Learning from investment mistakes is easier when you are already somewhat knowledgeable about the industry in which you invest. For example, if you know something about retailing and you invest in Target or Wal-Mart, you will have the opportunity to learn from your investments. In the late 1990s, I invested in Kmart because the stock looked cheap and I was expecting the company to grow. However, I suffered significant losses. I should have visited the stores more frequently to examine the quality of customer service and the availability of products. Later, I also learned that Kmart's low inventory turnover ratio was one indication that the company was not doing well. This mistake has nudged me to become better in using financial ratios. My knowledge in accounting and finance has helped me in this regard. Thus, expertise and learning from mistakes go hand in hand. This is one additional reason that investors should invest in their circles of competence.

The first step in learning from mistakes is to acknowledge that a mistake was made and by itself, making mistakes is not a bad thing.[4] To avoid future mistakes, I write down my errors in the privacy of my home. Second, I write potential reasons for my mistakes. Once I have analyzed the reasons, I take the third hard step of talking about my mistakes to my friends. I even hang the now-worthless Kmart share certificate on my office wall. I used to buy and sell frequently after reading an article in the *Wall Street Journal* or *Barron's*. But now, through this constant writing and evaluation process, I am much less likely to buy or sell on a whim. Most of my holdings are now long-term holdings. Whenever I feel like selling my long-term holdings of Berkshire Hathaway, Wal-Mart de Mexico, and American Express, I go back to the reasons I bought them in the first place and evaluate current conditions.

Mistakes of Commission and Mistakes of Omission

Berkshire Hathaway purchased 200 million shares of Coca-Cola for about $6.50 per share (split-adjusted) in the late 1980s. During the Internet bubble period in early 1998, the Coca-Cola stock price was $85 per share, which, by most valuation metrics, was overvalued. For example, the P/E ratio was over 50. Buffett has subsequently hinted that not selling Berkshire's Coca-Cola stock was a mistake. By 2003, the stock price had fallen to $40, and in early 2009, it was still trading at around $45 per share. We don't know why Buffett did not sell the stock, but we can speculate and possibly learn from this episode.

First, Buffett was a director on the Coca-Cola board of directors. Any director would find it difficult to sell a huge position in the company stock. Buffett resigned from his directorship in 2006 after 17 years on the board. Second, it is possible that when a company has significant cash flows as Berkshire does, even people like Buffett may not be attentive to the price of an investment. After all, the idea in long-term investing is not to focus on the day-to-day price. Finally, it is worth mentioning that if Buffett had sold the Coca-Cola stock at close to its peak, say in 1999 or 2000, and invested the after-tax proceeds in the market index, the losses by 2009 would have been about the same. This is a good example to think about when you look at your own mistakes; the main lesson probably is that you should sell a stock when it is clearly overvalued. I also do not know why Buffett bought ConocoPhillips stock and then sold it. My guess is that he realized that because of high volatility in oil prices, oil company stock prices are speculative in nature.

Buffett has often talked about mistakes of omission—the investments that should have been made but were not made. In one instance, he discussed not buying Wal-Mart stock, which was in his circle of competence. It was not a high-tech company, and it was growing successfully in the U.S. Midwest where his hometown of Omaha is located. I think it would help us all if we learned to evaluate our mistakes not only of commission but also of omission.

Conclusions

Everyone makes mistakes, and bad luck strikes everywhere. There is not much you can do about bad luck except to diversify and shy away from huge risks. When you do make mistakes, take the time to ponder them and find ways to avoid making the same ones again.

Part Nine

CORPORATE GOVERNANCE

H ow does Buffett successfully manage a large conglomerate? When you think about investing in the stock market, you should also consider the quality of corporate governance practices at the firm. In Chapters 27 through 30, I review several principles that Buffett has adopted in running Berkshire Hathaway.

Chapter 27

Dividends: Do They Make Sense in This Day and Age?

[D]ividend policy is irrelevant for the determination of market prices, given investment policy.[1]

—*Merton Miller and Franco Modigliani*

The practice of paying regular dividends is a long-standing puzzle. In a well-known article, two Nobel laureates in economics, Franco Modigliani and Merton Miller, wrote that a company's value does not depend on its dividend policy; rather, value depends on how the company invests its resources. After all, dividends are equivalent to transferring shareholders' money from their accounts with the company to their personal accounts. When a company pays a dividend, its share price drops by almost the same amount as the dividend.

Berkshire Does Not Pay Dividends

Buffett seems to agree with academic thought on the topic of dividends. Berkshire Hathaway has not paid any dividends for the past 42 years. MIT professor and Goldman Sachs partner Fischer Black argued that because of the U.S. double-taxation structure where corporations first pay taxes on earnings and then individuals again pay taxes on dividends, both corporations and individuals should prefer no dividends.[2] Corporations should only return earnings to their shareholders as cash dividends when they do not have projects with reasonable rates of return and their own share prices are high. If the share price is low, they should repurchase their own shares.

Consider Citigroup, a large financial institution with a market capitalization of about $200 billion in late 2007. Its common stock was among the highest dividend-yielding stocks, paying stockholders 7 percent. During 2007, the stock price declined by over 40 percent because the company suffered losses of about $10 billion in its housing-related investments. In the wake of Citigroup's decline, CEO Charles Prince had to resign. To regain its financial strength, Citigroup issued $7.5 billion of convertible securities, yielding 11 percent to the Abu Dhabi Investment Authority. By any yardstick, 11 percent is high, in light of the fact that the going rate of interest on 10-year Treasury notes at the time was only 4.25 percent and the 30-year mortgage rate, about 5.8 percent.

Although Citigroup's stock price had declined and the company was forced to raise funds, it continued to pay almost $10 billion a year in dividends. It was obvious that Citigroup needed cash in a hurry: The market did not think highly of Citigroup's financial strength because of the huge losses it had incurred. Why did Citigroup not cut its dividends immediately when it was obviously in serious financial trouble? Some have argued that once a company starts paying a dividend, the market expects the company to pay the dividend at regular intervals forever. This argument may have some justification in normal circumstances, but the logic is questionable in this case. Since the company already indicated that it was in financial trouble and needed to raise funds by issuing preferred stock, a dividend cut would have been a more logical choice than raising equity. While Citigroup is an extreme example (and it finally cut its dividend), it is common for corporations to raise equity and pay dividends at the same time. Such cases are often examples of poor financial management.

Receiving regular dividends is costly to you. First, if you own shares in your name, you receive checks every quarter that you then have to take to the bank, spending time on this chore. Depositing of dividends can be made automatic if you own shares in a brokerage account, but many people prefer to hold shares themselves because they are safer that way. Second, you have to spend more time and effort keeping track of your dividends for tax purposes. Finally, you have to pay taxes on these dividends, often at a rate higher than the capital gains tax rate. If some shareholders need regular infusions of cash, it is not clear that what they receive in dividends is the right amount for them. Shareholders can easily sell a few shares if they need cash. Also, shareholders can decide which shares to sell to minimize their tax burden. Perhaps some intermediaries and consultants who give advice on dividends earn fees, and that may be one reason most companies continue to pay regular dividends in this day and age.

So what should you look for in a dividend policy? A regular dividend payment from a company that generates regular free cash flows but does not have growth opportunities indicates a company with self-disciplined management. In academic finance, this is known as the *monitoring role of dividends*. Because of the commitment to pay regular dividends, such companies are less likely to waste resources and are good candidates for further analysis. Costco started in 1983 and used its cash flows for growth until 1994, when it started paying dividends. It was a good company to invest in before it paid any dividends and also after it started paying regular dividends. If you had focused only on dividend-paying companies, you would have not invested in Costco or for that matter in Berkshire Hathaway.

A regular dividend payment by itself is not a strong enough variable to characterize a company as a good investment. When a company paying regular dividends also raises funds in the financial markets and the balance sheet is not strong, you should be careful about investing in its stock. Dividend payment is just one possible use of free cash flows. What is most important is your comfort level with a company's usage of its free cash flows. Companies have many choices other than paying dividends: They can undertake new projects, repurchase their own shares, and invest in financial assets. If you are not comfortable with management decisions on its usage of cash flows, especially its investment policy, you should not buy the stock in the first place. If a company has excess cash without a reasonable probability of profitable new projects, it can do what Microsoft did.

Microsoft and a Special Dividend

Microsoft's policy presents a good example of what a company can periodically do with excess cash. It is clear that Microsoft has been highly profitable (see Table 27.1). Instead of paying regular dividends, the company repurchases its own shares. By repurchasing its own shares, Microsoft is effectively returning cash to its shareholders without making them liable for additional taxes. Second, Microsoft does not have to repurchase its shares very often; it does so only periodically when it has excess cash and the stock price is low.

By the end of 2002, Microsoft was in an enviable financial position with about $70 billion in cash and short-term investments. It was increasingly being criticized for not paying cash to its shareholders. In 2003, Microsoft paid its very first cash dividend: $857 million, or about 10 percent of its current earnings. Why did Microsoft start paying a

Table 27.1 Microsoft's Earnings and Return of Funds (Dividends and Share Repurchases) to Shareholders

Fiscal year	Earnings	Repurchase of own shares	Dividends paid to shareholders	Total returned to shareholders
1996	$ 2,195	$ 1,344		$ 1,344
1997	3,454	3,010		3,010
1998	4,490	2,631		2,631
1999	7,785	2,850		2,850
2000	9,421	4,896		4,896
2001	7,346	6,074		6,074
2002	5,355	6,069		6,069
2003	7,531	6,486	$ 857	7,343
2004	8,168	3,383	1,729	5,112
2005	12,254	8,057	36,112	44,169
2006	12,599	19,207	3,545	22,752
2007	14,065	27,575	3,805	31,380
1996–2007	$94,663	$91,582	$46,048	$137,630

Dollar amounts in millions.

regular cash dividend? The motive is uncertain, but Microsoft may have done so in response to demands from the media. The initiation of cash dividends certainly helped reduce criticism. The amount of the regular dividend is not large relative to Microsoft's earnings or its cash and short-term investments. In 2005, the company used $44 billion to repurchase shares and to pay a one-time dividend in excess of $36 billion. In recent years, I have not seen any criticism of Microsoft for its dividend policy. Maybe the main reason for a regular dividend payment is the misguided perception among many investors that dividends are always good for shareholders.

Conclusions

In most cases, companies pay regular dividends simply because it has been a long-standing corporate practice. There are no strong reasons to support paying regular dividends, however, especially when the balance sheet is not strong. Instead of focusing on the dividend policy, you should spend more time analyzing the sources and uses of a company's cash flows, which ultimately determine the stock price.

Chapter 28

Should You Invest in Companies That Repurchase Their Own Shares?

Companies in which we have our largest investments have all engaged in significant stock repurchases at times when wide discrepancies existed between price and value.[1]

—Warren Buffett

When a publicly traded company buys its own shares, the outcome is a smaller number of shareholders owning the business. Through repurchases, the company may signal that its shares are undervalued. Repurchases are also a tax-free method to return cash to shareholders. The academic literature supports the view that companies repurchasing their own shares are frequently undervalued. In an article in the *Journal of Business* published by the University of Chicago, Amy Dittmar concludes, "Firms repurchase stock to take advantage of potential undervaluation."[2]

Share Repurchasing Is Good News

Suppose you and John jointly own a tract of ancestral land. You divide it into two equal parts for farming purposes. Each of you can farm whatever you want and keep the outputs. In his piece of land, John cultivates cotton. You use it for sugarcane. After several years, John proposes to buy your piece of the land at an attractive price. Whether you sell or not, it should be immediately clear that his cotton farming is doing well. Through his desire to increase his landholding, he has revealed to you that he is in a profitable business. Share repurchasing is similar.

Investors can infer that a company that repurchases its shares frequently is unlikely to waste free cash flow in unproductive acquisitions. Consider the case of Coca-Cola, which has had significant free cash flows in recent decades. In 1982, it acquired Columbia Pictures. The Columbia acquisition did not work out and was sold in 1989. Buffett explained, "Corporate acquisition programs almost never do as well and, in a discouragingly large number of cases, fail to get anything close to $1 of value of each $1 expended."[3] Coca-Cola subsequently decided to invest its cash flows in itself by purchasing some of the shares back. From 1989 to 1999, the number of the company's common shares outstanding decreased from 2.79 billion to 2.49 billion—a drop of 11 percent, or about 1 percent per year. At current prices, this amounts to about $1 billion annually.

Share Repurchases by Companies in Which Berkshire Has Invested

In Table 28.1, I examine the repurchase practices of some Berkshire holdings. These data are for the five-year period from 2004 to 2008.

The five companies listed in Table 28.1 invested 34 percent to 76 percent of their net income in purchasing their own shares back. If their management quality had not been excellent, the managers would probably have used the cash to expand their empires by investing in other, potentially less profitable, projects. *Washington Post*, Wells Fargo, and Moody's have engaged in repurchase practices. In the case

Table 28.1   Buffett Likes Companies Buying Their Own Shares

Company	Net income (2004–2008)	Repurchases (2004–2008)	Repurchases as a percentage of net income
Coca-Cola	$26,587	$ 9,164	34%
American Express	17,597	13,314	76
Anheuser-Busch	9,907	6,518	66
Burlington Northern Santa Fe	8,153	4,317	53
Kraft	13,848	7,602	55

Dollar amounts in millions.

of *Washington Post*, the company made a significant investment in Kaplan, a commercial training company, and did not buy back shares in 2004 and 2005. However, it reverted to a share repurchase program in 2006.

Buffett writes:

> By making repurchases, when a company's market value is well below its business value, management clearly demonstrates that it is given to actions that enhance the wealth of shareholders, rather than to actions that expand management's domain but that do nothing for (or even harm) shareholders.[4]

He continues:

> Investors should pay more for a business that is lodged in the hands of a manager with demonstrated pro-shareholder leanings than for one in the hands of a self-interested manager marching to a different drummer.[5]

Sometimes, share repurchases can boost reported earnings because the number of shares go down due to repurchasing. Before investing in a company that is repurchasing its own shares, you should investigate the company fundamentals and its management quality.

Why Doesn't Berkshire Repurchase Its Own Shares?

In early 2000, when Berkshire Hathaway class A common stock was trading at about $40,000 per share, down from a high of $81,000 per share, many articles in the popular press suggested that Berkshire should consider repurchasing its own shares. Given what Buffett has expressed, it seemed to be a reasonable suggestion because the stock price was barely above its book value of $38,000 per share. The annual letter to Berkshire shareholders was widely anticipated, and when it finally appeared on March 11, 2000, it further clarified Buffett's thinking on share repurchases:

> There is only one combination of facts that makes it advisable for a company to repurchase its shares: First, the company has available funds—cash plus sensible borrowing capacity—beyond the near-term needs of the business and, second, finds its stock selling in the market below its intrinsic value, conservatively-calculated.[6]

If profitable investment opportunities exist, then management should not repurchase the company shares even when the price is attractive. This is probably one reason Buffett did not choose to repurchase Berkshire shares. Of course, even Buffett admits that he has made mistakes in the past, for which he has criticized himself: "At certain times in the past, I have erred in *not* making repurchases. My appraisal of Berkshire's value was then too conservative or I was too enthused about some alternative use of funds." Investors should also consider the potential value added. Buffett continues, "A repurchase of, say, 2% of a company's shares at a 25% discount from per-share intrinsic value produces only a 1/2% gain in that value at most." Thus, when management reputation is well established, as in Buffett's case, the advantage in repurchasing may not be substantial. Buffett further emphasizes his interest in shareholder wealth: "Please be clear about one point: We will *never* make purchases with the intention of stemming a decline in Berkshire's price. Rather we will make them if and when we believe that they represent an attractive use of the Company's money."[7] Overall, if a company purchases its own shares on a regular basis and its fundamentals appear sound, you should consider buying shares in the company.

Conclusions

When a company buys its own shares and you have confidence in the quality of that company's management, chances are that the stock is undervalued, and you should expect the stock price to rise over time. On the other hand, if the repurchase of stocks seems to be motivated by a desire to reduce the number of shares and, hence, increase earnings per share, you should avoid investing in the company.

Chapter 29

Corporate Governance: Employees, Directors, and CEOs

Warren Buffett's annual salary for 2008 was $100,000 and his total compensation was $175,000.

—Berkshire Hathaway Proxy Statement, 2009

arren Buffett has often remarked that he loves to run Berkshire Hathaway. Why? It is certainly not his $100,000 salary that motivates him in his roles as Berkshire Hathaway's CEO and chairman of the board. One necessary ingredient to ensure the success of any organization is to have motivated employees and top management. This chapter explains the salient features of Buffett's thinking on how to motivate employees, directors, and CEOs.

Employee Compensation at Berkshire

In 1996, Berkshire acquired the auto insurer GEICO. Immediately after the purchase, a focused compensation plan was put in place. Examining this simple but effective change by Buffett gives us insight into practices designed to motivate employees. The objective of the compensation plan was to keep employees focused on those aspects of the business that are under their control and that have an impact on profitability. Buffett writes, "At GEICO, the bonuses received by dozens of top executives are based upon two key variables: (1) growth in voluntary auto policies; and (2) underwriting profitability on seasoned auto business. *Everyone* at GEICO knows what counts."[1]

When a compensation plan is that simple and focused, dramatic results ensue. The following reflection by Buffett provides us with a set of principles in this regard:

> Berkshire's incentive compensation principles: Goals should be (1) tailored to the economies of the specific operating system; (2) simple in character so that the degree to which they are being realized can be easily measured; and (3) directly related to the daily activities of plan participants.[2]

Buffett also argues that compensation plans should encourage a high return on capital employed, not just a high level of profits, because it may be easy to increase the level of profits by simply increasing the amount of capital employed. In addition, the cost of capital must be taken into account. Recall Berkshire's highly successful subsidiary Scott Fetzer Company (discussed in Chapter 13) with Ralph Schey as its manager. Buffett explains how Schey's bonus plan gives him incentives to increase the profitability of capital employed.

Writes Buffett:

> If Ralph can employ incremental funds at good returns, it pays him to do so: His bonus increases when earnings on additional capital exceed a meaningful hurdle charge. But our bonus calculation is symmetrical: If incremental investment yields substandard returns, the shortfall is costly to Ralph as well as to Berkshire. The consequence of this two-way arrangement is that it pays Ralph—and pays him well—to send to Omaha any cash he can't advantageously use in his business.[3]

Note that it is not sufficient to reward managers only if performance is better than expected; managers should also receive incentives to avoid losses. This concept of symmetrical incentives is rare in practice. One consequence of the rarity of symmetrical incentive systems is that, when possible, managers manipulate accounting numbers to report higher numbers, in order to earn higher bonuses. However, these managers also attempt to report larger losses in years when they do not expect to earn bonuses.[4] When you study a company's incentive contracts, look for symmetrical incentive plans.

Buffett summarizes his overall management philosophy:

> At Berkshire, our managers will continue to earn extraordinary returns from what appear to be ordinary businesses. As a first step, these managers will look for ways to deploy their earnings advantageously in their businesses. What is left, they will send to Charlie and me. We then will try to use those funds in ways that build per-share intrinsic value. Our goal will be to acquire either part or all of businesses that we believe we understand, that have good, sustainable underlying economics, and that are run by managers whom we like, admire and trust.[5]

Buffett's philosophy suggests that people, rather than the type of industry, are behind extraordinary results. Berkshire gets extraordinary results from its subsidiaries, which range from auto insurance to honest-to-goodness traditional businesses, because Berkshire creates compensation plans tailored to those specific businesses. Unlike practices in most large corporations, compensation plans at Berkshire are *not* linked to Berkshire's overall performance.

Compensation for Directors and Executive Officers

Berkshire's program for compensating its directors also differs from compensation programs at most public companies. Berkshire pays nominal amounts to the directors to attend board meetings. A director who is not an employee or a spouse of an employee receives a fee of only $900 for each meeting attended in person, and $300 for participating in any meeting conducted by telephone. In comparison, directors in large corporations are frequently paid more than $100,000 in cash compensation and $200,000 in total compensation. Furthermore, the Berkshire Compensation Committee has established a policy that neither the profitability of Berkshire Hathaway nor the market value of its stock is considered in the compensation of any executive officer. Under the committee's compensation policy, Berkshire does not grant stock options to executive officers.

How does Berkshire attract outstanding directors? The key seems to be that, in identifying potential directors, Buffett looks for individuals who are "owner-oriented, business savvy, interested, and truly independent."[6] The last criterion, "truly independent," requires some elaboration. It is easy for a board member to meet the independence criteria set up by the National Association of Securities Dealers or other institutions. But for Buffett, what matters is "true independence." For example, suppose a university professor is appointed as a director of a publicly traded company and receives compensation of $100,000. Since the income derived from his board membership is likely to be a substantial portion of his or her total income, the company CEO can exert significant influence on that board member. According to Buffett, this board member cannot be considered truly independent. Most Berkshire board members are accomplished, wealthy business leaders who are likely to be "truly independent," by Buffett's standards. They are also owner-oriented, as Buffett explains, "Most of our directors have a major portion of their net worth invested in the company. We eat our own cooking."[7]

There is one caveat: When all directors think similarly, they may ignore new ideas that often come from outsiders, such as professors or entrepreneurs. In other words, a corporate board in which most members have similar backgrounds may fall victim to what is known as *groupthink*; they may try to minimize conflict and reach consensus without critically analyzing and evaluating ideas.

What Is Wrong with Compensation through Stock Options?

To motivate senior executives, many companies award stock options to top managers and CEOs. About stock options, Buffett has written, "Though options, if properly structured, can be an appropriate, and even ideal, way to compensate and motivate top managers, they are more often wildly capricious in their distributions of rewards, inefficient as motivators, and inordinately expensive for shareholders."[8] If the stock price increases after stock options are awarded, the value of stock options also increases. In most cases, the potential benefits to the executives are huge. It is not uncommon for some CEOs to reap millions or even hundreds of millions of dollars through stock options. However, when the stock price declines, the executives do not suffer much by way of direct monetary losses. From the shareholders' point of view, this is just not fair. Buffett believes that executives should participate in both the upside and the downside of stock price movements, just as the shareholders do.[9] For this reason, executives should be encouraged to own shares in the company.

When General Re, a large reinsurance company, was acquired by Berkshire Hathaway, Buffett changed General Re's compensation plan. In a special meeting of shareholders held to vote on the merger, which I attended, Buffett stated that he preferred to change the current plan at General Re, even though it would cost about a billion dollars to immediately vest the substantial benefits under existing plans.

In evaluating a company's prospects, an investor should look into executive compensation plans. Greedy executives prefer stock options over other forms of payments. Given the incentive structure arising from the existence of stock options, managers are more likely to care for their own interests, potentially at substantial cost to the shareholders. They also tend to care more about the short run rather than the long run; as stock options generally have a limited time to maturity.

CEOs often abuse the stock-option compensation system. David Yermack, a professor of finance at New York University, finds that the timing of stock options frequently coincides with movements in a company's stock prices.[10] At the end of 2007, 165 companies were under investigation in a wide-ranging federal probe of stock-option grants and practices. It appears that CEOs frequently receive stock-option awards shortly before favorable corporate news. Thus, CEOs benefit, but at the expense of shareholders. Evidence also suggests that managers, generally speaking, announce bad news prior to option grant dates and good news after.[11]

For example, Cendant Corporation's stock price declined dramatically during 1998 for many reasons, including an accounting scandal. When Cendant's stock price dropped, a large portion of CEO Henry

Silverman's 25.8 million stock options, originally priced between $17 and $31 a share, were repriced to $9.81—well under the then-current Cendant stock price of $15 per share. Silverman earned $63.9 million in 1998 and had about $400 million in the pipeline. It did not matter to him that the stock price declined. And, of course, he would have earned a large sum if the stock price had gone up. Wow! Heads I win, tails you lose. Not only did shareholders suffer because of the price decline; they suffered even more when the company's executives were handsomely paid.

How to Identify Good CEOs or Other Senior Managers

At Berkshire annual meetings, Warren Buffett sometimes mentions that he would forgo a profitable opportunity if pursuing it meant forging a partnership with someone whom he did not trust. In other words, if you are suspicious of the CEO, you should not invest in that company's stock. When investing for the long run, the quality of management—including integrity—is more important than current profitability, because profitability can't be sustained if management quality is poor. Here are a few signs of a good CEO, based on Buffett's thoughts.

First and foremost, track record matters a lot. To the best of my knowledge, all Berkshire subsidiary CEOs have a proven track record in their respective companies or in the same industry. Buffett is unlikely to hire a person from one industry to run a company in another industry. This coincides with his principle of staying in your circle of competence. Maybe this was one reason why Robert Nardelli was not successful at Home Depot. In 2000, he became CEO of Home Depot after successfully running General Electric's mines and locomotive businesses, but Nardelli lacked retail experience. In 2007, he was asked to resign from Home Depot—only to be appointed as the Chrysler CEO several months later! In 2009, when Chrysler filed for bankruptcy, he agreed to resign from his position by the end of the bankruptcy case.

Second, CEO compensation should be examined for abuse. Nothing is wrong with paying CEOs well, but to pay them exorbitantly may indicate a lax corporate governance culture. At Home Depot, Nardelli's problems probably started with the fact that he was from a different industry but that he had also negotiated a generous compensation contract. He had access to several corporate jets and other expensive benefits, for which he was criticized. Nardelli's compensation was so well designed that when he left Home Depot, he received a $210 million severance package, despite presiding over a 40 percent decline in the company's stock price. Highly paid CEOs also create a money-minded culture in the organization. Such CEOs do not command respect from employees, and when companies fall on hard times, they cannot possibly lead effectively. Such organizations are not likely to do well for shareholders in the long run.

Third, a CEO should have a conceptual framework that he or she can articulate well. You should listen carefully to a CEO's answers at public meetings or conference calls (all analyst conference calls are now open to the public). For example, if a CEO expands the company into a new business in which he or she lacks expertise, how does he or she explain this decision? You should examine the explanation carefully. Buffett also pays attention when CEOs forecast earnings: "We are suspicious of those CEOs who regularly claim they do know the future—and we become downright incredulous if they consistently reach their declared targets. Managers that always promise to 'make the numbers' will at some point be tempted to make up the numbers."[12] It may not be possible to avoid all companies that make forecasts, because most do. But avoid investing in companies for which CEOs claim to regularly accomplish seemingly impossible targets.

Fourth, you should read the company chairman's annual letters (frequently co-signed by the CEO) to the shareholders from several years. If letters generally offer excuses for weak results, you should certainly be suspicious of the quality of the management. In many of these letters, success is often attributed to management efforts, but failures are attributed to exogenous reasons, such as the weather or China's product dumping. Do you want to partner with company managers who have a habit of making excuses and avoiding responsibility?

Fifth, you should attend annual shareholder meetings. It gives you a unique opportunity to evaluate the company's managers by examining their responses to shareholder questions.[13] You may not learn more about company financials as they are already reflected in company financials. However, your objective should be to learn more about management attitude toward shareholders, which you certainly do in these meetings. You can develop a sense of whether you trust the management or not. Buffett and Munger have often emphasized the importance of trust and have mentioned that they would not invest in a company if they did not trust its management. To show his trust in various company managements, Buffett transferred his voting rights at different points in time in American Express, *Washington Post*, and Salomon Inc. to their respective management.

Last and probably overarching, a very high level of integrity among company employees and the CEO is important. When Bill Gates was asked what he admired most about Warren Buffett, he replied, "With Warren, there are a lot of things you could pick, . . . his integrity is an example for the world."[14] At various Berkshire annual shareholder meetings, a video clip of Buffett's 1991 testimony to Congress is shown to the shareholders to explain the company philosophy. At the time, Buffett was chairman of the investment banking firm Salomon, Inc. He told Congress that a letter was sent to all Salomon employees to obey all laws and to behave as if they were never ashamed of their actions. Buffett wrote to the employees, "Lose money for the firm and I will be understanding; Lose a shred of reputation for the firm and I will be ruthless."[15] Clearly, money is important but money alone must not be the main driving force for a CEO. Integrity is more important for the long-term survival of a company.

With some thought, you should be able to judge the quality and integrity of a company's CEO. These six points do not by any means constitute an exhaustive list to study company management. For example, I would rather invest with CEOs who do not lead an extravagant lifestyle. I am not claiming that identifying shareowner-oriented CEOs, like Warren Buffett, is easy. However, an investor should make sincere efforts in that direction. After all, you only need to find a few outstanding CEOs to be successful investor. It is indeed worth the trouble.

Conclusions

As an investor, you should look for companies in which CEOs own a significant interest in the company's stock and do not receive excessive compensation from the company, especially through stock options. If the top management is owner-oriented, fairly compensated, and has well-thought-out incentive plans, the consequences are likely to be transmitted down the ranks. All employees are then motivated to work hard, and the company will probably produce extraordinary results, just as Berkshire does.

Chapter 30

Large Shareholders: They Are Your Friends

Warren Buffett owns 26.91% of the shares in Berkshire Hathaway.
—*Berkshire Hathaway Proxy Statement, 2009*

Warren Buffett is the largest Berkshire Hathaway shareholder and effectively controls the company. Similarly, Wal-Mart is controlled by the Walton family, Charles Schwab Inc. is controlled by Charles Schwab, America Online (AOL) was controlled by Steve Case for a long time, Starbucks is controlled by Howard Schultz, Amazon.com is controlled by Jeffrey Bezos, Oracle is controlled by Larry Ellison, and Dell is controlled by Michael Dell. All these companies performed very well for 10 to 20 years or longer.

Founder Control Matters

While you may have missed joining the successful entrepreneurs just listed, plenty of others are likely to come to your attention if you keep looking for them. As an investor, you should investigate family-controlled or individually controlled companies for potential investment—they are usually well-managed and friendly to shareholders, especially when the founding CEO is still in charge. In a well-known study, Ron Anderson of American University and David Reeb of Temple University show that, among all firms in the S&P 500, family firms perform better than nonfamily firms.[1] Additional research shows that when the founder CEO is in charge, performance is even better. Why might this be the case?

Although Buffett did not establish Berkshire Hathaway, he has been a director since 1965 and its chairman of the board since 1970, and so, for all practical purposes, he is the founder. As CEO, he has worked hard and made a lot of money for Berkshire's shareholders. For an investor, it is clearly important to consider whether the firm will continue to do well after the initial success under a founding CEO. Since long-term successful entrepreneurs or founders are proud of their accomplishments, they have a strong desire for the firm to continue to perform well. It is personal for them. Just as most people would like their families to be successful, their universities to become prominent, and their children to be the best they can be, the founder of a company would like a long and successful life for the firm.

A passionate manager or business owner does not become satisfied simply because a goal is reached. Each success paves the way for achieving bigger goals. A successful high school football coach wants to become a college coach, and so on. Thus, you are typically in good hands when you invest with successful entrepreneurs, even if you invest with them after some success has already been reflected in the stock price. If you had invested in Wal-Mart in 1982, by which time it had been listed for 10 years on the New York Stock Exchange, you would have earned phenomenal returns—more than 1,000 percent over the next 10 years. Of course, you should do your company-specific analysis no matter when you invest.

During the second, third, or fourth generation, a family-controlled company may not be as successful as it was under the original entrepreneur. Motorola and Hewlett-Packard, now more than two generations old, have faced intermittent troubles. While both are still world-class companies, their recent performances have not equaled their early performances. Similarly, Henry Ford's and E. I. DuPont's legacies of entrepreneurship have not been duplicated, even though the families continue to maintain substantial interest in these companies. Thus, as an investor, you should investigate the company more thoroughly when the founding CEO is no longer influential.

In the S&P 500 universe, many companies are run by their founders. Anderson and Reeb found that founding families are involved in about one-third of the S&P 500 firms and own about 18 percent of the outstanding equity of these companies. Keep in mind that the stock prices of these companies fluctuate greatly; they are bid up very high in some years and pushed down substantially in other years. In part, this happens because owner-managers do not pay as much attention to the stock prices as hired managers do. But by the same logic, owner-managers are also not likely to engage in earnings management to manipulate stock prices. Overall, with other factors held constant, you are unlikely to go wrong if you invest in companies run by their founders.

A controlling interest is important to an owner-oriented manager because he or she cannot be influenced by corporate raiders in case the stock price goes down. Instead, he or she can remain focused on the long run. If so, a controlling interest in the hands of one or a few is beneficial to all shareholders.[2] A controlling interest is often maintained by a dual-class stock structure in which one class of shares has a higher voting power per unit of economic or cash flow rights. In Berkshire's case, class A stock has 30 times the economic interest per share of class B stock but has 200 times the voting power. Berkshire has announced a 50:1 stock split for its class B shares effective from a yet-to-be-announced date in 2010. Class A shares will not be split. Because Warren Buffett and Charlie Munger together effectively have a controlling interest in the company, they do not worry about an unfriendly takeover.

Google Inc. also has a dual-class common stock structure. CEO Eric Schmidt, Sergey Brin, and Larry Page together hold about 22 percent of the shares, but they control about 66 percent of the voting power. In 2004, when Google went public with a dual-class structure, several articles in the popular press criticized the company. Investors would have earned several hundred percent returns in a few years if they had ignored the criticism and invested in Google's stock.

Conclusions

Large shareholders in a company are likely to monitor the company's management in a way that is not possible when the shareholding is more dispersed. Similarly, CEOs with large shareholdings are likely to be shareholder friendly. Unless Warren Buffett decides to run for a political office, your money is generally safer in his hands, or in the hands of other entrepreneur-owner-managers, than with the hired managers who run the vast majority of other companies.

Conclusion

B = Baseball = Buffett

Warren Buffett frequently uses sports analogies to explain the game of investing. In this conclusion, I follow Buffett's refreshing simile between sports and investing to explain the key features for success in investing. In the appendix that follows this chapter, I present a short summary of the book.

When we play baseball—or, really, any sport—what motivates us? What about when we play bridge? What motivates us then? Is there a single most important principle that makes us better at any game, including the game of investing? If I have to point to a single characteristic, I would say that the survival instinct, which has been thoroughly explained in *The Selfish Gene* and earlier in *The Origin of Species*, leads players to victory more than anything else.[1] The survival instinct can be thought of as the mind-set to win. Once we see a game with this winning mind-set, the rest of our behavior follows naturally to put us in the best possible position to emerge victorious.

Don't Lose Money

The mind-set to win is the overarching principle that applies to life, sports, and investing. Other rules are generally derivatives of this fundamental notion. Let's start with baseball. Everyone has been told, "Keep your eyes on the ball." If your objective is to win the game and you have completely internalized the idea that you want to win, then your mind shuts out other thoughts, and you see the ball as clearly as possible. You automatically keep your eyes on the ball. Your body naturally reacts in a coordinated motion that may surprise you. This is because you have developed a mind-set to win. Furthermore, suppose you lose a game by hitting a fly ball that is caught just short of the fence, and you realize that you lost because you lacked the physical strength to drive the ball out of the park. If you have internalized the fundamental principle, you will be motivated to go to the gym and add the necessary muscle.

Let's apply the same ideas to winning in the stock market. Since the stock market is all about money, you win by earning good returns on your investments. At the very least, you don't want to lose the money you originally invested, the principal. Buffett puts it slightly differently, but the philosophy is the same. He says, "Rule number 1: Don't lose money."[2]

Thinking in terms of *not losing* and *winning* at the same time gives rise to most of the ideas that have been discussed in this book. When you plan to invest, you should look at Buffett's rule on not losing money and ask the question, "What are the chances that I will lose money?" By trying to decide the probability of losing, you are automatically beginning to think in terms of value investing, at a very basic level. If you find that you are still losing because you don't know enough about value investing, you will be motivated to learn more. Later, to win big or earn very high returns, you will start to take a harder look at the growth potential of companies and eventually grasp the principles of growth investing. At this point, by following the two principles of being careful not to lose and trying to win, you will learn to combine value investing with growth investing as I have discussed in this book. This is what I call Buffett investing.

Once you develop the mind-set to win, your subconscious will guide you to other rules for your success. You may indeed produce super-size returns just as Warren Buffett has. Buffett does not simply practice value plus growth investing but has a large repertoire. He participates in the market through judicious use of financial products such as options, futures, and swaps. He also manages one of the largest companies in the world with operations in the insurance, retail, manufacturing, utilities, and financial services sectors. He has developed a psychological bent that allows him to look at market movements objectively. For all these reasons, I call him a renaissance investor. Perhaps that should be your final goal: to become a renaissance investor. The good thing is that winning in the game of investing does not require a high IQ or magical mantras. Overall, once you decide you want to succeed, you will.

Stay in Your Circle of Competence

In the context of mind-set to win, one question has always appealed to me: "How do you beat world chess champion Bobby Fischer?"[3] Yes, it is a bit of a trick question. If you want to beat Bobby Fischer, you don't play chess with him. You find a game that you can win. Picking up the baseball analogy, assume that despite all your efforts, you still can't hit. Then you are playing the wrong game. You should find a new game, a game that you can win. If you are tall, maybe you should try basketball; if you have good endurance, maybe you should run a marathon.

Finding the right game is extremely relevant to investing. If the high-tech industry is not where you can win, then don't invest in it. Buffett does not invest in high-tech. Find an industry where you can win, and invest there. If you can't figure out how a company will probably shape up in 10 years, don't invest in it; find a company that you understand so you can project its likely future. You don't have to play every sport, and you don't have to have an opinion on every stock. In other words, the fundamental principle will keep you inside your circle of competence, an investing rule that Buffett has often discussed. In the booklet *Batting*, Babe Ruth wrote a simple rule for winning in baseball: "Learn not to swing at bad balls." Similarly, you should invest only when you understand the company and only when the market price is favorable in relation to the stock's intrinsic value. It is important to be patient. You wait and wait and wait for a fat pitch or a good stock, and when it comes, you swing away.

Find Good People

In sports, managers make key decisions, such as which prospects to draft and which coaches to hire. Effectively, high-quality management is a prerequisite to success—as Michael Lewis shows in his story of the general manager Billy Beane and his highly successful baseball team Oakland

A's, despite limited financial resources in *Moneyball*.[4] The same is true in investing. Buffett has emphasized the importance of management competence and integrity above other metrics in explaining his success. If you want to win in the game of investing, you should look for managers who have proven to be outstanding at running companies. Berkshire Hathaway is one such company I found. When you find outstanding people like Buffett, buy shares in their companies. If they head up money management firms, invest with them. Good luck!

Appendix

A Summary of the Book

Warren Buffett is a genius in the same league as Benjamin Franklin, Ernest Hemingway, and Henry Ford. Their ideas are simple to understand, but their successes are difficult to duplicate. However, geniuses abide by certain principles that we can learn from. In this book, I have tried to explain the principles that I believe Buffett follows. This appendix provides a succinct summary.

Table A.1 Summary of Warren Buffett's Investment Principles

Principle	Explanation
(i) Develop a Mind-Set to Win	You play a game because it's fun and even exhilarating when you win. You will win often when you play to your strengths. In the stock market game, this means staying within your circle of competence.
(ii) Stick with Value Investing	Examine historical records, price-to-earnings ratios (P/E), and other financial measures.
(iii) Combine Growth Investing with Value Investing	Management with integrity and competence is the key to growth. Make sure the quality of a company's management is outstanding.

(continued)

Table A.1 Continued

Principle	Explanation
(iv) Maintain Low Risk	Low debt level. Reread (ii). Learn some accounting to look for possible hidden risks.
(v) Act Rationally	Knowledge is the best antidote to irrationality. Know the company's business, and project what the company will look like in 10 years.
(vi) Do Not Pay a High Price	Estimate a company's intrinsic value by learning about the company's business. Invest only when the price is low compared with the intrinsic value.
(vii) Find Good People	Try to find and invest with outstanding people like Warren Buffett; they treat the shareholders' interests as their own.

Notes

Preface

1. Warren E. Buffett, "Up the Inefficient Market," *Barron's* (February 25, 1985), 11.
2. "Billionaires 2008," *Forbes* (March 24, 2008), 80.
3. Berkshire Hathaway *Annual Report* 1996, 16.
4. There are at least two excellent Buffett biographies: Roger Lowenstein, *Buffett: The Making of an American Capitalist* (New York: Random House Trade Paperbacks, 2008), and Alice Schroeder, *The Snowball: Warren Buffett and the Business of Life* (New York: Bantam Books, 2008).

Chapter 1 The Thrill of Investing in Common Stocks

1. Roger Lowenstein, *Buffett: The Making of an American Capitalist*, 20.
2. "Mr. Market" is a fictitious character created by Benjamin Graham to represent market indices and has often been discussed by Warren Buffett. See Benjamin Graham, *The Intelligent Investor* (New York: HarperCollins Publishers, 1996, originally published by Harper & Row in 1973), 108.
3. Peter Lynch with John Rothchild, *Beating the Street* (New York: Simon and Schuster, 1993), 20.
4. Warren E. Buffett, "Buy American, I am." *New York Times* (October 17, 2008, Op-ed).
5. Lauren C. Templeton and Scott Philips, *Investing the Templeton Way* (New York: McGraw-Hill, 2008), x.

Chapter 2 1965–2009: Lessons from Significant Events in Berkshire History

1. Berkshire Hathaway *Annual Report* 1980, 7.
2. Berkshire Hathaway *Annual Report* 1984, 12.
3. Berkshire Hathaway *Annual Report* 1985, 8.
4. Ibid., 9.
5. Berkshire Hathaway *Annual Report* 1986, 18.
6. Benjamin Franklin, *Autobiography of Benjamin Franklin* (New York: Simon and Schuster, 1993), 28.
7. Berkshire Hathaway *Annual Report* 1988, 13.
8. Ibid.
9. Berkshire Hathaway *Annual Report* 1989, 16.
10. Ibid., 14.
11. Ibid.
12. Berkshire Hathaway *Annual Report* 1990, 17.
13. Ibid.
14. Berkshire Hathaway *Annual Report* 2008, 5.
15. Berkshire Hathaway *Annual Report* 1991, 17.
16. Ibid.
17. Berkshire Hathaway *Annual Report* 1992, 20.
18. Berkshire Hathaway *Annual Report* 1993, 19.
19. Berkshire Hathaway *Annual Report* 1994, 8.
20. Ibid.
21. Berkshire Hathaway *Annual Report* 1995, 7.
22. Ibid., 6.
23. Ibid., 10.
24. Ibid., 6.
25. Ibid.
26. Berkshire Hathaway *Annual Report* 1997, 5.
27. Ibid.
28. Berkshire Hathaway *Annual Report* 1999, 3.
29. Berkshire Hathaway *Annual Report* 2000, 3.
30. Berkshire Hathaway *Annual Report* 2001, 61.
31. Berkshire Hathaway *Annual Report* 2002, 15.
32. Berkshire Hathaway *Annual Report* 2008, 3.

Chapter 3 Value Investing—It's Like Buying Christmas Cards in January

1. Berkshire Hathaway *Annual Report* 1985, 19.
2. Benjamin Graham, *The Intelligent Investor* (4th ed.) (New York: HarperCollins, originally published by Harper & Row in 1973), 54.
3. Ibid.

4. Data are obtained from Professor Robert Shiller's Web site at Yale University. These data are updated frequently.
5. John Neff, *John Neff on Investing*, with S. L. Mintz (New York: John Wiley & Sons, 1999), 122.
6. Berkshire Hathaway *Annual Report* 1985, 19.
7. Berkshire Hathaway *Annual Report* 2008, 5.
8. Ibid., 280.
9. Warren Buffett, "The Superinvestors of Graham-and-Doddsville," in Graham, 1973, appendix.
10. Graham, 82.
11. Josef Lakonishok, Andrei Shleifer, and Robert W. Vishny, "Contrarian Investment, Extrapolation, and Risk," *Journal of Finance* (1994): 1541–1578.
12. Benjamin Graham discusses glamour-type stocks in *The Intelligent Investor* on page 182. He points out that in the short run, glamour stocks may do well and common-stock investment policy must depend on the individual investor.
13. Eugene Fama and Kenneth French, "The Cross-section of Expected Stock Returns," *Journal of Finance* (1992): 427–466.
14. David Dreman, *Contrarian Investment Strategies: The Next Generation* (New York: Simon and Schuster, 1998).
15. Ibid., 61.
16. For this analysis, the value portfolio is composed of the stocks in the two deciles (i.e., about 20 percent of the total number of stocks) with the smallest market-to-book ratio, while the glamour portfolio is composed of the corresponding largest market-to-book ratio stocks.
17. Louis K. C. Chan and Josef Lakonishok, "Value and Growth Investing: Review and Update," *Financial Analysts Journal* (2004): 71-86.

Chapter 4 Growth Investing

1. Philip A. Fisher, *Common Stocks and Uncommon Profits* (New York: John Wiley & Sons, 1996), 15.
2. Benjamin Graham, *The Intelligent Investor* (4th ed.) (New York: HarperCollins, originally published by Harper & Row in 1973), 57.
3. Wal-Mart's Web site, www.walmart.com.
4. Jay R. Ritter and Ivo Welch, "A Review of IPO Activity, Pricing, and Allocations," *Journal of Finance* (2002): 1795–1828. For results on recent years, see updates by Jay Ritter at the University of Florida Web site.
5. Sam Walton, *Made in America*, with John Huey (New York: Bantam Books, 1993).
6. Michael Dell, *Direct from Dell: Strategies That Revolutionized an Industry*, with Catherine Freidman (New York: Harper Collins, 1999).

7. Clayton M. Christensen, *The Innovator's Dilemma: When New Technologies Cause Great Firms to Fail* (Boston: Harvard Business School Press, 1997).

8. Fisher, 35.

Chapter 5 Intrinsic Value

1. Benjamin Graham and David Dodd, *Security Analysis* (New York: McGraw-Hill, 1934), 17.

2. Berkshire Hathaway *Annual Report* 1999, 60.

3. Wesco Financial Corporation *Annual Report 2008,* 7.

4. Myron J. Gordon, *The Investment Financing and Valuation of the Corporation* (Homewood, IL: Richard D. Irwin, 1962).

5. Berkshire Hathaway *Annual Report* 2008, 5.

6. The assumption of a growth rate smaller than the discount rate implies that Berkshire may sell some shares to invest in wholly owned subsidiaries that generate earnings or that the stock market growth rate in the coming 10 years will be about 5.5 percent plus dividends.

Chapter 6 Buffett Investing = Value + Growth

1. Berkshire Hathaway *Annual Report* 1992, 13.

2. Gerald S. Martin and John Puthenpurackal, "Imitation Is the Sincerest Form of Flattery: Warren Buffett and Berkshire Hathaway," American University working paper, April 2009.

3. Buffett's letter to his partners in Buffett Partnership, October 9, 1967.

4. Berkshire Hathaway *Annual Report* 2008, 7.

5. Columbia University, "Warren Edward Buffett," http://c250.columbia.edu/c250_celebrates/remarkable_columbians/warren_edward_buffett.html.

6. Berkshire Hathaway *Annual Report* 1996, 6.

7. Berkshire Hathaway *Annual Report* 1998, 49.

8. Berkshire Hathaway *Annual Report* 1999, 9.

9. Berkshire Hathaway *Annual Report* 2007, 14.

10. Berkshire Hathaway *Annual Report* 1999, 5.

11. In 1999, the pretax operating profits of $225 million on revenues represent a 12 percent margin on revenues and a 12.5 percent return on identifiable assets. This certainly seems satisfactory.

12. *Fortune* published a cover story on BYD, "Buffett's Electric Car," April 27, 2009, pp. 44–60.

13. Charlie Munger has had a considerable influence on Buffett, especially in thinking about growth investing. Munger was also the main person in convincing Buffett to invest in BYD. Thus, this style of combining value investing with growth investing may also be called Buffett-Munger investing.

Chapter 7 Insurance: Other People's Money

1. Berkshire Hathaway *Annual Report* 1999, 6.
2. Berkshire Hathaway *Annual Report* 1995, 9.
3. Berkshire Hathaway *Annual Report* 2008, 8.
4. Berkshire Hathaway *Annual Report* 1998, 6.
5. Berkshire Hathaway *Annual Report* 1967, 2.
6. Charlie Munger, "Letter from the Chairman and the President of Blue Chip Stamps, 1981," in Berkshire Hathaway *Annual Report* 1981, 47.
7. Charlie Munger, "Letter from the Chairman and the President of Blue Chip Stamps, 1982," in Berkshire Hathaway *Annual Report* 1982, 59.

Chapter 8 Reinsurance: More of Other People's Money

1. Berkshire Hathaway *Annual Report* 1998, 9.
2. Ibid., 10.
3. Berkshire Hathaway *Annual Report* 2008, 8.
4. Ibid., 9.
5. Berkshire Hathaway *Annual Report* 1996, 8.
6. Berkshire Hathaway *Annual Report* 2002, 8.

Chapter 9 Tax Deferment: Interest-Free Loans from the Government

1. Wesco Financial Corporation *Annual Report* 2000, 6.
2. Berkshire Hathaway *Annual Report* 1989, 6.

Chapter 10 If You Don't Know Jewelry, Know Your Jeweler

1. Berkshire Hathaway *Annual Report* 1989, 6.
2. Berkshire Hathaway *Annual Report* 1990, 8.
3. Berkshire Hathaway *Annual Report* 1989, 9.
4. Berkshire Hathaway *Annual Report* 1995, 7.
5. Barnett C. Helzberg, *What I Learned before I Sold to Warren Buffett* (Hoboken, NJ: John Wiley & Sons, 1993), xx.
6. Ibid., xvii.

Chapter 11 Compete Like Mrs. B

1. Berkshire Hathaway *Annual Report* 2000, 11.
2. Berkshire Hathaway *Annual Report* 1983, 3.
3. This Mrs. B quote is from Nebraska Furniture Mart's web site, www.nfm.com/ourstory_history.aspx?ID=1a.
4. Berkshire Hathaway *Annual Report* 1996, 20.

5. Peter Lynch with John Rothchild, *One Up on Wall Street* (New York: Penguin Books, 1989), 123.
6. Berkshire Hathaway *Annual Report* 1995, 8.
7. Ibid., 9.
8. Berkshire Hathaway *Annual Report* 1997, 13.
9. Berkshire Hathaway *Annual Report* 1999, 11.
10. Wesco Financial Corporation *Annual Report* 2008, 14.

Chapter 12 Why Invest in Utility Companies?

1. Berkshire Hathaway *Annual Report* 1989, 6.
2. MidAmerican Energy press release, October 25, 1999.
3. Ibid.
4. Berkshire Hathaway *Annual Report* 1999, 11.
5. A MidAmerican subsidiary, HomeServices (previously HomeServices.com), is a collection of many small local real estate firms and has grown steadily. Interestingly, its philosophy of keeping the individual units independent is similar to Berkshire's model for its subsidiaries. I owned shares in HomeServices.com before it was acquired.
6. I made some adjustments to the reported accounting numbers for them to be comparable across years. For example, I do not include gains from investment in Constellation Energy and the break-up fee as explained in the Berkshire Hathaway 2008 annual report.

Chapter 13 High Profits in Honest-to-Goodness Manufacturing Companies

1. Berkshire Hathaway *Annual Report* 1994, 8.
2. Since Shaw Industries was acquired after the beginning of 2001, some of the numbers for the year 2001 in the table have been adjusted slightly to make them comparable for the other full-year numbers.
3. *Tribune Business News*, July 21, 2006.
4. Lorraine D. Miller, "Scoring the Board Company Profile," *Flooring* (August 1, 1977).

Chapter 14 Risk and Volatility: How to Think Profitably about Them

1. Berkshire Hathaway *Annual Report* 1993, 14.
2. See the previously mentioned article in Chapter 3 by Eugene Fama and Kenneth French (1992) and additional insight by S. P. Kothari, Jay Shanken, and Richard Sloan, "Another Look at the Cross-Section of Expected Returns," *Journal of Finance* (1995): 185–224.

3. The Orange County example is not unique. In March 2008, Jefferson County, Alabama, failed to produce $200 million in collateral for its swaps. See *Wall Street Journal* online edition, March 22, 2008.
4. Berkshire Hathaway *Annual Report* (10-K) 1999, 18.
5. Berkshire Hathaway *Annual Report* 1993, 15.
6. Robert J. Shiller, *Market Volatility* (Cambridge, MA: The MIT Press, 1999).
7. *Forbes*, "The Money Men," November 1, 1974, pp. 41–42.
8. Berkshire Hathaway *Annual Report* 1985,19.
9. Berkshire Hathaway *Annual Report* 1993, 15.
10. Ibid.

Chapter 15 Why Hold Cash: Liquidity Brings Opportunities

1. Berkshire Hathaway *Annual Report* 1990, 19.
2. Morgan Stanley *Equity Research Report on Insurance-Property and Casualty*, New York, World Trade Center Special Issue, September 17, 2001.
3. As reported in a press release by Wrigley on April 28, 2008, available on Wrigley.com.

Chapter 16 Diversification: How Many Baskets Should You Hold?

1. See Chapter 13 in Stephen A. Ross, Randolph W. Westerfield, and Bradford D. Jordan, *Fundamentals of Corporate Finance* (New York: McGraw-Hill Irwin, 2006). For a detailed academic discussion of this topic, see Eugene Fama, *Foundations of Finance* (New York: Basic Books, 1976).
2. For this purpose I assumed a typical stock to have a covariance of 0.18 with other stocks. This is typical of an exchange traded stock.
3. Benjamin Graham, *The Intelligent Investor* (4th ed.) (New York: HarperCollins, originally published by Harper & Row in 1973), 54.
4. Philip A. Fisher, *Common Stocks and Uncommon Profits* (New York: John Wiley & Sons, 1996), 108.
5. Peter Lynch with John Rothchild, *One Up on Wall Street* (New York: Penguin Books, 1989), 242.
6. Ibid.
7. Ibid., 150.

Chapter 17 When to Sell

1. Berkshire Hathaway *Annual Report* 1996, 16.
2. Berkshire Hathaway *Annual Report* 1988, 13.
3. Berkshire Hathaway *Annual Report* 1997, 15.
4. Berkshire Hathaway *Annual Report* 1998, 12.
5. See, for example, *Washington Post*, October 31, 2007.

Chapter 18 How Efficient Is the Stock Market?

1. Berkshire Hathaway *Annual Report* 1988, 18.
2. See Hemang Desai and Prem C. Jain, "An Analysis of the Recommendations of the 'Superstar' Money Managers at *Barron's* Annual Roundtable," *Journal of Finance* (1995): 1257–1273. In this article, we show that even the stock recommendations published in *Barron's* by the so-called superstar money managers do not produce excess returns.
3. For a summary of this research, see Andrei Shleifer, *Inefficient Markets* (Oxford University Press, 2000).
4. Andrew W. Lo and A. Craig MacKinlay, "A Non-Random Walk Down Wall Street" (Princeton, NJ: Princeton University Press, 2001).
5. Several papers in recent years try to explain deviation of prices from fundamentals. For a recent paper, see Henk Berkman, Valentin Dimitrov, Prem C. Jain, Paul Koch, and Sheri Tice, "Sell on the News: Differences of Opinion, Short-Sales Constraints, and Returns Around Earnings Announcements," *Journal of Financial Economics* 92 (June 2009): 376–399.
6. See, for example, Hemang Desai and Prem C. Jain, "Firm Performance and Focus: Long-run Stock Market Performance Following Spinoffs," *Journal of Financial Economics* (October 1999): 75–101. Also see Hemang Desai and Prem C. Jain, "Long-Run Common Stock Returns following Stock Splits and Reverse Splits," *Journal of Business* (1977): 409-433.
7. Narasimhan Jegadeesh and Sheridan Titman, "Cross-Sectional and Time-Series Determinants of Momentum Returns," *Review of Financial Studies* 15 (2002): 143–157.
8. Werner DeBondt and Richard Thaler, "Further Evidence on Investor Overreaction and Stock Market Seasonality," *Journal of Finance* 42 (July 1987): 557–581. Several other similar papers are explained in Richard Thaler, *Advances in Behavioral Finance, Volume II* (Princeton, NJ: Princeton University Press, 2005).
9. Louis Chan, Narasimhan Jegadeesh, and Josef Lakonishok, "Momentum Strategies," *Journal of Finance* 51 (December 1996): 1681-1713.
10. Berkshire Hathaway *Annual Report* 1988, 18.

Chapter 19 Arbitrage and Hedge Funds

1. Berkshire Hathaway *Annual Report* 1989, 16.
2. Berkshire Hathaway *Annual Report* 1988, 15.
3. For a detailed account, see Roger Lowenstein, *When Genius Failed: The Rise and Fall of Long-Term Capital Management* (New York: Random House Trade Paperbacks, 2001).
4. Burton G. Malkiel and Atanu Saha, "Hedge Funds: Risk and Return," *Financial Analysts Journal* (2005): 80–88.
5. Andrew W. Lo, *Hedge Funds: An Analytic Perspective* (Princeton, NJ: Princeton University Press, 2008).

6. Ludovic Phalippou and Oliver Gottschalg, "The Performance of Private Equity Funds," *Review of Financial Studies* 22 (2009): 1747-1776.
7. Steve Kaplan and Antoinette Schoar, "Private Equity Performance: Returns, Persistence and Capital," *Journal of Finance* 60 (August 2005): 1791–1823.

Chapter 20: M = Monopoly = Money

1. Berkshire Hathaway *Annual Report* 2001, 61.
2. While it is tempting to compare the two companies using return on equity (ROE), I do not do so because both Microsoft and IBM repurchased significant amounts of common stock in recent years. These transactions made book values of equity very small and ROE comparisons meaningless. This also shows that mindless comparison of financial ratios may not yield useful results.
3. An insightful history of *Buffalo News* is presented by Murray B. Light in *From Butler to Buffett: The Story Behind the* Buffalo News (Prometheus Books, 2004). In the foreword to the book, Buffett describes Murray Light to be a brilliant and tireless editor who successfully pulled off a Sunday edition of the newspaper.
4. Berkshire Hathaway *Annual Report* 1981, 46.
5. Peter Lynch with John Rothchild, *One Up on Wall Street* (New York: Penguin Books, 1989), 266.

Chapter 21 Who Wins in Highly Competitive Industries?

1. Berkshire Hathaway *Annual Report* 1999, 8.
2. Buffett explained this point in a question–answer session at Columbia University on November 12, 2009. He said, "The Burlington Northern last year moved . . . a ton of freight 470 miles on one gallon of diesel. That is far, far more efficient than what takes place over the highways. I'm willing to bet . . . on the fact that 10 years from now, 20 years from now, 50 years from now, there will be more goods being moved by rail and it will be better for the country and for the shareholders." The transcript is available on www.cnbc.com.
3. Berkshire Hathaway *Annual Report* 2008, 6.

Chapter 22 Property, Plant, and Equipment: Good or Bad?

1. Wesco Financial Corporation annual meeting, May 9, 2007.
2. Net PPE and total assets as of September 28, 1963, were $12.8 million and $39.5 million, respectively.
3. Berkshire Hathaway *Annual Report* 1989, 21.

Chapter 23 Key to Success: ROE and Other Ratios

1. See Benjamin Graham, David L. Dodd, and Sidney Cottle (4th ed.), *Security Analysis* (New York: McGraw-Hill, 1962), 231.

2. Ibid., 464.
3. Probably the most well-known accounting research paper that influenced the way hedge funds invest in long-short strategies is Richard G. Sloan's "Do Stock Prices Fully Reflect Information in Accruals and Cash Flows about Future Earnings?" *Accounting Review* (1996): 289–315.
4. Berkshire Hathaway *Annual Report* 1992, 17.
5. *WorldCom 8-K*, Securities and Exchange Commission, Washington, DC, August 8, 2002.

Chapter 24 Accounting Goodwill: Is It Any Good?

1. Berkshire Hathaway *Annual Report* 1983, 4.
2. Berkshire Hathaway *Annual Report* 1996, 66.

Chapter 25 How Much Psychology Should You Know?

1. L. J. Davis, "Buffett Takes Stock," *New York Times,* April 1, 1990.
2. Peter Lynch with John Rothchild, *One Up on Wall Street* (New York: Penguin Books, 1989), 155.
3. Benjamin Graham, *Intelligent Investor* (4th ed.) (New York: HarperCollins, originally published by Harper & Row in 1973), 94.
4. George Soros, *The Alchemy of Finance* (New York: John Wiley & Sons, 1987).
5. George A. Akerlof and Robert J. Shiller, *Animal Spirits* (Princeton, NJ: Princeton University Press, 2009). Also see Hersh Shefrin, *Beyond Greed and Fear* (New York: Oxford University Press, 2002).
6. Terrance Odean, "Are Investors Reluctant to Realize Their Losses?" *Journal of Finance* 53, no. 5 (October 1998): 1775–1798.
7. Brad Barber and Terrance Odean, "Trading Is Hazardous to Your Wealth: The Common Stock Investment Performance of Individual Investors," *Journal of Finance* 55, no. 2 (April 2000): 773–806.
8. Prem C. Jain and Joanna Shuang Wu, "Truth in Mutual Fund Advertising: Evidence on Future Performance and Fund Flows," *Journal of Finance* 66, no. 2 (April 2000): 937–958.
9. For further readings, see Michael J. Mauboussin, *More Than You Know: Finding Financial Wisdom in Unconventional Places* (New York, NY: Columbia Business School Publishing, 2008). Charlie Munger has often convincingly argued the importance of psychology in his dialogues at the Berkshire and Wesco annual meetings. He has also recommended books by Robert B. Cialdini. I have benefited from his recommendations and his talks. Several of Munger's very well-articulated talks and thoughts are published in *Poor Charlie's Almanack: The Wit and Wisdom of Charles T. Munger*, edited by Peter D. Kaufman (Marceline, MO: Walsworth Publishing Company, 2008).

Chapter 26 How to Learn from Mistakes

1. Berkshire Hathaway Shareholders' annual meeting, 2005.
2. Tom Dowdell, Suresh Govindaraj, and Prem Jain, "The Tylenol Incident, Ensuing Regulations, and Stock Prices," *Journal of Financial and Quantitative Analysis* (1992): 283–301.
3. Michael J. Mauboussin, *Think Twice: Harnessing the Power of Counterintuition* (Boston, MA: Harvard Business Press, 2009).
4. Richard H. Thaler and Cass R. Sustein, *Nudge: Improving Decisions About Health, Wealth and Happiness* (New Haven, CT: Yale University Press, 2008). The authors argue that it is sometimes helpful to make mistakes, since that is how we learn.

Chapter 27 Dividends: Do They Make Sense in This Day and Age?

1. Merton Miller and Franco Modigliani, "Dividend Policy, Growth, and the Valuation of Shares," *Journal of Business* (1961): 411–433.
2. Fischer Black, "The Dividend Puzzle," *Journal of Portfolio Management* 2 (Winter 1976): 72–77.

Chapter 28 Should You Invest in Companies That Repurchase Their Own Shares?

1. Berkshire Hathaway *Annual Report* 1984, 5.
2. Amy K. Dittmar, "Why Do Firms Repurchase Stock?" *Journal of Business* (2000): 331–355. For long-run performance following repurchases, see David Ikenberry, Joseph Lakonishok, and Theo Vermaelen, "Market Underreaction to Open Market Share Repurchases," *Journal of Financial Economics* 39 (1995): 181–208.
3. Berkshire Hathaway *Annual Report* 1984, 5.
4. Ibid., 6.
5. Ibid.
6. Berkshire Hathaway *Annual Report* 1999, 16.
7. Ibid., 17.

Chapter 29 Corporate Governance: Employees, Directors, and CEOs

1. Berkshire Hathaway *Annual Report* 1996, 10.
2. Ibid.
3. Berkshire Hathaway *Annual Report* 1994, 10.
4. Paul M. Healy, "The Effect of Bonus Schemes on Accounting Decisions," *Journal of Accounting and Economics* (1985): 85–107.
5. Ibid.
6. Berkshire Hathaway *Annual Report* 2006, 18.
7. Berkshire Hathaway *Annual Report* 2008, 89.

8. Berkshire Hathaway *Annual Report* 1998, 14.

9. Academic research evidence also does not suggest that stock options improve company profits significantly. See David Larcker, "Discussion of Are Executive Stock Options Associated with Future Earnings?" *Journal of Accounting and Economics* 36 (2003): 91–103.

10. David Yermack, "Good Timing: CEO Option Awards and Company News Announcements," *Journal of Finance* (1977): 449–476.

11. David Aboody and Ron Kasznik, "CEO Stock Option Awards and the Timing of Corporate Voluntary Disclosures," *Journal of Accounting and Economics* 29 (2000): 73–100.

12. Berkshire Hathaway *Annual Report* 2002, 21.

13. Randy Cepuch describes his experiences from attending a large number of annual shareholder meetings in the United States, Europe, and Australia. See Randy Cepuch, *A Weekend with Warren Buffett: And Other Shareholder Meeting Adventures* (New York: Basic Books, 2007). You should also be aware that managers often announce good news prior to or during the annual shareholder meetings. See Valentin Dimitrov and Prem C. Jain, "It's Showtime. Do Managers Manipulate Stock Prices before Annual Shareholder Meetings?" Working paper, McDonough School of Business, Georgetown University, 2009.

14. A question and answer session with students at Columbia University on November 12, 2009.

15. Roger Lowenstein, *Buffett: The Making of an American Capitalist* (New York: Random House Trade Paperbacks, 2008), 395.

Chapter 30 Large Shareholders: They Are Your Friends

1. Ronald C. Anderson and David M. Reeb, "Founding-Family Ownership and Firm Performance: Evidence from the S&P 500," *Journal of Finance* (June 2003): 1301–1328.

2. Valentin Dimitrov and Prem C. Jain, "Recapitalization of One Class of Common Stock into Dual-Class: Growth and Long-run Stock Returns," *Journal of Corporate Finance* (2006): 342–366.

Conclusion B = Baseball = Buffett

1. See Richard Dawkins, *The Selfish Gene* (New York: Oxford University Press, 1990); and Charles Darwin, *The Origin of Species* (New York: Gramercy Books, 1979, originally published in 1859).

2. Janet Lowe, *Warren Buffett Speaks* (New York: John Wiley & Sons, 1997), 85.

3. John Train, *Money Masters of Our Time* (New York: Harper Paperbacks, 2003), 47.

4. Michael Lewis, *Moneyball: The Art of Winning an Unfair Game* (New York: W. W. Norton and Company, 2004).

About the Author

Prem C. Jain, Ph.D., C.P.A., began his academic career in 1984 at the Wharton School of the University of Pennsylvania, followed by a move in 1991 to the Freeman School of Business at Tulane University in New Orleans. In 2002 he accepted his current position as the McDonough Professor of Accounting and Finance at Georgetown University's McDonough School of Business.

Jain has also taught at Monterrey Tech in Mexico and the China Europe International Business School (CEIBS) in Shanghai, and was a visiting scholar for two summers at INSEAD in France. He has taught graduate-level courses in corporate finance, investments, international finance, and financial statement analysis. He has also worked as a financial economist for the Commodity Futures Trading Commission (CFTC) in Washington, D.C.

Over his 25-year academic career, Jain has traveled across the globe to present his research at various conferences and universities. He has published extensively in the most prestigious finance and accounting journals, including the *Journal of Finance*, *Journal of Financial Economics*, and *Journal of Accounting Research*. His work includes several scholarly articles analyzing stock market and stock futures data. He has also been referenced in the *Wall Street Journal* and other news media. His research subjects include stock splits, spin-offs, mutual fund advertising, performance of Wall Street superstars, and market efficiency.

At Tulane, Jain developed a course for MBA students to study traditional value and growth investment strategies, initially developed by
Benjamin Graham, David Dodd, and Philip Fisher. The students also
study Warren Buffett's writings and decisions along with contemporary
finance research and manage a two-million-dollar portfolio as part of the
University endowment. He frequently takes students and other faculty
members with him to Berkshire's annual shareholders' meetings.

Jain received a bachelor's degree in engineering from Birla Institute
of Technology and Science in India and worked as an engineer for two
years at Hindustan Motors, an Indian car manufacturing company. He
received an MBA from the Indian Institute of Management, Calcutta and
worked for two years as a financial analyst for Novartis. He received a
Master's degree in Applied Economics from the University of Rochester,
a Ph.D. from the University of Florida, and his C.P.A. license from the
State of Florida.

Index